THE ENCYCLOPEDIA OF
ITALIAN
COOKING

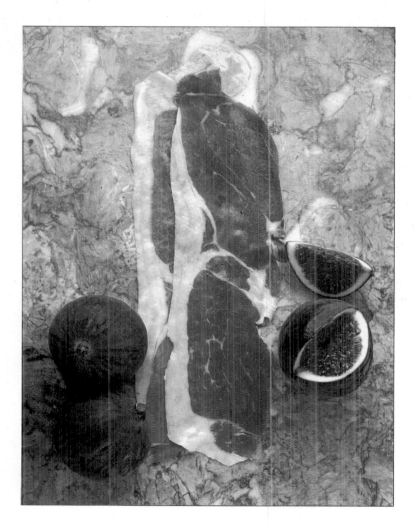

THE ENCYCLOPEDIA OF
ITALIAN
COOKING

General Editor: JENI WRIGHT

CRESCENT BOOKS
New York

CONTENTS

INTRODUCTION

RECIPES

General Editor: Jeni Wright

Consultant Editor: Giovanni Parmigiani

Authors:

Susanna Agnelli   Riccardo Di Corato   Maria Casati

Ilaria Rattazzi   Bruno Roncarati   Jeni Wright

Translator: Erica Propper

Library of Congress Catalog Card No: 80-70677
Wright, Jeni
The encyclopedia of Italian cooking
NY: Crescent Books 192p. 8106. 80112a
ISBN 0 517 34141 7

Produced by Mandarin Publishers Limited
22a Westlands Road,
Quarry Bay, Hong Kong
Printed in Hong Kong

History

Italy is described in *Larousse Gastronomique* as 'the mother of all European Latin cuisines'. With its roots in Greek, Roman and Arab cultures, the cuisine of Italy is indeed responsible for influencing many of the cuisines of Western Europe. When Catherine de Medici travelled to France in 1533 for her marriage to the Dauphin (later to become Henri II), no other cuisine in Europe had reached such a level of sophistication and expertise as that of the Florentine court. Catherine's chefs passed on their knowledge to the French, who are not always keen to admit this, and here lie the roots of French culinary tradition.

To go back to the beginning, life for the ancient Romans was simple and rustic, and so too was their daily food. Most men were farmers or shepherds and, in early pre-Christian times, grain or *pulmentum* as it was called, formed the staple diet. It was not usually eaten as bread, but as a kind of porridge, or it was left to harden into a cake, similar to today's *polenta*. Meat was not normally eaten, as sheep and goats were bred primarily for their milk, and cattle were extremely rare. Protein was provided by milk and many different kinds of cheese. *Pecorino* cheese for example, was known in pre-Roman times, when it was believed to have been made from a combination of sheep's and goat's milk.

Trade in salt brought new found wealth to the Roman Empire, and as the Empire became increasingly powerful, tastes became more sophisticated. With the avid interest in conquering new territories developed a desire to cultivate land, and new varieties of fruit and vegetables were introduced into Roman cuisine. The excesses of the Romans in their eating and drinking habits are well documented, and there is little doubt that this style of Roman cuisine has left its mark on modern Italian cooking. It must however be remembered that few Romans could actually afford such ostentations of wealth and the majority of people at this time lived on a frugal diet of grain, fruit, vegetables and nuts – with fish as an added bonus for those living in coastal regions.

Those few Romans who enjoyed the Empire's wealth developed a mania for food and wine. The Central Market in Rome became their centre for importing and trading foodstuffs, and incredibly high prices were paid for rare game birds, fish and other delicacies. Lavish banquets were frequently staged, where vast dishes of exotic meat, game and poultry were served in the most elaborate style. Not only was the food noted for its quantity, the dishes were remarkable in their richness, spiciness and complexity.

The decline and eventual downfall of the Roman Empire brought with it a deterioration in cooking, and there were few new developments for several centuries to come. Barbarism and austerity became the order of the day, and what was left of Roman cuisine seemed only to survive in the monasteries of the Middle Ages. The monks could hardly afford meat and therefore learnt to concentrate on the use of vegetables in cooking, with less emphasis on herbs and spices.

With the Islamic invasion of southern Europe in the ninth century, came yet another foreign influence on Italian cuisine. In Sicily and southern Italy, the Arabs introduced the art of making ices and sorbets, which they in turn had learnt from the Chinese, together with a variety of other Arabic desserts. These southern regions of Italy are still noted for their delicious sweets, cakes and pastries.

As the Middle Ages drew to a close, changes could be seen throughout Europe as lifestyles became less rural and more urbanized. The food became less austere and new ingredients were introduced. The Crusaders brought sugar cane back from the Holy Land and for the first time Europeans tasted sugar; they had previously used honey as a sweetener. Although the flavour of this 'new sugar' was readily accepted, it was a long time before its full potential was realized.

When Marco Polo opened the spice route to the East via his native town of Venice, the use of spices was re-introduced into Italian cooking. The spice-traders of the day enjoyed untold wealth, particularly in Venice and Genoa. This route was closed in 1453 when Constantinople fell, but the traders retained the monopoly on spices and sugar by importing them overland. They continued to make handsome profits until Vasco da Gama discovered the sea route to India at the end of the century, and the centre of the spice trade switched to Lisbon.

RIGHT: **Early 18th century oil painting of the Piazza del Verziore in Genoa by Allesandro Magnasco, depicting the food market at the height of activity**

BELOW LEFT: **Early Roman fresco retrieved from the ruins of Pompeii**

Up until this time, the only records of 'recipes' since the Romans were kept by the monks in the Middle Ages. The birth of the Renaissance in the fifteenth century saw a revival in culinary matters, and the first book of recipes to be printed was written by Bartolomeo Sicci in 1474–5. Sicci was a librarian at the Vatican, and his book, commonly referred to as Platina's book (from the title *Platine de honesta voluptate et valitudine*), proved so popular that there were six editions in 30 years.

During the Renaissance interest in gastronomy grew, particularly in the homes of wealthy families where lavish banquets and feasts were staged in an effort to outdo each other. Yet despite the efforts of such groups as the Doges of Venice, the Borgia and the Visconti, it was the Medici of Florence who far outshone the others. The Florentines had for a long while led the rest of Italy in their thirst for culinary knowledge. They were unique amongst their fellow Italians, as not only did the nobility enjoy good food, but also the merchants and the middle classes.

Many of the characteristics of the Renaissance are very much in evidence in Italy today. The extensive use of vegetables is still a predominant feature. Of these, spinach, broccoli, truffles, artichokes and petits pois are native to Italian soil; tomatoes, sweet peppers (pimientos) and haricot (navy) beans were introduced from the New World. As far back as the Renaissance there were pasta factories in Naples, although the Florentines insisted on making it at home, as they still do today. There is also a strong emphasis on sweets and desserts, particularly in the south.

These last two examples introduce the most important aspect of Italian cuisine – that it is strongly regional in character. This is because Italy did not become a united nation until 1861. Although one can pinpoint common characteristics between regional cuisines, it is essential to look at each region in order to understand the cuisine of the country as a whole. Regional differences create a fascinating national cuisine that has immense variety, character and colour.

Regional Cooking

Each area has its own distinctive cuisine, owing to geographical and historical differences between the regions. In addition to this, there is a marked difference between the north and south. Regions in the north tend to be more industrial and more prosperous than those in the south, and the northern soil tends to be more fertile.

The most obvious differences as far as cooking is concerned are that the pasta eaten in the north is usually the flat variety, freshly made with eggs; the fat used for cooking is generally butter. In the south, manufactured tubular varieties of pasta are more common and olive oil is used for cooking. Flavours are stronger in the south, where herbs and aromatics predominate, especially in sauces and pizza toppings.

Piemonte & Valle d'Aosta

Literally translated, *piemonte* means 'at the foot of the mountains', and it is true to say that the Western and Central Alps, which dominate the north-west frontier of Italy, have made their mark on the cuisine of the region. Not all of the region is mountainous, however, as the mountains give way to hills, plains and cities. These also influence Piedmontese cooking, and the cuisine can be described as one of contrasts, from the more simple rustic mountain fare, through to the more sophisticated style found in the capital of Turin.

High in the mountain areas that border France and Switzerland, food is hearty and substantial to combat the long severe winters. Stews and casse-

BELOW LEFT: **Piedmontese cattle grazing in Val Ferret, which borders on Val d'Aosta. In this area cattle are bred primarily for their milk which is used to make the popular creamy cheese** *fontina*

roles are highly seasoned and garlic is a favourite ingredient; so too is cheese, which is always a predominant feature of sub-alpine cooking. The best-known cheese of the area is *fontina*, a rich, creamy cheese made with milk from two special breeds of local cattle. It is used extensively in cooking, but is best known for its inclusion in the famous Piedmontese dish *Fonduta* (see page 46). Truffles are also found in the mountain areas of Piemonte and occupy a prominent position in the cuisine of the area. They are the rare white variety and are considered to be a great delicacy. The most highly coveted ones come from the forest around Alba.

Game also features extensively in everyday Piedmontese cooking, as well as in the sophisticated restaurants of Turin. Most highly prized is the chamois or wild mountain antelope, whilst wild goat, white hare and wild boar are also to be found. These rare game are seldom eaten outside the mountain areas where they are caught, although pheasant and partridge are enjoyed elsewhere in the region.

As the mountains give way to hills and plains, dishes become less homely and bread changes from coarse rye to white. One of the better known specialities of this part of the region is *Bagna caôda* (see page 46) – a 'hot sauce' of oil, garlic and anchovies, into which raw vegetables are dipped. There are numerous variations of this regional speciality, although originally it was used as a dip for the Piedmontese delicacy, *cardo* or cardoon, an edible white thistle that is cultivated in the area.

Another characteristic feature of the hills is the abundance of vineyards. The climate is milder and the soil is richer here than in the mountains, making the area one of the greatest wine-producing regions of Italy. Piemonte is famous for its robust red wines – Barolo, Barbera, Barbaresca and Nebbiolo being perhaps the best known. Vermouth and sparkling white wine take the place of red wines around Turin and on the plains of the region. Italian vermouth was produced commercially in Turin in the 18th century, although it had been drunk for its supposed medicinal properties as far back as the Middle Ages. Nowadays there are vast factory complexes in and around Turin for the manufacture of Italian vermouths, such as Cinzano and Martini, and the celebrated sparkling white wine Asti Spumante.

The plains of Piemonte also produce rice for the region's numerous rice dishes As the streams flow down from the mountains they are used to irrigate the paddy fields, which make the Po valley the greatest rice-producing area in Italy. This whole area is rich and fertile and vegetables such as asparagus, celery, artichokes, peppers and onions flourish. Tench, carp and frogs are caught in the streams that serve the rice fields.

Turin itself, the industrial capital of Piemonte, is probably best known for its vermouth, pâtisserie, confectionery and *grissini* – those thin crisp bread sticks found in Italian restaurants all over the world. Turin has also had a significant influence on the cuisine of Italy as a whole; in the days before Italy was united in 1861, the aristocrats at the court of Turin were rich and powerful, with sophisticated tastes in food. Over the centuries, this sophistication has spread throughout the region. Even the cuisine of France bears evidence of Piedmontese influence, for several French dishes are described 'à la piémontaise'!

Liguria

Often called the 'Italian Riviera', this narrow stretch of land between the Ligurian Sea, the French Alps and the Appenines, is rich in natural resources, and the Genoese people use them to the full. The fish and shellfish from the sea, combined with the herbs and vegetables from the land, result in a cuisine that is considered by many connoisseurs of Italian food to be amongst the best.

The region has a long and successful maritime tradition, centred upon the port of Genoa. Fish is, of course, a staple food and the sea provides an abundance of different varieties. Many of these are unobtainable outside the Mediterranean waters, and for this reason Ligurian fish dishes tend to be difficult to imitate in other countries. Local fish include anchovies, sardines, whitebait, cuttlefish, squid and *datteri di mare* – a variety of mussel shaped rather like a date. These are used to make bouillabaisse-type fish soups or stews, such as *burrida* and *zimino*, or served deep-fried as a starter.

Fresh vegetables and herbs have always featured prominently in the cuisine of the region; many people believe this stems from the days when the sailors craved for fresh green produce during their long sea voyages. Unlike the Venetians, Genoese sailors never used the exotic spices of the East which they transported in their holds. Whether this was because they did not like the flavours, or because they realized these spices were far too valuable a commodity to use themselves, remains open to question. To this day the Genoese cuisine still relies quite heavily on locally grown herbs.

Many herbs are used in Ligurian dishes, including rosemary, marjoram, sage, thyme, oregano, dill and the flat-leaved variety of parsley, but it is the sweet, distinctive flavour of freshly picked basil that characterizes Ligurian cooking. This herb is used extensively in the cooking of the area, but is perhaps best known for its inclusion in *pesto* – the classic Genoese sauce. *Pesto* appears in many different forms throughout the region, although its basis is usually basil, olive oil, garlic, Parmesan and *pecorino* cheese. The ingredients are pounded together to make a thick paste, using a pestle –

hence the name *pesto*. The Ligurians serve *pesto* with the pasta *trenette* (see page 64), with a potato gnocchi called *trofie*, and on top of their minestrone soup.

Minestrone is another speciality of this region and, despite the fact that it is served all over Italy and most regions have their own version, it is the Genoese who claim to have created it in the first place. *Minestrone alla genovese* is a thick soup made with rather more vegetables than other versions, and pasta rather than rice.

Veal is a popular meat in the region and one veal speciality – *Cima alla genovese* (see page 127) has become one of the most celebrated of all Italian dishes. *Cima* is breast of veal rolled around a stuffing of offal (variety meats), vegetables and nuts, although the choice of stuffing ingredients depends very much on what is to hand. Beef is sometimes used instead of veal.

Another well-known regional speciality is *Sardenaira* (see page 95), a kind of pizza made with onions, tomatoes, anchovies and olives. The Ligurians pride themselves on their abundant green olives which are often pressed locally to yield a thick, green olive oil. This imparts a distinctive aroma and flavour to the majority of Ligurian dishes.

It must not be forgotten that Liguria is reputed to be the birthplace of ravioli. Legend has it that these pasta envelopes were made to enclose leftovers for the sailors on board ship, in the hope that they would not be able to identify what was inside. True or not, it seems a fair explanation for their invention. The ravioli of today doesn't usually rely so heavily on leftovers for its filling. *Ravioli Genovese* (see page 65) can be stuffed with numerous delicacies, including lean veal or pork, sweetbreads, cheese, freshly chopped herbs and mushrooms.

Lombardy

The large region of Lombardy stretches from the Alps in the north to the Po valley in the south. It is the size of the region, coupled with the varied landscape, that gives the cuisine of the area a rich diversity that is almost unequalled elsewhere in Italy. There are many outstanding culinary specialities, particularly in and around the city of Milan.

One of the main features of the cuisine is slow cooking. Stewing, pot roasting, simmering and braising are preferred to faster cooking methods, with the result that meat served in Lombardy is usually tender and succulent, having been cooked for hours in thick, flavoursome sauces. Modern stoves and fuels have obviously accelerated the old-fashioned methods of cooking, but the principle of slow cooking still holds good today.

The region is a fertile one and provides lush pasture land for grazing the excellent dairy herds and beef cattle of the region. Oil is rarely used as a cooking fat in Lombardy, due no doubt to the abundance of locally churned butter. Veal is the preferred meat in the region, with beef the second favourite. There are numerous local recipes using both these meats, particularly rich stews and casseroles containing plenty of herbs, tomatoes and sometimes wine. Typical of such dishes is the regional speciality *Ossibuchi alla milanese* (see page 128), which is traditionally served with the classic *Risotto alla milanese* (see page 88). Controversy surrounds another local dish – *Costelette alla milanese* (see page 128) – a cutlet of veal which is coated in egg and breadcrumbs, then fried until crisp and golden brown. It is very similar to the famous Austrian *Wiener schnitzel*, but whether the Austrians copied the Milanese or vice versa, is open to question.

In southern Lombardy the Po valley yields good quality rice, which forms the staple cereal throughout the region, except in the Alpine districts of the north, where polenta is more common. Along with Piemonte, Lombardy is the home of the risotto, and almost every Lombardian housewife has her own special way of making it. *Risotto alla milanese* is justifiably famous all over the world, for its distinctive flavour and creamy texture.

Vegetables are also grown in Lombardy and these play an important part in the cuisine of the region. Vegetable soups are typical regional fare, as is the vegetable dish *Peperonata*, a mixture of sweet peppers (pimientoes), tomatoes and onions. This is often served hot with roast or grilled (broiled) meat. It can also be served chilled as an antipasto.

The Lakes – Lugano, Como, Iseo and Garda – provide many varieties of freshwater fish, most of which are only eaten locally. The eel, bass and *alborello* deserve a mention. Lombardy is also noted for its smoked meats, sausages and salamis. Exported varieties include salami from Brianza, goose sausage from Lemellina, liver mortadella from Valtellina and the spiced, smoked meats from Cremona – which is also famous for its *mostarda di frutta* (fruit pickle).

The best known cheeses of the region are undoubtably *Gorgonzola* and *Bel Paese*, but there are numerous other local ones – particularly *stracchino* and *grana* cheeses.

Two of Italy's most famous export products from Lombardy are Campari and *panettone*. The fashionable apéritif, Campari, was first concocted by Caspare Campari in the late 19th century, and the Campari family have been manufacturing it on an increasingly large scale ever since. The Milanese *panettone* is a delicious rich yeast cake containing candied fruit. Traditionally it is eaten at Christmas, but nowadays *panettone* is often served with coffee throughout the year. At Easter it is also made in the shape of a dove and called *Colomba*.

RIGHT: **Harvesting in Lombardy. In many parts of rural Italy oxen are still used as working animals**

Trentino–Alto Adige

Sandwiched between Austria and Switzerland to the north, Lombardy to the west and Veneto and Friuli-Venezia Giulia to the south and east, this is a region of many contrasts. Northern Alto Adige is just south of the Tyrol and the Brenner Pass through the Alps, so it is hardly surprising to find that the cuisine is strongly Germanic in character. The whole of Trentino-Alto Adige was once in the hands of the Austro-Hungarian Empire, and this too has left its mark.

In true German tradition, pork and pork products feature prominently amongst the specialities of the area, and the art of preserving meat has a long tradition here. Smoking and curing processes are often closely guarded family secrets and individual 'recipes' are passed down from one generation to another.

Another characteristic of this region is the number of dishes which contain *canderli* or *knoedel* (see page 89). These are a type of *gnocchi* (or dumpling) usually made with bread and any other ingredient which happens to be at hand – bacon, liver, spinach or brawn, for example. *Canderli* are served dry, or added to soup to give extra bulk, or served in goulash, which is another popular local dish.

In Alto Adige sour flavours are common. Sauerkraut and similar cabbage dishes like *Cavolo rosso alla bolzanese* (see page 160) are popular, so too is the condiment *kren* – or horseradish. The combination of sweet and sour flavours also appeals to the northern palate, and sweet sauces are often served with roast meats.

The southern part of the region, centred around the town of Trento, is more Italian than the north, being influenced by the neighbouring region of Veneto. Polenta is common fare here, but whereas Italian polenta is usually made of maize and thus yellow in colour, the polentas of this region are often made from buckwheat and are black or grey, or mixed with potato flour which gives them an unusual texture and colour.

The lakes in this region supply numerous different species of freshwater fish, which feature prominently in the local cuisine. Tench, eel, trout, salmon trout, grayling and pike are amongst those caught. The locals usually grill (broil) or fry the fish, sometimes marinating it in lemon juice or wine vinegar beforehand.

RIGHT: **Typical restaurant front in Venice, displaying the fresh foods on its menu to entice any hungry person off the street**

BELOW: **A lone fisherman on Lake Garda. The picturesque lakeside town of Bardolino is situated in the background**

Friuli-Venezia Giulia

Occupying part of the Dalmatian coast around the port of Trieste, bordering on Austria in the north and Yugoslavia in the east, this region boasts a cuisine that is best described as varied. It has been influenced by Austro-Hungary, the Slavs and the Balkans, but the Venetian influence is perhaps the strongest of all, and the cuisine of the region as a whole is Italian.

Trieste was once the Adriatic seaport for the Austro-Hungarian Empire. Here sophistication has crept into a cuisine that in the surrounding countryside is more homely and basic, relying as it does on local produce. The people of Trieste have learnt to combine local produce and traditional fare with imported and exotic ingredients, particularly spices. They have adopted many culinary skills from the Hungarians, the Greeks and the large Jewish community in the town.

Goulash is a popular local dish, learnt from the Hungarians, of course. Called *golas* locally, it is made sweet and strong with onions, cumin and paprika. From the Greeks, the Triestines copied the idea of serving rice in soup with eggs and lemon juice – a dish similar to the Greek *avgolemono*. *Jota* (see page 52) is probably one of the most famous dishes from this region.

As is to be expected with a seaport, fish also features prominently on the menus of Trieste. Spider crabs, *datteri di mare* ('sea dates') and inkfish are caught locally.

Leaving the exotic tastes of the Triestine townspeople behind, the simple cuisine of the rest of the region provides a sharp contrast. Soups are common fare, made with local vegetables and beans. There is beef and dairy farming on the lush pastures of the Alpine slopes and the region boasts some excellent smoked sausages and hams, notably the thin *Luganega* sausage and the famous San Daniele ham.

Veneto

Stretching from the Dolomite mountains in the north, the region of Veneto has a long coastline curving around the Adriatic Sea. The illustrious port of Venice in the centre of this coastline holds the key to the cuisine of the whole area, for it was through Venice's trade with the East that wealth came to this part of Italy, together with the ingredients and culinary knowledge that have made such an indelible mark on the whole of European cuisine.

The cuisine of Veneto is remarkably uniform throughout the whole area. There is even an old Italian saying that 'the cooking of Veneto can be reduced to four basic elements – rice, beans, baccalà and polenta'. Whatever the cooking of Veneto may lack in variety – and this is debatable – it more than compensates for in its use of colour. From the brilliance of the red, green and yellow peppers to the purple-black sheen of the

aubergines (eggplants), colour is very much a predominant characteristic of the food of Veneto. The towns of the region are alive with colourful bustling markets, such as the famous Piazza San Marco in Venice, and the less renowned market squares of such towns as Treviso, Verona and Padua.

In each market square, the number of stalls and the choice of merchandise is endless. Venice is noted for its splendid fish market, where obscure Mediterranean species can be bought. Treviso specializes in local vegetables – in winter the unique Italian *radicchio*, a bitter-tasting salad vegetable, is a feature here. (See *Radicchio alla Trevisana* on page 163.) Verona sells just about everything, including the deep-fried gnocchi known as *Bombolini* (see page 180), and Padua sells bunches of courgette (zucchini) flowers which are used for making fritters, a Paduan speciality.

Rice is the staple cereal of the region and is frequently served in the form of a risotto, such as *Risotto alla sbiraglia* (see page 90). A Venetian risotto is quite unique for it has a delicious creamy taste and a rather liquid consistency known as '*all 'onda*'. Different ingredients are added to the rice for colour and flavour. Inkfish pigment makes for black rice; pork sausage, tomato and beans lend the rice a brick red or ochre colour, and milk and raisins turn it speckled white in appearance. One of the prettiest of the Venetian rice dishes is *Risi e bisi* (see page 54). Correctly made with the finest Italian rice and freshly picked green peas in spring, this dish should be the most delicate shade of pale green. The Venetians regard it as a feast for the eyes as well as the palate.

Polenta is eaten throughout Veneto, though not quite to the same extent as rice. It is this region which gave the dish its beautiful golden yellow colour, for Venetian sailors brought the first maize grains to Italy. The new grain, *gran turco*, was quickly adopted throughout most of northern Italy in preference to the ordinary flour previously used for polenta.

Beans are another food which the Venetians have imported and made their own. The common *cannellini* bean was only introduced to Italy after the discovery of America. It soon became popular and is now cultivated throughout the entire region.

Along the coast of Veneto, fish is the most important food, for the Mediterranean provides an abundant supply for locals and visitors alike. Most of the regional fish specialities originated within the port of Venice. Not surprisingly, for red and grey mullet, octopus, squid, eels and sardines are caught and brought here; so too are scampi, mussels, oysters, crabs and other lesser known varieties of fish and shellfish.

Scampi served with *Risi e bisi* is a popular local dish, but perhaps the best known of all Venice's fish dishes is *Baccalà mantecato* (see page 109). *Baccalà*, or salt cod as it is otherwise known, is popular throughout Veneto and each locality has its favourite way of serving the fish. For *Baccalà mantecato* the fish is cooked, then pounded to a creamy consistency – a method frowned upon by the people of Vicenza, who cook their *baccalà* in milk flavoured with onion, garlic, anchovies, cinnamon and other spices.

It is impossible to leave the region of Veneto without mentioning another local speciality – *Fegato di vitello alla veneziana* (see page 146). Few would wish to claim credit for creating the simple dish of fried liver and onions but the Venetians do. The delicate combination of onions and parsley cooked with wafer-thin slices of prime calf's liver bears little resemblance to the rather coarse dish of liver and onions that is frequently served outside Italy today.

Finally, we should thank the Venetians for coffee, because it was the Venetian sailors who imported the coffee bean from the East, and the Italians who taught us the art of making *espresso* and *cappucino*.

Emilia-Romagna

Situated at the top of the 'leg' of Italy, this region is divided into Emilia in the north and Romagna in the south, with Bologna the capital situated roughly in the middle. The entire region is rich in natural resources, from fertile agricultural soil and lush pastures, to the well-stocked lagoons and fishing waters of the Adriatic Sea. It is therefore not surprising that the region hosts an array of gastronomic specialities.

Bologna has become one of the most famous gastronomic centres in Italy and is frequently referred to as '*Bologna la grassa*' – 'Bologna the fat'. Within the region there are even '*mangismo*' contests to see who can eat the most; according to the records, one Enrico Busi ate 3.25 kg/$7\frac{1}{2}$ lb *tortellini al burro* in just $1\frac{1}{2}$ hours!

Probably the most famous product to come from this region is Parmesan cheese. It is made in the area just north-west of Bologna and takes its name from the town of Parma. Mature Parmesan is of course used extensively in cooking, but few people outside Italy realize that Parmesan can also be eaten as a young cheese, when its flavour is much less strong.

Parma is also famous for its raw cured ham, *prosciutto di Parma*, which is served in restaurants all over the world as a starter with melon or figs. It has a sweet flavour and a tender texture – the result of a special curing and air-drying process that takes place in the hills of the area around Parma. These hills are believed to have exactly the right climate and air for curing hams, and hams are brought from all over Italy to benefit from such favourable conditions.

Pork and pork products feature prominently amongst the specialities of the area, and the delicatessens of Bologna sell numerous different kinds of sausage. Best known amongst these is *mortadella*, a large cured sausage usually flavoured with coriander, which is sometimes simply called 'Bologna sausage'. *Mortadella* is most frequently eaten cold, sliced very thinly, but it is also used in cooked dishes, such as *Fave stufate* (see page 163). *Zampone* is another well-known sausage: a speciality of Modena, it is the foot of a pig with the bone removed and replaced by a stuffing of minced (ground) and spiced pork. Originally this sausage had to be boiled before eating, but nowadays most Italian specialist shops and delicatessens sell it as *zampone lampo*, either partially or totally pre-cooked. *Cotechino* is the same as *zampone*, except that it is not encased in a pig's foot, but in a conventional sausage skin.

Emilia-Romagna is also renowned for its egg pasta, *tortello*. The varieties are numerous and the same basic dough is used to create such well-known shapes as *tagliatelle, stricchetti, cappelletti, garganelli, anolini, lasagne* and *tortellini*. The pastas of Emilia-Romagna are almost always served with a *ragù* (meat sauce). Varieties such as *cap-*

BELOW: **Vineyards and olive groves on the fertile hillsides and plains of Tuscany**

pelletti and *tortellini* have a filling of minced (ground) meats, vegetables, cheese, eggs, herbs and spices, etc. The famous *ragù bolognese*, served with the *tagliatelle* of the region, makes one of the best known of all Italian pasta dishes.

Although meat and pasta dishes feature prominently in the cuisine of this region, fish is by no means excluded from local menus. *Brodetto*, or fish soups, and stews are popular. These contain many different kinds of fish – red mullet, eel, brill, cuttlefish and shrimps – with oil, garlic, tomatoes and parsley included for additional flavour. Another speciality of the region are the *anguille* (eels) from Comacchio in the Ferrara district. These are usually served cooked with tomatoes or tomato purée (paste) and vinegar, as in the recipe for *Anguille alla comacchiese* (see page 109). They are also served pickled in vinegar.

The local vinegar 'aceto balsamico' is a speciality in itself, for it was once valued so highly that it used to figure in the dowries of noble ladies. Delicately flavoured with herbs, this vinegar is still highly regarded today.

Tuscany

At the 'heart' of Italy lies the region of Tuscany, or *Toscana*, flanked in the north and east by the Appenine mountains. It is a region of hills, river valleys and fertile plains, and the natural produce of these feature prominently in the local cuisine. Beef, vegetables, olive oil, herbs and wine form the bulk of the Tuscan diet.

Tuscan dishes are aptly described as traditional, plain and wholesome, for food is generally served as simply as possible. Meat, for example, is more likely to be served plain rather than in a sauce. Tuscan cooking has never been influenced to any great extent by any other cuisine, and for this reason traditional peasant styles of cooking still predominate.

Nowadays, it is often said that Tuscany has only three culinary virtues – beef, beans and Chianti. Beef from the Chiana Valley to the south-east of Florence, is some of the most highly prized meat in the world. The distinctive Chianina cattle are an ancient breed with a remarkably quick growth rate – they reach

maturity and an extraordinary size before they are two years old. Chianina meat is unbelievably tender and succulent, and the steaks are famous throughout the world. Following tradition, the Florentines cook their steaks simply, over charcoal and flavoured only with olive oil, salt and pepper.

The term 'alla fiorentina' or 'Florentine' is misleading. It is often incorrectly applied to any dish that contains spinach; it should in fact be used to denote any dish that comes from Florence. Very few Florentine dishes contain spinach and it is difficult to explain this misconception.

Beef is not the only meat to be consumed in the region, although it is undoubtedly the most popular. Pigs too are reared, and there are a few local pork specialities, such as Braciole di maiale ubriache (Pork chops with fennel seeds – see page 139) and Arista di maiale alla fiorentina (Loin of pork with rosemary – see page 139). Tuscany also produces a number of sausages, salamis and cured hams; the best known of these are arezzo ham and finocchiona salame which is flavoured with fennel.

The small white beans or fagioli of Tuscany are eaten in large quantities throughout the region, appearing in different guises at almost every meal. Indeed Tuscans are frequently given the rather disparaging nickname of 'mangiafagioli' (the bean-eaters) by their fellow countrymen. The beans are served simply – in soups, starters, main courses and as a vegetable dish in their own right. In one of the most unique Tuscan recipes, Fagioli nel fiasco (Beans in a wine flask), the beans are actually cooked in an empty Chianti wine flask. The narrow stem restricts the amount of steam escaping so that the beans retain maximum flavour and aroma. When tender, the beans are left to cool in the flask, then served with olive oil, lemon juice and seasoning.

Another excellent product is the olive oil from Lucca in the north of Tuscany. Used in cooking, together with freshly picked herbs, it gives Tuscan food its characteristic aromas and unique flavours.

Chianti must be the most famous wine to come from Italy, and the familiar straw-covered Chianti bottle is one of the most recognizable wine bottles in the world.

Umbria

Just north of Rome, situated between Lazio, Marche and Tuscany, lies the tiny region of Umbria. It is the only region in the Italian peninsular without a sea coast, but as if to compensate for this, it has one of the largest lakes in the country, Lake Trasimeno. Most of the region is hilly or mountainous, so the scenery is quite spectacular, but agricultural resources are poor. The economy of the region is mostly based on rearing livestock, especially pigs.

Pork and pork products are to be found all over the region, but particularly around the town of Norcia where the black Umbrian pigs feed on acorns, chestnuts, mushrooms and truffles. The pork of Norcia is so celebrated that the Italian word *norcino* has come to mean 'pork butcher's shop'. Equally famous are the *salumi* – the sausages, hams and smoked meats that come from this area. Most everyday family meals include a dish of *salumi*.

Spit-roasting over an open fire is the favourite method for cooking fresh meat in Umbria and whole young lambs as well as pigs are cooked in this way. The renowned local speciality is *porchetta*, a whole pig stuffed with rosemary, garlic and pepper, and spit-roasted over coal embers. It is normally only served on high days and holidays.

Small game are hunted in the woods of the region; woodcock, wild pigeon, partridge, pheasant and quail being the most common species. The woods are also the home of the classic black truffles – Spoleto, Norcia and Cascia. When the truffles can be found, they are used to make the local speciality omelet, *Frittata di tartufi* (see page 104), or to impart flavour to practically any savoury dish.

Vegetables grow in the green valleys of the region, particularly along the Tiber. The wild local asparagus is considered a great delicacy, so is the white celery from Trevi. Chicory, chard, mushrooms, peas, beans and onions are also grown. Olives from Trevi are pressed to make fine quality Trevi olive oil.

Lake Trasimeno provides a variety of freshwater fish, notably *lasca* or European roach, a fish that was praised by Dante. Carp, eel and pike are found in the same lake. Locally the highly prized carp is stuffed whole with a mixture of rosemary, fennel, bacon and garlic, then spit-roasted over an open fire. Trout are caught in the streams and rivers of the region.

For such a small region, Umbria is blessed with a cuisine with a strong family tradition, and many fine dishes have come from this area. Chocolate from the capital city of Perugia makes Umbria a famous name all over the world, as does the dry white wine Orvieto. This is made from local trebbiano grapes and named after the cathedral town Orvieto.

Marche

This region is situated immediately north of Umbria, with a beautiful coastline along the Adriatic Sea. The peasant-style cuisine of Marche is similar to that of its neighbour Umbria, the most obvious difference being that Marche has a coastline, whereas Umbria does not. Excellent fish are caught along the coast of Marche, and there are numerous recipes for *brodetto*, a thick fish soup. *Brodetto all'anconetana* (see page 111) is deemed to be one of the best of these. Stockfish – cooked with onion, garlic, tomatoes, oil, pepper and pounded anchovies – are popular, and so are *datteri* ('sea dates') marinated in olive oil, vinegar, sage and garlic.

The main crop of Marche is wheat, but maize, beetroot, tomatoes, cauliflower and peas are also grown. Maize is used to make polenta and the people of Marche are almost as fond of the dish as the Venetians.

Apart from the celebration dish of *porchetta* (whole spit-roasted pig), which is said to have originated from this region, there are few other dishes of note. *Vincisgrassi* (see page 73) is an exception. A kind of lasagne with pasta made from semolina, it is believed to have taken its name from the Austrian Prince Windisch-Graetz, who came to the region in the 18th century and had *vincisgrassi* cooked specially for him. In those days the dish always contained truffles, gathered from the woods. Nowadays the dish does not include truffles, but is still considered special enough to be the traditional dish for feast days and Sundays.

Lazio

With the city of Rome at its centre, the region of Lazio, or Latium, lies in the centre of the country and together with Umbria and Marche, seems to form a natural dividing line between the north and south, both in the geographical and culinary sense.

The old adage 'all roads lead to Rome' is certainly true in the gastronomic sense. The cuisine of Rome has drawn from each of the distinctive cuisines of north and south Italy, but it has also retained a character of its own. One small example of the way in which Roman cooking is quite distinct is in its choice of cooking fat; whereas butter is used mainly in the north and olive oil in the south, in Rome lard or bacon is most common. The ancient Romans were firmly convinced that butter was only good for smearing on the delicate skins of new-born babies!

As a capital city, housing the Papal seat, Rome has absorbed many influences from other countries, and her cuisine has something of an international air about it. In the celebrated *ristoranti* of Rome one can savour dishes found in international restaurants throughout the world, but to taste true 'Roman' cooking, it is essential to eat in

BELOW: **Everyday scene in the fishing village – Marino di Campo – on the island of Elba, off the Tuscan mainland. A local fisherman weaves his lobster pot on the quayside**

the small homely *osterie* or *trattorie*. There are hundreds of these, tucked away down sidestreets and alleyways. Here the cooking is hearty, robust and highly seasoned, a far cry from the sophisticated menus of the international *ristoranti*.

The pasta of the region has a character of its own, being neither exclusively the flat type as in the north of Italy, nor the tubular variety found in the south. *Fettuccine*, a ribbon pasta, is a regional speciality; it is usually served with melted butter or a mixture of butter and cream, and always sprinkled liberally with freshly grated Parmesan cheese. Roman cannelloni is a special dish, made by rolling rectangles of flat pasta around a stuffing, rather than putting the stuffing into tubes of cannelloni as in the south. Spaghetti is eaten in large quantities, as can be seen by the number of local spaghetti recipes (see pages 74–5). Roman gnocchi are also popular, made with flour, as in the recipe *Gnocchi di semolino* (see page 92).

Local cheeses include the classic Roman *pecorino*, a sheep's milk cheese which is sharp in flavour and usually grated over cooked dishes, like the better known Parmesan. In the dairy district around the Sabine mountains, cheeses of the *mozzarella* type are made. *Provatura* is an old Roman buffalo cheese which is virtually unobtainable nowadays. Recipes including this cheese are still found on *trattorie* menus in Rome but they are more likely to be made with *mozzarella* than *provatura*. The soft ewe's milk cheese, *ricotta*, is also widely used in Roman cooking – in tarts, pizzas, pasties, cakes and biscuits (cookies).

Although pork is probably eaten more frequently, lamb is popular and spit-roasted baby lamb is a great delicacy. Another speciality of this region is *Saltimbocca alla romana* (see page 131), a delicious combination of slices of ham on slices of veal, cooked with herbs and wine.

There are vegetable dishes in abundance in Lazio, one of the most famous of which is *Carciofi alla giudea* (see page 165). A speciality of the Jewish community in Rome, this is a dish of fried artichokes, flattened out to look like large, crisp roses. As already mentioned, Roman food is highly seasoned, and the exotic spices of the East are as well liked as locally picked herbs. Onions and garlic are common ingredients, along with basil, rosemary, sage, parsley, bay leaf and mint. A classic Roman dish, *misticanza*, a kind of mixed salad, uses no less than 11 different herbs.

Abruzzi & Molise

These two central regions of Italy, each with an Adriatic coastline, are predominantly mountainous and farming is the main occupation. Modern technology has made very little impact here, and cooking has therefore remained old-fashioned, relying as it does almost entirely on local resources.

Of the few resources in the region, grain is perhaps the most important. It is made into pasta, most notably into macaroni, which is everyday fare. The local *macaroni alla chitarra*, unique to this area, is made at home on guitar-shaped frames with thin steel wires. The thick ribbon pasta is pressed through the frame, then flattened with a rolling pin and left to dry. When cooked, the macaroni is served with a meat sauce and grated cheese.

Cattle, sheep and pigs are bred, but it is pork and pork products which make the greatest impact on local cuisine. Smoked meats include hams, liver sausage flavoured with garlic and orange peel, smoked loin of pork, garlic-flavoured *mortadella*, salami and small sausages.

Goats are also reared, and *scamorza* cheese is made from a mixture of goat's and cow's milk. *Scamorza* is a soft cream cheese, varying in flavour from one district to another, according to the aromatic herbs that grow in such profusion in the

river valleys. Other local cheeses include *caciocavallo di pescocostanzo*, a highly spiced cheese with a strong flavour, and *ricotta* made from cow's or sheeps' milk.

Vegetables are grown in the fertile valleys for pimentos, aubergines (eggplants) and tomatoes are quick to ripen in the hot sun. Artichokes, celery, cabbage, chard and cauliflower are also grown, but it is the pimentos that appear in so many of the local dishes, either the sweet type, or the hot variety known locally as *diavolillo*.

Along the coast, fish takes pride of place, both in everyday menus and for festive occasions. The region has its own version of the customary *brodetto*, a fish stew flavoured with onion, garlic, tomatoes, herbs and white vinegar. This white vinegar is another local speciality; it is also used in the traditional Abruzzi dish *scapece* – fish marinated in vinegar, seasoned with saffron and fried. Octopus and cuttlefish are also popular, particularly cooked in spicy tomato sauces.

Campania

The administrative region of Campania, known to the Romans as *Campania felix*, the happy country, surrounds the Bay of Naples in the Mediterranean Sea, and includes the idyllic holiday islands of Capri and Ischia. Vegetables, fruit and vines grow in abundance and the local cuisine is full of character and colour.

Neapolitan cuisine is perhaps the best known of all Italian cuisines, for it was the emigré Neapolitans who took their pasta and pizzas around the world with them – opening Italian restaurants all over Europe and America. Indeed the familiar dishes we casually term 'Italian' are most likely to be of Neapolitan origin.

The port of Naples is the culinary capital of southern Italy, for it provides the mother cuisine which influences the style of cooking covering the entire 'foot' of Italy. The main characteristics of southern cuisine are tubular pasta, the use of olive oil for cooking and the extensive use of tomatoes

LEFT: **Typical Italian smallholding situated at the foot of the Appenines in central Italy**

and garlic – particularly in sauces. This part of Italy is considered poor, at least in relation to the north. The basic foodstuffs are often described as humble, but the Neapolitans transform them into a vast number of different dishes.

No Neapolitan meal would seem complete without a dish of macaroni or spaghetti. Both pastas were invented in the region. Although known elsewhere in Italy as *maccheroni*, macaroni is the spelling used in Naples and throughout Europe. Pasta is always served with a sauce in the south, and this invariably includes tomatoes, onions and garlic amongst its ingredients – a combination aptly described as *alla napoletana*. Similar mixtures are also known as *alla pizzaiola* and *al pomodoro* (with tomato sauce). Of course there are other sauce ingredients, including excellent clams, mussels and other shellfish.

If the region is frequently described as poor, it is probably because the Neapolitan diet does not include much meat. *Bistecchine alla napoletana* (see page 123) and a similar dish called *Bistecca alla pizzaiola* are the only two beef dishes of note to come from this area.

To compensate for the lack of meat, the Neapolitans have plentiful supplies of Mediterranean fish, including clams, mussels, oysters, mullet, sea bass, cuttlefish, anchovies, sardines and octopus. Fish is frequently served deep-fried, as in the two local specialities *fritto misto* and *fritto di pesce*, or cooked in a fish soup or stew, with tomatoes, onion, garlic and parsley.

The region is also justifiably famous for its cooking cheese, *mozzarella*. This soft cheese was originally made with buffalo milk, but as this is rarely available nowadays, ordinary cow's milk has to suffice. Naples is of course the home of the Italian pizza, although pizzas of all shapes and sizes are to be found throughout the region. *Pizza Napoletana* (see page 98), with its familiar topping of tomatoes, *mozzarella* cheese, anchovies and herbs, is perhaps the most famous. There are countless other recipes, including the well-known *Pizza Campofranco* (see page 98), with its topping of ham and cheese.

The majority of the region's dishes rely on locally grown tomatoes for both their colour and flavour. Hardly a day goes by when tomato sauce is not served with pasta or vegetables. Aubergines (eggplants), courgettes (zucchini) and pimentos are grown throughout Campania and are frequently served stuffed and baked. Other less exotic vegetables to be found in this area are beans, cauliflowers and broccoli.

Southern Italy is more than justifiably proud of its ice creams and water ices, for it is the Neapolitan Tortoni whom we have to thank for the invention of the ice cream as we know it today. Pastries, cakes and candies are popular throughout southern Italy and the towns of this region are dotted with bars and pastry shops.

Apulia & Basilicata

No geographical boundary exists between these two regions, situated at the southernmost tip of Italy, but in gastronomical terms they are quite distinct from each other. Apulia is a region of plains and arable land, with a cuisine based on pasta made from local wheat. Basilicata is mountainous, with few natural resources apart from the vine, and the usual smoked meats and cheeses normally associated with rugged landscapes.

Both regions have a seaboard, although Apulia has been blessed with a much longer coastline than Basilicata, together with the magnificent Gulf of Taranto, famous for its oyster beds. Taranto provides breeding grounds for mussels, clams and many other shellfish besides the famous oyster. Around the Gulf shellfish dishes are common, but all along the coast of both regions fish soups and stews are made with different Mediterranean fish.

The different varieties of pasta in Apulia are too numerous to mention, but they include *troccoli* (rather like the pasta made with the guitar-shaped frame in Abruzzi), *orecchiette* and *recchietelle* (ear-shapes) and *turcinielli* (spiral-shapes), as well as the

pungent sauces, such as in *Cutturiddi* (see page 135). Ginger is included in many such dishes, as the people of Basilicata have an extraordinary liking for this spice. It is even used to flavour the many varieties of local sausages. Of these, *soppressata* is undoubtedly the best known; it is a highly seasoned salami, sometimes preserved in oil.

Basilicata boasts many cheeses, including *provolone* and *caciocavallo*. *Provole*, the Apulian version of *provolone*, is sometimes smoked. Numerous soft *ricotta*-type cheeses are made in both regions and these can be sweet, salted, fresh or dried; there are also buttery cream cheeses. Cheese is sometimes used in sweet dishes, as in *Ricotta fritta* (see page 185). Sweet pastries appear at every opportunity, particularly on high days and holidays.

Calabria

Calabria forms the 'toe' of Italy, and is surrounded on three sides by sea, with Basilicata its neighbour in the north. It is predominantly a mountainous region, with very few natural resources. An extensive coastline is undoubtedly Calabria's greatest asset and locally caught fish are a dominant feature of the region's cuisine. There are *fritto misto* and numerous fish soups made with a variety of Mediterranean fish, including fresh tuna, sardines and swordfish.

In true southern tradition, the many forms of pasta are the mainstay of the local cuisine. Substantial dishes are favoured, where the pasta is layered with other ingredients and baked in the oven, as in *Sagne chine* (see page 81), a kind of lasagne with a rich *ragù*. The macaroni-types of pasta are most common to this region, and *rigatoni* is a local favourite, stuffed and baked as in *Rigatoni alle pastore* (see page 80) and *Rigatoni al forno* (see page 82). Pasta also finds its way into substantial vegetable soups, which frequently form part of Calabrian family meals; *Millecosedde* and *Licurdia* (see page 58) are examples of these.

Another typical everyday dish is *Pitta* (see page 101), a pie made with a yeast dough and filled with eggs, cheese and ham. In this recipe the filling is baked inside the dough, but the dough is also often baked on its own, then split as soon as it comes out of the oven and filled with anything that comes to hand – meat, vegetables, etc. *Pitta* made in this way is often eaten first thing in the morning, when it is called *morseddu*.

Aubergines (eggplants) and pimentos are the main vegetables grown in the region, and they can be found virtually everywhere, ripening in the hot southern sun. Pimentos range from pale yellow through to cool green and fiery red, and are even eaten at breakfast – stuffed into *pitta*. Both pimentos and aubergines (eggplants) are prepared in numerous ways, but stuffing and baking seems to be the most popular cooking method.

Although pigs, sheep and goats are reared on

more usual forms of spaghetti and macaroni. The Apulians are said to be so keen on their pasta that a 17th century legend tells how the Spaniards imposed a tax on flour to prevent the Apulians from making pasta. The Apulians were so incensed that they apparently rose up in revolt against the Spaniards, who hastily had to lift the tax. All manner of *ragù* are made to serve with the pasta: meat, fish and vegetables being added to the basic tomato sauce.

The Apulians are also very fond of savoury breads and pasties made from pizza dough. Two local specialities are *Calzone alla pugliese* (see page 100), which are literally 'little trousers' stuffed with onions, olives, anchovies and cheese amongst other things, and *Penzerotti* (see page 100), a kind of deep-fried ravioli filled with *mozzarella* cheese and tomatoes.

Meat is eaten in both regions, to a greater extent than in other parts of southern Italy. Lamb, pork, goat and small game seem more common than beef, particularly in the hills and mountains of Basilicata. Meat is generally roasted, although lamb is often served in stews and casseroles with the hills, the average Calabrian housewife provides for her family without a great deal of meat. The majority of people live on pasta, soup, vegetables and fish. The region also produces a number of local cheeses of the *ricotta* type. There is also *pecorino, provole, mozzarella* and *caciocavallo*. Pastries, cakes and other confections are popular throughout Calabria.

Sicily

Situated just three miles off the Italian mainland is the island of Sicily, the largest of all the Mediterranean islands. It is predominantly a mountainous country, with spectacular scenery and a wealth of sandy beaches.

It is the Sicilians whom we have to thank for Italian cuisine as we know it today, for it was to Sicily that the Greeks first came over 2,000 years ago, bringing with them a whole new world of culinary knowledge. Over the centuries the Greeks were followed by Romans, Byzantines, Arabs, Normans and Spaniards who all left their mark on the local cuisine, that was in turn to find itself imitated by the Romans and later other Europeans.

A cuisine with such an illustrious history must surely live up to its past, and given that mountains and volcanos do not provide a wealth of natural resources, the cuisine of Sicily is far from disappointing in this respect. It is basically a peasant style of cooking, with bread and pasta forming the staple diet, but there is nevertheless plenty of character, flavour and colour in the food, with a number of noteworthy specialities.

Many Sicilian housewives still make their own bread – a custom that is dying out in other parts of Italy – and everyday family meals usually include a portion of freshly baked bread, or a dish of homemade pasta. Most of the island's pasta dishes combine spaghetti, macaroni and other tubular varieties with a strongly flavoured sauce.

The landscape does not lend itself to stock-breeding, but a number of sheep, goats, small game and pigs ensure a limited supply of fresh and smoked meats, hams and sausages. The average Sicilian family is more likely to live off the vegetables, fruit and wheat from the land, and fish from the sea; here the Sicilians are spoilt for choice. Spring comes early so the growing season is longer than in mainland Italy; the Sicilians take full advantage of this by growing an enormous variety of vegetables, including aubergines (eggplants), pimentos, tomatoes, fennel, broccoli, pumpkin, asparagus and mushrooms.

Vegetable dishes often constitute a main meal when served together with bread, pasta or fish; such a dish is *Caponata* (see page 172). The Sicilians are also fond of combining sweet and sour flavours – a habit they are said to have acquired from the Spanish; pumpkin cooked in this way, called *Zucca all'agrodolce* (see page 172), is another

popular local dish. Groves of citrus fruit, olives and grapes can be seen all over the island; indeed Sicily is often described as a 'paradise' for the vine.

Fish is a major source of protein in the Sicilian diet, for large quantities of sardines, swordfish, tuna and grey mullet are caught locally. Shellfish is popular, so too is *baccalà* or salt cod. There are a large number of fishing ports dotted around the coast, and the tuna fishing industry is particularly important to the island's economy. Local fish specialities include *Sarde a beccafico* (Marinated sardines – see page 114) and *Agghiotta di pesce spada* (Swordfish with tomatoes and olives – see page 115); the latter being a type of fish stew.

When it comes to the dessert course, the Sicilians excel themselves, for ices, pastries and gâteaux are their forte. The famous ice cream cake, *Cassata Siciliana* (see page 37) and *Zabaione* (see page 186) are both of Sicilian origin. Ice creams made with fresh fruit or fruit juice, such as *Mantecato di pesche* (see page 186), are popular too. The Sicilians are equally proud of their pastries, although some credit for these is due to their Saracen invaders, who introduced such delicacies to the island way back in the 9th century.

Sardinia

The second largest of the Mediterranean islands, Sardinia faces the Bay of Naples but it is situated some distance from the mainland, and only a few miles south of the French island of Corsica. Sardinia is a hilly country, with rolling plains and a rocky coastline. The distance from the mainland has helped to keep the island's ancient customs and cooking techniques intact, but centuries of foreign colonization have left their traces on the local cuisine. The Phoenicians arrived over 2,000 years ago and were followed by a succession of Arabs, Africans, Spanish, Romans and Piedmontese, all of whom have affected the Sardinian style of cooking.

The majority of Sardinians are peasant farmers working on the land, or tending their flocks of sheep, and cooking is still basically peasant-style. Meat is more plentiful in Sardinia than Sicily, and the favourite Sardinian way to cook it is in the open air over a spit. This method is called *a furia furia*, and whole lambs, goats and sucking pigs (called *porceddu*) are spit-roasted in this way. Another similar method of cooking whole young animals is *carraxiu* or 'roast-in-the-hole': the meat is cooked between layers of myrtle leaves, on a bed of glowing embers and covered by more glowing embers. For celebrations such as feast days and weddings, large animals are often stuffed with smaller ones, which in turn are stuffed with game birds of various sizes until as many as five different meats are roasted together as one. Wild boar, hare and game birds such as partridge, quail and thrush are all hunted locally.

Fish is as important to the Sardinians as meat, if

ABOVE: **The old fishing harbour of Cefalu in Sicily**

not more so, for there are plentiful supplies of sardines, swordfish, tuna, eel and shellfish – the local lobster being particularly good. Around the coast, one finds numerous recipes for *Cassola* (see page 117), the Sardinian version of fish stew; there is also a delicacy known as *buttariga*, which is the compressed dried eggs of mullet or tuna fish, eaten as a starter with olive oil and lemon juice.

Inland, more frugal meals of bread and local cheeses sustain the Sardinian farmers. The bread will invariably be *carta di musica* (music paper), a very thin crisp bread which makes a crackling sound when broken, hence its name. Local cheeses are usually made with sheep's milk; *pecorino* and various kinds of *ricotta* being the most common.

Little cheese puppets and animal figures, known as *gioghittus de casu*, originally made for the local children, have proved such a tourist attraction that they are now made almost exclusively for visitors to the island.

Ravioli, macaroni and spaghetti are the most popular varieties of pasta on the island. The Sardinians have their own version of ravioli called *Culingiones* (see page 85), which can be made with any number of different fillings. Other typical everyday dishes include hearty vegetable soups, such as *Minestra di farro* (see page 58) and *Minestra di fave* (see page 58), and *Favata* (see page 141), a substantial casserole of beans with sausage and spices

Introduction:Regional Cooking/23

Special Ingredients

It is not necessary to invest in a whole storecupboard of special ingredients to cook *alla Italiana* but certain basic items are required. Delicatessens and good supermarkets stock an ever-increasing number of Italian products, and most essential ingredients can be bought at these, or a simple substitute can be used. To obtain an authentic flavour, however, it is best to use the exact ingredient wherever possible; less common ingredients can usually be obtained from Italian specialist shops.

Herbs

Herbs are an important flavouring in Italian cooking and fresh ones are normally used, because most Italians either grow their own or have easy access to fresh herbs. In the winter months home-dried herbs are used. Herbs can be grown easily in pots on the windowsill or in the garden – they should be picked in the summer at the height of the growing season, then either stored in the freezer or hung up to dry in a cool, airy place, away from damp. Once dry, they should be stored in airtight containers.

Basil *Basilico*
There are numerous varieties of this spicy, aromatic herb, but sweet basil and bush basil are the most common. It is used mostly in dishes that contain tomatoes, and in salads, soups and on pizzas. Freshly chopped basil should be used whenever possible, as dried basil makes a poor substitute. If buying dried basil, however, always choose the sweet kind; its flavour is much less pungent than other varieties.

Bay Leaves *Lauro*
Bay leaves are used as a flavouring for casseroles, soups and sometimes roasts.

Borage *Borragine*
Borage has a flavour not unlike cucumber. It grows all over Italy, and is used both as a flavouring and as a vegetable. Ravioli is stuffed with borage in Genoa. Borage leaves are also served like spinach or dipped in batter and deep-fried as fritters.

Fennel *Finocchio*
Fennel is used in three ways in Italian cooking. The bulb, known as Florence fennel or *finocchio*, is used whole, sliced or quartered as a vegetable, and either braised or baked au gratin. It is also chopped raw in salads. Wild fennel stems (*finocchiella*) and the frondy leaves, which have the slightly bitter tang of aniseed, are used in cooking to flavour sauces, particularly in fish and sometimes pork dishes. They are also chopped and added to mayonnaise, eggs and cold fish dishes. Fennel seeds are a common flavouring in spiced sausages and other cooked meats, *Finocchiona salame* being the best known of these.

Juniper *Ginepro*
The berries of the juniper bush are used in pork and game dishes and in marinades. If they are to be included in a dish such as a stuffing they should always be crushed first. Use juniper berries sparingly as their flavour can be bitter if used in too large a quantity.

Marjoram, Sweet *Maggiorana*
This herb is sometimes used in soups, stews, vegetable and fish dishes. If necessary it can act as a substitute for origano.

Marjoram, Wild
SEE **Oregano**.

Myrtle *Mirto*
The Sardinians make full use of myrtle to flavour meats, particularly when spit-roasting young animals. This herb is used elsewhere in Italy, but not to the same extent.

Oregano *Origano*
This is also known as wild marjoram. It is an essential ingredient in many Italian dishes, including pizzas, sauces and casseroles, but its flavour differs slightly from one region to another.

Parsley *Prezzemolo*
Italian parsley is the flat-leaved variety as opposed to the curly 'moss' variety common in Britain and the United States. Flat-leaved parsley can usually be found at continental stores, where it is often called 'continental parsley'. Its flavour is far more pungent than curly parsley, and for this reason it is generally used as a flavouring in Italian dishes rather than as a simple garnish. For Italian recipes where parsley is specified, try to obtain the flat-leaved variety; other parsley can be used as a substitute, but the flavour of the finished dish will not be quite the same.

Rosemary *Rosmarino*
The Italians are very fond of flavouring lamb and sucking pig with rosemary. It is also used liberally in soups and stews. However it is wise to treat this herb with a little caution, since its distinctive flavour can easily overpower ingredients with more subtle flavours.

Sage *Salvia*
Sage is commonly used in liver and veal dishes.

Spices and Seasonings

Spices have been used in Italy since Roman times, when if anything they were used to excess, drowning the flavour of other ingredients. Nowadays spices are used in smaller quantities but they are present in many dishes. The following list describes those spices most frequently used in Italian recipes.

ABOVE: **Selection of typical Italian ingredients: cherries, dried tomatoes, peppers, marjoram, quince, salsiccia, mozzarella, grapes, garlic, chilli peppers, figs, oranges, lemons, paprika, Ciro–Sicilian wine, olives and chestnuts.**

Cinnamon *Canella*

Ground cinnamon is mostly used in sweet dishes, although it is occasionally added to meat dishes.

Coriander *Coriandolo*

Crushed coriander seeds are used in various meat dishes, particularly lamb and pork.

Ginger *Zenzero*

This spice is rarely used in Italian cooking, except in the region of Apulia and Basilicata in southern Italy, where it is very popular.

Nutmeg *Noce moscata*

The Italians are fond of this spice, both in sweet and savoury dishes. Ground nutmeg has none of the fresh flavour and aroma of the freshly grated kind, therefore whole nutmegs should be bought and grated directly into the dish at the time of cooking. Nutmeg is a common ingredient in ravioli and dishes which contain spinach or cheese.

Pepper *Pepe*

Black peppercorns should always be used. Grind them fresh at the time of cooking or serving; never use ready-ground pepper.

Saffron *Zafferano*

This is used mostly in risotto and in fish soups and stews. Saffron is very expensive and therefore used sparingly. Saffron threads are probably the easiest and most economical way of using saffron: they should be steeped in a little warm water until the colour and aroma are extracted; the water should then be strained and added to the dish.

Salt *Sale*

Sea salt is used throughout Italy. Coarse sea salt rather than table or cooking salt is the type to use.

Vanilla *Vaniglia*

Vanilla is a popular flavouring in sweet dishes, and vanilla sugar sold in sachets is frequently used with ordinary sugar to give flavour to cakes and

pastries. The Italians use vanilla pods (beans) rather than essence (extract).

Pulses (Legumes)

The Italians use pulses (*legumi secchi*) in cooking, dried *borlotti* and *cannellini* beans being the most common types. All pulses (except lentils) should be soaked in cold water overnight, then rinsed well before use. For convenience, canned Italian beans are now becoming widely available. They are more expensive than the loose variety, but they do cut down on soaking and cooking times. Their tenderness is also guaranteed – something which cannot be relied upon with loose dried beans. If these are old, they will never become tender, no matter how long they are soaked or cooked. For this reason, always buy pulses from a shop which has a quick turnover.

Borlotti

These are dried beans from the same family as red kidney beans. They vary in colour considerably, from pale pink to dark red, but are always speckled in appearance. They can be bought fresh in Italian specialist shops, or ready-cooked in cans from good supermarkets and delicatessens. The latter are preserved in brine and should be rinsed well before use, when they only need heating through. Red kidney beans, which are more widely available outside Italy, can always be used as a substitute for *borlotti*.

Cannellini

Cannellini are probably used more than any other dried beans in Italian dishes, and any recipe that calls for 'dried beans' invariably means the elongated, small white *cannellini*. They are like a smaller version of dried white haricot (navy) beans, which can always be used as a substitute if *cannellini* are difficult to obtain. Cannellini are available ready cooked in cans like *borlotti*.

Chick Peas (Garbanzos) *Ceci*

The Italians use chick peas (garbanzos) in thick soups with other pulses and pasta or rice. They are also traditionally served with *baccalà* (salt fish) on Good Friday. Chick peas are available at Italian, Middle Eastern and Indian specialist shops.

Fave Secche

These are the Italian equivalent of dried broad (lima) beans and are most frequently used in soups. They are sometimes difficult to obtain, although some Greek or Arab stores stock them.

Haricot (Navy) Beans *Fagiolo Secco*

Dried white haricot (navy) beans are widely available in supermarkets. Although not strictly Italian, they can be used as a substitute in any recipe calling for 'dried beans'.

Lentils *Lenticchia*

The lentils used in Italian dishes are the green or 'continental' variety, as opposed to split or red lentils. They have an unusual earthy flavour and do not disintegrate on cooking as do some other varieties. There is no need to soak them before cooking. They are often stewed with onions, garlic and seasonings as a vegetable accompaniment to meat, and are traditional with such dishes as *bollito misto*, a dish of boiled mixed meats, and sausages such as *cotechino* and *zampone*. *Cotechino con lenticchie* is traditional at New Year. Green or continental lentils are available at Italian and Indian specialist shops, health food stores and some good supermarkets

Other Flavouring Ingredients

The following items are commonly used in Italian dishes and it is useful to keep a stock of them.

Garlic *Aglio*

Garlic is used throughout Italy, but not to quite the extent that some people imagine. Certain dishes rely heavily on garlic, such as the Genoese sauce *pesto* (see page 64), *Bagna caôda* (see page 46) from Piemonte, and the tomato sauces of southern Italy. Otherwise it is used no more in Italian cooking than in other Mediterranean countries. When using garlic, adjust the quantity according to individual taste and size of the cloves, which can vary considerably. The strength also depends on the variety and age of the garlic. Garlic sold by the kilo in continental stores is fresher than the packaged varieties sold in supermarkets, and is well worth obtaining. Purple-skinned varieties tend to be sweeter and less strong in flavour.

Mushrooms, Dried *Funghi*

These are used frequently in Italian sauces, soups, stuffings and omelets, since their flavour is quite strong and only small quantities are needed. They are convenient to use when fresh mushrooms are expensive or unobtainable – Italian cooks rely on them heavily in winter. Dried mushrooms must always be soaked for about 20 minutes in warm water before use, then drained or squeezed dry and sliced. They should be added to cooked dishes shortly before the end of the cooking time, since they lose their flavour if overcooked. Dried mushrooms called *porcini* are available at all Italian specialist shops, some good delicatessens, health food stores and supermarkets. If an Italian recipe specifies dried mushrooms it is pointless using fresh cultivated ones instead for they lack the flavour and aroma of *porcini*

Oil *Olio*

Olive oil is an essential ingredient in most Italian cooking, although vegetable oil can sometimes be used as a less expensive alternative. In northern Italy butter is used more frequently because the cattle there provide sufficient milk for butter production. In the regions around Rome in central Italy, half oil and half *strutto* (see below) is used.

In southern Italy, Tuscany and along the Ligurian coast, olive oil is the basis for cooking. The finest is said to come from Lucca in Tuscany, although some connoisseurs will argue that Trevi olive oil from Umbria is better. Sassari from Sardinia is also reputed to be good. Many of the olive oils in Italy are made locally from freshly picked olives, pressed by peasants and villagers for their own use. Italian housewives could never imagine cooking without good quality olive oil, whereas outside Italy we have to rely on commercially produced oils. Cheap olive oil is false economy; it is far better to buy the best and use it sparingly, than to buy cheap oil which has little flavour or aroma.

Pine Kernels *Pinoli*

These are taken from the seeds of the pine cone. They are small and elongated in shape, creamy white in colour. Their flavour is distinctive, quite unlike that of any other nut, and therefore it is difficult to find a substitute. The Italians are fond of using them in meat dishes, particularly game, and in sweet and sour sauces. They are also used in sweet dishes, sometimes chopped into the mixture, other times as a decoration on fancy cakes and pastries. Pine kernels are usually sold ready shelled and are available at health food shops, Italian specialist shops and some good delicatessens and supermarkets.

Strutto

Strutto is an Italian version of lard (shortening), sold in tubs in specialist shops. Most Italians would not dream of using any other kind – in fact many Italian recipes specify *strutto* in the ingredients list. It is a refined lard (shortening) with a neutral flavour, excellent for roast meats and potatoes and some cakes and pastries.

Tomatoes, Canned and Tomato Purée (Paste) *Pomodori*

Italian housewives, particularly those in the south, use large ripe homegrown tomatoes to make tomato sauce and *ragù*, and there is really no substitute for this type of tomato. It is possible to grow or buy Italian or other continental varieties in the summer months. When not available, use canned peeled plum tomatoes, with cans or tubes of tomato purée or paste, rather than fresh English tomatoes. While canned Italian tomatoes never equal their fresh counterparts, they make a very acceptable alternative in cooked dishes, and are used by Italians in the winter months.

Vinegar *Aceto*

Red or white wine vinegar is used, particularly in salads. Some meats, particularly game, are often brushed with vinegar before cooking. Malt and distilled vinegars are uncommon and never used in cooking.

Wine *Vino*

Both red and white wines are used for cooking purposes. Wine for cooking should be of the same good quality as table wine; cheap wine can ruin a dish, whereas a good wine can transform an ordinary dish into something special – this is particularly true of sauces. Barbera is an excellent red wine for use in cooking; Soave, Frascati and Orvieto are equally good whites. Dry Marsala is used a great deal in Italian food and is a traditional ingredient in veal dishes and in *Zabaione* (see page 186). *Marsalauovo* (Egg Marsala) is a very sticky dessert wine, and is not used in cooking.

Cured Meats & Sausages

Sausages, cooked meats, salami and hams are very much a feature of the local cuisine in Italy. They are eaten at different times of day, depending on the region, but they mostly appear as part of the *antipasto* course. There are countless different varieties of salami and sausage and many of them are purely local to the particular area in which they are made. The main meat products exported from Italy, including all those that are mentioned in the recipes in this book, are listed below. Some are obtainable at delicatessens and supermarkets; all are available at Italian specialist shops.

Bologna

Bologna is the capital of Emilia-Romagna and the heart of the sausage-making industry. Sausage or cooked meat referred to as *Bologna* is likely to be *mortadella*; it should not be confused with 'boloney' or 'polony' sausage, which although believed to have been a corruption of the name Bologna, is not a Roman sausage at all.

Bresàola

This is raw beef which has been salted in much the same way as *prosciutto di Parma*. It goes through a long curing process and is very expensive to buy, but there is little or no waste and therefore a little goes a long way. It is served in very thin slices as an *antipasto*, sprinkled with olive oil, lemon juice and pepper.

Coppa/Capocollo

This is a salted raw ham like *prosciutto di Parma*, but it is the shoulder (*spalla*) cut rather than the rear leg. It is just as expensive as Parma and some connoisseurs actually prefer it because its flavour is sweeter. However, it does not have such a good, uniform shape as Parma. The most highly prized *coppa* ham is *coppa di Zibello* from the village of Zibello, near Parma.

Cotechino

This is a speciality of Emilia-Romagna. It is a fresh pork sausage which should be cooked soon after purchase. *Cotechino* has a spicy flavour and is usually served sliced with lentils or mashed potatoes, *cotechino con lenticchie* being a traditional New Year's Eve dish in Rome. To cook *cotechino*, prick the sausage casing all over, then wrap in a cloth and boil for about 3 hours, depending on size. Pre-cooked *cotechino lampo* is now available; it is sold in foil vacuum packs and only needs simmering for about 20 minutes before it is ready to eat – instructions are given with each pack.

Finocchiona

A spicy salame flavoured with fennel seeds, from the region of Tuscany.

Lardo

This is the Italian pork back fat which is sold by the kilo. It is used in savoury dishes as a cooking fat and is well worth buying to give dishes an authentic 'Italian' flavour and aroma, because it is stronger than other cooking fats. It is used most often in central and southern Italy. To use *lardo*, first cut off any hard skin or rind, then dice the fat and add to the pan. When fried or simmered, *lardo* is broken down and absorbed into the other ingredients in the dish.

Luganega

SEE **Salsiccia a metro**

Mortadella

Mortadella di Bologna, also known as *Bologna* in Italy, is one of the most famous Italian sausages. The best *mortadella* is made of pure pork, but there are many variations, some with a mixture of pork and beef, others contain offal (variety meats). Spices and flavourings also vary although black peppercorns are usually included. *Mortadella* is the largest Italian cured sausage and is widely available nowadays, although the quality and flavour varies; it is best bought in specialist Italian shops. It is usually eaten cold, sliced very thinly; occasionally it is diced and used in cooked dishes.

Pancetta

This is salted raw belly of pork which is used in many Italian dishes. It is bought by the kilo in slices, then diced and fried with onions and garlic. This is used as a basis for *ragù* and soups to give extra flavour and body. It can also be used in stuffings. Italian housewives use a great deal of *pancetta*, in the same way that streaky (fatty) bacon is used in Great Britain and the United States.

Prosciutto

There are three kinds of *prosciutto* available outside Italy – boned *prosciutto di Parma* which is sold, sliced, *prosciutto di Parma* on the bone which is carved fresh when bought, and *prosciutto di San Daniele*, which is also sold on the bone. All three are similar in flavour, appearance and price, it is merely a matter of personal preference which one you choose. Parma ham on the bone is more difficult to obtain and is usually only available in the best Italian specialist shops. *Prosciutto di San Daniele* is a leaner ham, but its flavour is less sweet. All Parma hams come from the area around the town of Parma in the region of Emilia-Romagna. San Daniele hams come from the region of Frinli.

The high cost of these hams is determined by the fact that only the best quality hams are used, and the salting process is an extremely lengthy one. Certain importers will occasionally sell some hams cheaper than usual, but it is often inferior quality meat which has not been left for a sufficient length of time for the ageing process to be completed.

ABOVE: **Pork butcher's shop, known as *norcino* in Umbria. Cooked meat is often sold, as well as salami, spiced sausages and fresh meat.**

Salame

The salami of Italy are far too numerous to mention, since each region has its own speciality, most of which are unknown and unavailable outside the tiny area in which they are made. These purely local salami are known as *casalingo*, which can be roughly translated as 'homemade'. They are mostly coarse in texture and often highly spiced or seasoned. There are a few *casalingo*-type salami available outside Italy in Italian shops, and it is well worth asking for them. Two such types are *salame Napoli* and *salame Genova* – but there are others sold under different brand names.

The most common types of salami to be seen in delicatessens and supermarkets outside Italy are *salame Milano* and *salame Varzi*. *Salame Milano* is fairly large and is made of finely minced (ground) pure pork or a mixture of pork and beef with seasonings. *Salame Varzi* is coarser and more highly spiced; it comes from a village called Varzi in the Parma-Piacenza area. *Cacciatore* is a small salame, about 175 g/6 oz in weight, which is bought whole. Its name derives from the Italian word for 'hunter' because it was originally made for hunters to carry as a ready-to-eat snack.

Salamelle

SEE **Salsiccia a metro**

Salsiccia a metro

Salsiccia a metro or *luganega* is the long thin spiced sausage sold by the kilo in Italian specialist shops. In Italy, it is traditionally sold in one long piece,

hence *a metro* (by the metre). Italians either grill (broil) or fry it for lunch or supper, often with mashed potatoes or lentils. *Salsiccia a metro* is also used in Italian stuffings and other recipes which call for sausagemeat; the skin is simply cut and the meat squeezed out. *Salamelle* is often the same mixture as *salsiccia a metro*, but is sold tied in short links like our conventional sausage. It is also available in many different varieties, some of which are peppery hot. They should be grilled (broiled) or fried, but they can be boiled if preferred.

Soppressa

This is a loaf-shaped mixture of pressed cooked meats, mainly pork and brawn. It is eaten cold, thinly sliced, with other cooked meats, usually for lunch or a snack.

Soppressata

This is a speciality of the region of Apulia and Basilicata. It is fairly small in size and usually bought whole. The meat is coarsely pressed, rather than minced (ground) as for salame. It is very spicy, with a fairly high proportion of fat.

Zampone

Zampone is a fresh sausage made with the same mixture as *cotechino*, but it is stuffed into a pig's trotter rather than a conventional sausage casing. It is a fairly fatty sausage, and it is recommended to soak it in cold water overnight before making indentations in the skin at the foot end, then cooking it in the same way as for *cotechino*. It is also possible to buy pre-cooked *zampone lampo* in Italian specialist shops.

KEY

1 Prosciutto di San Daniele	9 Salame Cremona
2 Salame cacciatore	10 Pancetta di Zibello
3 Coppa di Parma	11 Cotechino
4 Luganega	12 Soppressata
5 Prosciutto di Parma	13 Bresàola
6 Salsiccia a metro	14 Mortadella
7 Zampone	15 Salame Genoa
8 Salame Napoli	16 Salame Bindone

Cheeses

Cheeses are enjoyed throughout Italy. In the northern sub-alpine regions and the plains of the Po, where the pastures are rich and lush for cattle rearing, cheeses are more likely to be made of cow's milk, whereas in central and southern Italy they are made from the milk of sheep and goats.

Many of the best Italian cheeses are the country cheeses, made locally by peasants and farmers. In most Italian villages, there is at least one shop packed with unusual cheeses rarely seen outside Italy. However, the Italians do export a large number of excellent cheeses, and it is becoming increasingly easy to obtain these in good delicatessens and supermarkets, as well as in specialist Italian shops. Listed below are the main Italian cheeses.

Asiago

From the region of Veneto, this hard cheese impregnated with small holes was originally made on the foothills of the Dolomite mountains. There are two types: *Asiago d'Allievo* is made from a combination of skimmed evening milk and fresh morning milk, then left to mature. It is piquant in flavour and suitable for grating; *Asiago grasso di monte* is a younger and therefore softer cheese, and is more often eaten as a table cheese.

Bel Paese

The name '*Bel Paese*' means 'beautiful country', for this popular cheese comes from the beautiful countryside of Lombardy. *Bel Paese* is fairly mild in flavour and soft and creamy in texture. It is most frequently used as a table cheese and provides an excellent contrast to the sharper Italian varieties. It is also a good melting cheese, and for this reason is useful in cooking, particularly as a substitute for *mozzarella*, which can be more difficult to obtain than *Bel Paese*.

Bitto

A Lombardy cheese made from both cow's and goat's milk.

Caciocavallo

This is a variety of *formaggio di pasta filata* or plastic-curd cheese, of which the better known *provolone* is also an example. It is made in Calabria by a process that involves warming the whey to a temperature that allows it to be stretched and kneaded into different shapes. It is a smooth, compact cheese with a spicy tang, and is sometimes smoked after shaping. The Italian word *caciocavallo* means 'on horseback', and the cheese is so called because it is always sold strung together in pairs, as if for carrying astride a horse.

Dolcelatte

SEE **Gorgonzola**

Fior di Latte

SEE **Mozzarella**

Fontina

A semi-hard cheese from Val d'Aosta, *fontina* takes its name from Mount Fontin near the town of Aosta. It is one of the most famous of all Italian cheeses, and many cheese connoisseurs rank it amongst the top cheeses in the world for its sweet, nutty flavour and deliciously creamy texture. Although it is classed as a table cheese, it is most often found in the celebrated Piedmontese speciality *Fonduta* (see page 46) and in other rich cooked dishes.

Gorgonzola

The blue-veined, yet mild, *Gorgonzola* is one of the most famous cheeses throughout the world. It takes its name from the town of the same name in Lombardy, where it was originally made in damp caves. These provided the right conditions for the mould to develop and mature naturally – a process that could take up to a year.

Nowadays the cheese is made in factories where, with the help of the bacteria *penicillium gorgonzola*, the whole process usually takes as little as three months. Pricking and turning the cheese in a specially controlled atmosphere also helps accelerate its ageing process.

Dolcelatte is a type of *gorgonzola*. It is mild and creamy – as its name suggests, like 'sweet milk'.

Grana

SEE **Parmesan**

Groviera

This cheese is similar in flavour and texture to the French gruyère. It is either eaten fresh or allowed to mature and used in cooking.

Manteca

SEE **Mozzarella**

Mascarpone

A fresh cheese originally from Lombardy, *mascarpone* can now be found in many other regions. It is made from fresh cream and sold in muslin bags as a dessert cheese to be served with fruit and sugar. For special occasions it is sometimes flavoured with a liqueur.

Mascarpone is also sold as a dessert cheese layered with *gorgonzola*; confusingly, this cheese is often simply called *mascarpone*.

Mozzarella

This cheese is traditionally made with buffalo's milk, but nowadays it is more frequently made with cow's milk, or a mixture of both. In its native Campania, *mozzarella* comes in many unusual shapes and it is frequently eaten fresh, when it is moist and dripping with whey. Unless it is completely fresh like this, it is only suitable for cooking, because it soon becomes dry and loses some of its flavour. It is commonly used as a topping for Neapolitan pizzas, but it can also be

fried and baked – southern Italy has countless different ways of using it. *Mozzarella* available outside Italy is often wrapped in waxed paper ready for use; it is a good quality cheese which compares favourably with the Italian varieties.

Scamorza is a similar kind of cheese to *mozzarella*, but it is rarely obtainable outside Italy. It is made with cow's milk and so has a less distinctive flavour. *Fior di latte* and *menteca* are also similar, although inferior in flavour. In cooked dishes, *Bel Paese* is the best substitute for *mozzarella*.

Parmesan

Parmesan, or *Parmigiano*, is the most famous of all the *grana* cheeses which are produced in northern and central Italy. *Grana* is simply the collective term used by Italians to describe matured hard (grainy) cheese, of which there are many different types. These cheeses are believed to have originated in Roman times. Other types of *grana* include *grana Lodigiano* (from the region of Lodi in Lombardy) and *grana padano* (from the plain of Lombardy). Only *grana* that has been made around the town of Parma can actually bear the name of *parmigiano reggiano*.

Parmesan cheese takes at least two years to come to maturity, although the flavour of a good Parmesan will improve with age. Generally the longer the cheese has been matured, the more expensive it is. During the long maturing process, usually after the first year, the cheese is often coated with a mixture of earth and oil which acts as a protective coating. The skilled cheesemaker constantly taps this coating to ascertain the quality of the cheese inside, and he knows instantly from the sound of his hammer whether the cheese is right. In Italy, fresh Parmesan or *grana* cheeses are often eaten as table cheeses, but exported Parmesan cheese is rarely of such good quality as this.

Parmesan should always be bought in a piece to be freshly grated over sauces, pasta and rice, or added to cooked dishes. Drums and sachets of ready-grated Parmesan cannot in any way compare in flavour with the freshly grated cheese.

Pecorino

This is a hard country cheese, often used instead of Parmesan for grating and cooking. Unlike Parmesan, *pecorino* is a quick-maturing cheese – it is usually ready to eat within eight months.

There are several varieties of *pecorino*, each with a slightly different flavour, texture and appearance. *Pecorino Romano* is considered to be one of the best; *pecorino sardo* is made in Sardinia, where its manufacture has become a thriving industry for the island.

When selecting *pecorino*, look for a straw-coloured, hard cheese with a compact texture and a black or reddish brown rind. The Sardinian *pecorino pepato* is speckled with black peppercorns. All make excellent grating and cooking cheeses, and are rarely eaten as table cheeses.

Provatura

This is an ancient country cheese which has almost disappeared inside Italy, and is certainly impossible to obtain elsewhere. If a recipe calls for *provatura*, substitute *mozzarella* or *Bel Paese*.

Provola

SEE **Provolone**

Provolone

Originally meaning 'large oval', *provolone* must be one of the most famous of all Italian cheeses, although this is probably due as much to its shape as to its flavour. *Provolone* is particularly familiar to tourists in Italy, for no cheese shop is complete without its quota of *provolone* suspended by their cords from hooks on ceilings. *Provolone* is another of the *pasta filata* cheeses like *caciocavallo*, and although it is still made in a simple oval shape into which the cord makes deep grooves, it is more often 'kneaded' into fanciful shapes. There are two kinds of *provolone*, both eaten as table cheeses: *provolone dolce*, which is young and mild, and *provolone piccante*, which is mature and strong. In recipes calling for *provola*, use a mild *provolone*.

Robiola

This is an alpine cheese from northern Italy, similar in type to the *stracchino* cheeses and usually sold on straw mats or in straw-lined boxes. *Robiola* is a quick-ripening, soft cheese that does not travel well and is therefore only found locally. Originally it was only made in Lombardy on the foothills of the Alps, but nowadays it is made throughout northern Italy. *Robiolina* is a smaller version of *robiola*.

Ricotta

Ricotta is a soft white cheese with a crumbly texture made from the whey of ewe's or cow's milk. It is most frequently used in cooking, both in sweet and savoury dishes, for like curd or cottage cheese its mild rather bland flavour combines well with other ingredients. There are different types of *ricotta*, from fresh ones through to salted, dried and well-matured varieties. *Ricotta* is usually fairly easy to obtain outside Italy, at least in Italian specialist shops. Curd or cottage cheese can be used as substitutes in dishes that specify *ricotta*, although the results will not be so good.

Scamorza
SEE **Mozzarella**

Stracchino
This is a generic name for a group of Alpine cheeses made in northern Italy, particularly in the regions of Lombardy and Piemonte. *Taleggio* is perhaps the best known of the *stracchino* cheeses, which are soft and quick to mature. *Gorgonzola* is also of the same family, but *stracchino* cheeses are not generally blue-veined. Most of them are not very well known outside Italy, since they mature too quickly to travel any distance, and it is therefore unusual to see them outside their place of origin. *Crescenza* is another type, a dessert cheese from Milan which is highly prized by cheese connoisseurs.

Taleggio
Another of the *stracchino* cheeses *taleggio* is named after the valley outside Milan. It is an ancient cheese like all the *stracchino* cheeses, but is little known outside Italy, since it is very quick to mature and therefore not suitable for export. It is a soft, creamy cheese and one that should be eaten as fresh as possible, otherwise it tends to become sour.

Toma
There are many Alpine country cheeses that go under the name of *toma*. Made in the region of Piemonte, they are not found outside the locality in which they are made, but are well worth searching for if visiting the region. Some of the *toma* cheeses are so sharp that they seem to burn the throat when swallowed!

KEY

1 Mozzarella	7 Emmenthal
2 Fontina	8 Robiola
3 Dolcelatte	9 Ricotta
4 Parmesan	10 Pecorino
5 Provolone	11 Bel Paese
6 Caciocavallo	12 Gorgonzola

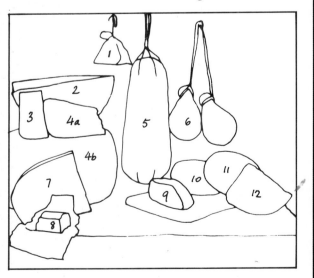

Festive Cooking

The Italians welcome any excuse for a festive occasion, and all that such an event brings in the way of special dishes. Quite apart from the universal celebrations of Christmas and Easter, the Catholic calendar also celebrates numerous feast days and Saints' days throughout the year. Special celebration feasts are served on such days, not only throughout Italy – and particularly in Rome – but also by Italians all over the world. Wine festivals are also common in many regions throughout the autumn when the grapes are harvested. Here the food eaten at the major festive occasions in the Italian year are described and traditional festive recipes from the different regions are provided.

Lent
Sweet fritters, called *fritole di Carnevale* (see page 179), are eaten the day before Lent – called Carnival Night in Italy.

St Joseph's Day March 19 ·
This festival is celebrated throughout Italy. The traditional fare on this day are *Bignè di San Giuseppe*, deep-fried puffs something between a choux bun and a doughnut. *Bignè* are usually served piled into a pyramid and sprinkled with icing (confectioners') sugar.

Easter
The Easter holiday signals the arrival of many different specialities. Fish is always eaten on Good Friday, in particular *baccalà* (salt cod), which is prepared in numerous different ways. Perhaps the best known of Easter specialities is the Milanese *Colomba Pasquale*. This is a sweet yeast cake made with a similar mixture to the Christmas *panettone*, except that *colomba* is baked in the shape of a dove and traditionally has a crust of sugar and whole almonds. Most Italians buy rather than bake it at home these days. It is available in Italian specialist shops in this country.

The reason for the cake being baked in the shape of a dove dates back to the 12th century. During a battle between the armies of Milan and the Holy Roman Empire, two doves are said to have landed near the standards of the Milanese army. The Milanese won the battle, and have venerated the two doves ever since – as a symbol of good fortune.

As in many European countries, lamb is the traditional meat at Eastertime. In and around Rome, whole baby lambs (*abbacchio*) are roasted in the open air over spits. *Capretto* – whole

Weddings, christenings and confirmations all warrant special celebration dishes in Italy, but occasions such as these are private family ones. Religious festivals throughout the year bring everyone out into the streets for the public celebrations – and Easter is one of the main events in the Italian calendar. Shop windows and stalls are crammed full with special Easter food; for Italian bakers it must be one of the busiest times of the year.

LEFT: **A baker's shop celebrating Easter in the town of Bergamo, near Milan. Loaves are baked in the shape of baskets, flowers and the symbolic doves *Columba*.**

sucking kids – are also cooked in this way at Easter.

Torta Pasqualina (see recipe below) is an Easter speciality from Genoa. It is a kind of vegetable pie made with a simple dough. The filling ingredients can be varied according to what is available, although traditionally it is made with spinach or artichokes and *ricotta* cheese. The original recipe is believed to be one of the most ancient of Ligurian recipes: the dough used to be rolled into 33 separate layers, presumably to symbolize the age of Christ at the time of his death. This has now been reduced to 18 or 14 layers, a more practical, if less symbolic, number.

The Sicilians need no excuse for a celebration feast. The famous *Cassata Siciliana* (see recipe below), was traditionally an Easter speciality, but nowadays is served at weddings and other family celebrations, as well as on high days and holidays. *Cassata Siciliana* is a chilled dessert cake made with layers of *ricotta* cheese and sponge. It should not be confused with *cassata gelata*, a Sicilian ice cream flavoured with pistachios and candied fruit.

TORTA PASQUALINA
Spinach, Cheese and Egg Pie

Metric/Imperial	American
DOUGH:	DOUGH:
575 g/1¼ lb plain flour	5 cups all-purpose flour
salt	salt
4 tablespoons vegetable oil	¼ cup vegetable oil
250 ml/8 fl oz warm water	1 cup warm water
FILLING:	FILLING:
1 kg/2 lb fresh spinach	2 lb fresh spinach
100 g/4 oz Parmesan cheese★, grated	1 cup grated Parmesan cheese★
pinch of dried marjoram	pinch of dried marjoram
9 eggs	9 eggs
400 g/14 oz ricotta cheese★	1¾ cups ricotta cheese★
salt and freshly ground black pepper	salt and freshly ground black pepper
4 tablespoons olive oil	4 tablespoons olive oil

To make the dough: sift the flour and a pinch of salt into a bowl, add the oil and enough lukewarm water to obtain a soft dough. Knead for 5 minutes until smooth, then divide into 14 equal pieces. Shape the pieces into small rolls, sprinkle lightly with flour, then cover with a clean cloth (napkin). Leave to stand for 1 hour.

Meanwhile, make the filling: put the spinach in a large heavy pan with just the water clinging to the leaves after washing. Cook until tender, drain thoroughly, then chop finely. Place in a large bowl and add half the Parmesan, the marjoram, 3 beaten eggs, the ricotta and salt and pepper to taste. Beat well.

Knead two of the rolls of dough together, then roll out into a thin sheet and use to line the base and sides of an oiled 25 cm/10 inch springform pan. Brush the dough lightly with oil. Flatten another 6 rolls into circles the same diameter as the mould, then put inside the mould, one on top of the other, brushing each one with oil. Spread the spinach mixture on top of the dough, then make 6 hollows in the surface of the mixture, using the back of a spoon. Break 1 egg into each hollow, then sprinkle with salt and pepper and the remaining Parmesan.

Flatten the remaining 6 rolls of dough, then place on top of the filling, one on top of the other, brushing each one with oil as before. Make lines on the surface of the dough with a fork, then pinch the edge to seal and brush with more oil. Bake in a preheated moderately hot oven (200°C/400°F/Gas Mark 6) for 1 hour. Leave to cool before removing from the mould. Serve cold.
SERVES 8

CASSATA SICILIANA
Chilled Cheese Dessert Cake

Metric/Imperial	American
675 g/1½ lb ricotta cheese★, sieved	3 cups ricotta cheese★, sieved
250 g/9 oz caster sugar	1 cup plus 2 tablespoons sugar
150 ml/¼ pint Maraschino liqueur (approximately)	⅔ cup Maraschino liqueur (approximately)
100 g/4 oz bitter chocolate, finely chopped	⅔ cup finely chopped bitter chocolate
200 g/7 oz mixed candied peel, chopped	1 cup chopped mixed candied peel, firmly packed
400 g/14 oz 'pan di Spagna' (sponge cake), cut into 1 cm/½ inch thick slices	14 oz 'pan di Spagna' (sponge cake), cut into ½ inch thick slices

Put the ricotta in a bowl with the sugar, 7 tablespoons liqueur, the chocolate and candied fruit. Stir well.

Line a tall 1.5 litre/2½ pint mould with foil, then sprinkle with a few drops of liqueur. Dip the cake in more liqueur, then use three-quarters of the cake to line the bottom and sides of the mould. Spoon in the ricotta mixture and level the surface. Put the remaining cake on top of the ricotta mixture, pressing down well. Cover with foil and tie firmly around the top edge of the mould.

Chill in the refrigerator for at least 2 hours, then unmould onto a serving platter and remove the foil. Serve chilled.
SERVES 4

St John's Eve Midsummer Night – 24 June
Snails are the traditional food in Rome for this occasion that celebrates the birth of St John the Baptist. The Romans observe the custom by serving snails in a sauce of tomatoes, garlic, olive oil, mint, onion and chilli.

Festa di Noantri July
This festival, which literally translated means 'Our Festival', is celebrated in the famous Trastevere quarter of Rome. It lasts for a whole week, and was created by the celebration-loving Romans exclusively for themselves. The streets are lined with stalls selling *porchetta*, whole spit-roasted pig. Usually the pig is rubbed with a mixture of wild fennel, garlic, rosemary, nutmeg, mulled wine, salt and lots of pepper, then brushed with olive oil and roasted on the spit. Dry white wine is used to baste the pig during cooking, and pine and oak branches are placed on the fire to give the cooked meat a wonderful aroma and flavour. It is served sliced and often sandwiched between slices of bread.

Christmas
Traditional Christmas celebrations start on Christmas Eve; the custom is to eat fish, *baccalà* (salt cod) or eels being most popular. *Capitone* eels from Grosseto in Tuscany, or eels from Comacchio in Emilia-Romagna, are considered to be the greatest delicacy for this occasion.

The Christmas Day feast begins with an antipasto; this is invariably followed by *tortellini* (see recipe opposite) – the traditional pasta for Christmas. *Tortellini* are always served stuffed – with anything from minced (ground) meats, ham and sausage to cheese. Some Italian housewives make a batch of stuffing to use for both the *tortellini* and the capon or turkey on Christmas Day. There are several ways of serving *tortellini*, but at Christmastime it is customary to serve them *in brodo* – in a clear broth like consommé.

Roast stuffed capon is the traditional main course (see recipe opposite), although more and more modern Italian cooks are taking to serving turkey. Stuffings vary considerably, but minced (ground) pork, giblets, sausagemeat and bread are usually included, together with grated Parmesan cheese. For the evening meal, particularly in northern Italy, boiled meats (*bollito misto*) are traditional, and they are usually served with *mostarda di frutta*, the famous pickled fruit from Cremona in Lombardy. The best known of all Christmas specialities is of course *panettone*, a rich yeast cake which contains dried fruit, candied peel and sometimes pine nuts. Commercial bakers in Milan make *panettone* for shops and restaurants all over Italy at Christmas; they also export it abroad in large quantities. In northern Italy, *panettone* does not confine itself to Christmas these days, for some Italians eat it thoughout the year at breakfast or with coffee in bars. On Christmas morning, one tradition is to serve it with mugs of hot chocolate – the idea is to dunk it into the chocolate.

BELOW: **A tempting array of festive dishes prepared for an Italian family celebration. Foods include salami, parma ham and olives for an antipasta; stuffed pasta, stuffed roast meat, vegetables and fruit.**

Torrone is a traditional sweet at Christmastime. A nougat-type confection made of ground almonds or other nuts, butter, sugar, biscuits (cookies) and sometimes chocolate, *torrone* is said to be of Lombardian origin, although the Sicilians also lay claim to it and there is even evidence that, like most nougats, it is of Saracen origin.

New Year

New Year celebrations include eating *cotechino con lenticchie*, a dish of spiced pork sausage, boiled, sliced and served with lentils. *Panettone* is also eaten over the New Year period, but *pan pepato di cioccolato* is the traditional New Year cake. From the Emilia-Romagna region, it is a sweet yeasty bun made with honey, almonds and spices, and is often served topped with a chocolate icing.

CAPPONE FARCITO AL FORNO

(Stuffed Roast Capon)

Metric/Imperial	American
1 capon, weighing 2.5 kg/ 6 lb	1 capon, weighing 6 lb
2 tablespoons olive oil	2 tablespoons olive oil
STUFFING:	STUFFING:
225 g/8 oz lean pork	½ lb lean pork
150 g/5 oz salsiccia★	5 oz salsiccia★
100 g/4 oz chicken breast meat	¼ lb chicken breast meat
100 g/4 oz chicken livers	¼ lb chicken livers
2 thick slices of white bread, crusts removed	2 thick slices of white bread, crusts removed
75 g/3 oz smoked streaky bacon, chopped	4 smoked fatty bacon slices, chopped
1 bunch of parsley, finely chopped	1 bunch of parsley, finely chopped
50 g/2 oz Parmesan cheese★, grated	½ cup grated Parmesan cheese★
1 egg, beaten	1 egg, beaten
pinch of dried marjoram	pinch of dried marjoram
salt and freshly ground black pepper	salt and freshly ground black pepper
1 wine glass of dry Marsala (approximately)	1 wine glass of dry Marsala (approximately)

To make the stuffing: put the pork, salsiccia, chicken, livers, bread and bacon twice through the fine blades of a mincer (grinder). Add the parsley, cheese, egg, marjoram and salt and pepper to taste. Beat well to mix, then add enough Marsala to bind the mixture together.

Stuff and truss the capon, then place on an oiled rack in a roasting tin (pan). Brush all over the capon with olive oil and sprinkle liberally with salt and pepper. Cover the capon with foil, then cook in a preheated moderately hot oven (200°C/400°F/Gas Mark 6) for 2 to 2¼ hours until tender, turning halfway through cooking.

Serve hot, with the strained cooking juices.
SERVES 8

TORTELLINI ROMAGNOLI

(Tortellini with Turkey Filling)

At Christmas in Italy, tortellini are usually served in brodo, i.e. floating in beef or chicken broth like a soup. If you prefer, tortellini can also be served with melted butter and grated Parmesan or in a ragù rather than in brodo, but this will make them more of an everyday dish, not a Christmas speciality.

Metric/Imperial	American
PASTA:	PASTA:
400 g/14 oz plain flour	3½ cups all-purpose flour
salt	salt
4 eggs, beaten	4 eggs, beaten
FILLING:	FILLING:
25 g/1 oz butter	2 tablespoons butter
350 g/12 oz turkey breast meat, roughly chopped	¾ lb or 1½ cups roughly chopped turkey breast meat
50 g/2 oz ricotta cheese★	¼ cup ricotta cheese★
50 g/2 oz Bel Paese cheese★, grated	½ cup grated Bel Paese cheese★
25 g/1 oz Parmesan cheese★, grated	¼ cup grated Parmesan cheese★
finely grated rind of ½ lemon	finely grated rind of ½ lemon
2 eggs, beaten	2 eggs, beaten
pinch of grated nutmeg	pinch of grated nutmeg
salt and freshly ground black pepper	salt and freshly ground black pepper
TO SERVE:	TO SERVE:
750 ml/1¼ pints hot beef or chicken stock, or 25 g/1 oz melted butter and 75 g/ 3 oz Parmesan cheese★, grated	3 cups hot beef or chicken stock, or 2 tablespoons melted butter and ¾ cup grated Parmesan cheese★

To make the pasta: sift the flour and a pinch of salt onto a work surface, then make a well in the centre. Add the eggs and mix together to form a smooth dough. Shape into a ball, wrap in a damp cloth then leave to stand for about 30 minutes.

Meanwhile, make the filling: melt the butter in a heavy pan, add the turkey and cook over moderate heat for 15 to 20 minutes. Mince (grind) the mixture, then combine it with the remaining filling ingredients.

Flatten the dough with a rolling pin and roll into a thin sheet. Cut into 5 cm/2 inch rounds with a rotary cutter or pastry cutter. Put a little filling in the centre of each circle, then fold the dough over the filling into a semi-circle. Wrap this around a finger and press the ends together, forming a ring.

Cook the *tortellini* in plenty of boiling salted water for 5 minutes or until they rise to the surface. Remove from the pan with a slotted spoon, then pile into a warmed serving dish and pour over the hot stock. Alternatively, serve sprinkled with melted butter and Parmesan. Serve immediately.
SERVES 4

The little circles of stuffed pasta known as *tortellini* are a speciality of Bologna in Emilia-Romagna, one of the regions in Italy where this kind of pasta is very common. They are not confined to just Emilia-Romagna at Christmas, however, since Italians all over the world like to observe the Christmas custom of eating *tortellini* before their main course of roast capon or turkey.

Wines

Italy produces more wine than any other country in the world. Italian soil and climate lend themselves perfectly to viticulture and every region produces wine.

In some areas of Italy, wine production can be traced back to the Bronze and Iron Ages when shepherds cultivated wild plants to produce small quantities of wine. The Greeks first introduced an organized form of viticulture to Italy between 800 and 600 BC when they colonized the area from Naples to Sicily – *Magna Graecia* as it was called then. Their methods soon spread to the surrounding areas. A little later the Etruscans settled in Tuscany and introduced wine-making to northern Italy.

With the rise of the Roman Empire this knowledge of wine-making spread far afield to Gaul and Britain, but wine was not plentiful at the time and only men were allowed to drink it. The popularity of wine increased; so too did the vineyards, to such an extent that Italy became known as *Enotria* or land of vines. Centuries later Italy is still worthy of this title.

In 1963, a long awaited set of regulations was issued to control wine production throughout Italy. Under this law three classifications of wine were outlined. *Denominazione semplice* states the region of production but there are no set standards for production or quality. *Denominazione di Origine Controllata* (DOC) denotes that wines are registered and must wear a DOC label, as well as their own. The area where the wine is produced and the quality must be agreed by the wine-growers and government. Other technical stipulations must be adhered to and the wines are tested regularly. *Denominazione di Origine Controllata e Garantita* (DOCG) is reserved for the top wines. These wines must be bottled and sealed with a government seal which guarantees the quality of the wine.

The northern region of Piemonte is one of the most prolific wine-producing areas; it is particularly noted for its red wines. The best known of these is Barolo – an austere, full-bodied, yet harmonious wine with a potent bouquet that ages well. It makes a perfect accompaniment to game or red meat. Like Barbaresco and many of the other Piemonte wines, it is made from the Nebbiolo grape, known locally as 'Spanna'. Barbaresco is similar to Barolo yet softer and more delicate; it is normally drunk much younger, but is equally suited to red meat dishes.

Barbera is another of Piemonte's famous red wines. Named after the grape it is made from, this wine is produced in different denominations: Barbera d'Asti is the best, but Barbera d'Alba and del Monferrato are produced in greater quantities. Although it is sometimes said that Barbera lacks the distinction of the other reds of the region, it is a superb accompaniment to typical Italian dishes like minestrone, risotto and lasagne.

A Piemonte wine which ages well is Nebbiolo. It is similar to Barolo as it is made from the same grape variety, and like Barolo it is best drunk between five and ten years old. It is a perfect accompaniment to *Pollo alla diavola* (see page 148). Gattinara is another fine red wine from this region. Made in the province of Vercelli from Nebbiolo grapes, this wine is aged for a compulsory minimum of four years.

One of the best known Italian wines to come from Piemonte is undoubtedly Asti Spumante, a sweet white sparkling wine made in vast quantities and exported all over the world. It is the ideal wine to finish the meal and is particularly delicious with *panettone*.

From the gentle slopes of Piemonte we move to the steep terraces of Valtellina in northern Lombardy, where the Nebbiolo grape has found yet another ideal habitat in which to thrive. Known locally as Chiavennasca, it produces some of the best red wines of Lombardy. The wines are named after the valley itself, but those of superior quality are given geographical subdenominations: Inferno, Sassella and Grumello. They are long lived and develop slowly in the bottle to become excellent full-bodied wines with a superb bouquet. They are a good accompaniment to grilled (broiled) mushrooms, beef stews such as *Costata di manzo alla valtellinese* (see page 119) and *bresàola*, the local speciality.

Besides Valtellina, viticulture is very active to the west of Lake Garda and in the Oltrepo Pavese, to the very south of the region. The best known are the red wines of the Oltrepo Pavese. This area also provides a good rosé wine – Riviera del Garda – ideal with fish or rice dishes, such as *Ossibuchi alla milanese* (see page 128).

On the far shore of Lake Garda is the province of Verona in the Veneto region, which produces such famous wines as the red Valpolicella and Bardolino, and the white Soave. These are all excellent table wines – fruity and light enough to accompany any meal. Much more challenging is Amarone, whose full denomination is Recioto Amarone della Valpolicella. This full-bodied red wine is made from the same variety of grape as Valpolicella. For Amarone, the grapes are picked and left to dry on wooden frames for several weeks, to increase the amount of sugar in them. Vinification eventually begins in winter, and it is a long process that takes place at nearly

freezing temperatures. The resulting product is a superb wine of 14/15° that ages well and does justice to a *fiorentina* steak or any other rich red meat dish or game.

North of Verona in the Trentino-Alto Adige some excellent wines are made. Lago di Caldaro and Santa Maddalena are the two most popular reds. Terlano, a scented and delicate white wine, is less well known but equally good.

Further to the east and bordering on Yugoslavia is the Friuli-Venezia Giulia region where some outstanding wines are made. The Collio range of red and white wines includes Pinot Grigio, a superlative white wine that is becoming more and more popular. Another distinguished white wine is Picolit, usually sold under the denomination of origin as Colli Orientali del Friuli. It is a golden dessert wine, full-bodied and warm, described by some as the *Château d'Yquem* of Italy.

Further south in the Po valley Lambrusco is made. This red wine varies from sweet to dry, but is always sparkling and slightly acidy, and makes a perfect companion to the rich foods of Emilia-Romagna, especially *cotechino* and *zampone*. The Po valley is probably the only place where Lambrusco wines are really appreciated for what they are.

On the other side of the Appennines is the region of Tuscany where nearly 3,000 years ago the Etruscans settled and made wine. The region still produces outstanding wines, including – of course – Chianti.

Chianti is made mostly with the red and white Sangiovese and Trebbiano grape varieties. Young Chianti is an exceptionally delightful wine, for it is both fragrant and fruity. When aged in vats for some years, the wine becomes austere and can reach outstanding quality. This is particularly so with Chianti Classico which only comes from the small area of Florence and Siena. Young Chianti is just right for light chicken dishes and vegetable soups, whilst older Chianti, which is referred to as *Vecchio* after two years and *Riserva* after three, is perfect with *fiorentina* steaks.

Another important Tuscan wine is Brunello di Montalcino. Montalcino is a small area some fifteen miles south of Siena and within its boundary a type of Sangiovese grape called Brunello di Montalcino is grown. The wine made exclusively from this grape is aged for a minimum of four years before it is sold. It is a deep ruby red colour, which is inclined to garnet with age and the taste is dry, warm and slightly tannic. This is probably the most expensive Italian wine, with a history that barely dates back a century. It is exceptional and should be reserved for important occasions as an accompaniment to special game and red meat dishes.

Nobile di Montepulciano is an excellent red from this region which has been produced for a

LEFT: **Spraying the vines to protect them from disease. Oxen are used to draw the cart holding the canister of liquid.**

BELOW RIGHT: **Black grapes ripening in the hot sun.**

century by the aristocracy of Montepulciano. A favourite of Pope Paul III and originally used for Holy Mass when it was first produced by the Jesuits during the 13th century, this wine is inclined to turn brick red with age. It has a delicate bouquet of violets, is dry and slightly tannic and improves with age.

In Umbria, the mystical land of St Francis of Assisi, the well-known white wine Orvieto is produced. Named after the town of the same name it is available in two versions: a dry and a semi-dry. The latter, known as Abboccato, has been famous since the town of Orvieto was a Holy See. The dry wine has only been made for a few decades and was introduced purely to meet the Italian demand for dry table wines.

Further west, on the Adriatic coast, is the region of Marche. Here the distinctive white, Verdicchio dei Castelli di Jesi, is made. An excellent wine for fish dishes, it is dry, balanced and delicate and should be drunk very young for full appreciation. The wine is usually sold in amphora-shaped bottles.

In central Italy a variety of white wines are made and those from Lazio are well worth a mention. Est! Est!! Est!!! di Montefiascone is particularly good and is made in the communities near Lake Bolsena. The wine is either dry or semi-dry and has been produced for many centuries. An amusing story about its name exists. In the year 1100 an Austrian bishop on his way to Rome for the coronation of Henry V, sent his quartermaster on ahead of him to select suitable inns, food and wine. The quartermaster was so enthusiastic about this white wine that, having had rather too much of it, he wrote on a wall Est ('this is it') three times to make sure there was no misunderstanding. Since then the white wine of the area has been called Est! Est!! Est!!! The dry

version is excellent with *Anguille alla comacchiese* (see page 109) – stewed eels from Lake Comacchio, a local speciality.

Frascati is another well-known white wine from this region, named after a town to the east of Rome. It is one of the famous *vini dei castelli romani*, the wines of the Roman hills. Frascati is a straw yellow colour and ranges from dry through semi-sweet to sweet, the latter being known as Canellino. Canellino is good with *fave* (beans) and gnocchi. But the better known Frascati is the dry one which is excellent with the specialities of the area, *Saltimbocca alla romana* (see page 131) and *Spaghetti all'amatriciana* (see page 74) and with other white meat and fish dishes. Other good white wines in Lazio include Velletri, Marino and Colli Albani. The Romans like to drink their wines in the local *trattorie* as well as at home.

The Romans' love for leisure is inherited from their ancestors. But in those days Romans preferred to retreat to Campania, the fertile region south east of Rome, to relax. One of their favourite wines was Falernum which was much praised by Horace and Pliny. A sound table wine by the same name is still produced in that region today, but its qualities are by no means exceptional.

Just outside the bay of Naples is the island of Ischia where two interesting wines are made. Both are named after the island, one a red, the other a white wine. The white is better and is characterized by a fruity, lightly aromatic bouquet and a balanced dry taste. It should be drunk young and goes well with the local pasta dishes and pizzas.

On the far side of the peninsula, along the Adriatic coast, lies the region of Apulia. In contrast to Lazio and Campania's delicate wines, here one finds some of Italy's most robust wines.

The strong sunshine and heavy soil of this area encourage the grapes to mature fully and acquire high levels of sugar. These give the wines a considerable natural alcoholic strength, sometimes in the region of 16° or 17°. Castel del Monte is a denomination of origin which applies to red, white and rosé wine produced in the Minervino Murge community and surrounding areas in the province of Bari. The red is the most well known and has a good bouquet and a balanced taste with a light burnt undertone.

Particularly interesting is the powerful wine of this region – Primitivo di Manduria. This is some 14° strength and is available as a naturally sweet or fortified wine. When fortified it can be either sweet or dry. The dry version, known as Liquoroso secco, has an alcoholic content of about 17°. More wine is produced in Apulia than in any other region, but most of it is sold in bulk and exported. A large percentage goes to France where the deep colour and high alcohol levels are appreciated for blending.

The viticulture of Calabria, the southernmost region on the mainland of Italy, bears evidence of Greek and Arab influence. The first viticulturists here were the Phoenician settlers, followed by the Greeks who shipped the local wines back to Greece. Cremissa was their favourite wine – it was awarded to the winning athletes at the Olympic Games. Its direct descendant is Ciro which is considered to be one of the world's oldest wines. There is a sweet red, a rosé and a white Ciro. The white wine is considered to be one of the best table wines of the region.

Across the Messina strait is Sicily, the largest of the Mediterranean Islands and known in the past as *Trinacria* because of its triangular shape. Many countries have fought over this beautiful island and all the cultures have left their mark in some form or another. The climate and the fertile land greatly contribute to the success of the Sicilian wines which are produced in large quantities. The most famous must be Marsala, a fortified wine which has been made from Grillo and Catarratto grapes for well over two centuries. The British take some credit for this wine for it was John Woodhouse, a Liverpool merchant, who travelled to Sicily and recognized its potential. He later set up a large scale business dealing in Marsala, and even supplied Lord Nelson's fleet with the wine.

Marsala is named after a town on the extreme west of the island, where it is made. It is basically a fortified white wine, but there are various types from very dry to sweet, all with an alcoholic content in the region of 18°. Marsala is essentially a dessert wine, but some types are also drunk as apéritifs. Perhaps its greatest virtue is that it does not deteriorate after opening. It is used a great deal in cooking – in both savoury and sweet dishes. Blended with egg yolks it makes the famous Italian dessert, *Zabaione* (see page 186).

Sicily produces a large amount of wine, the majority of which is exported. A large percentage is also used by the vermouth industry. On the whole the table wines are not well known at the moment but more and more are appearing outside Italy. Alcamo is a fruity dry white with a pronounced bouquet of Catarratto grapes. The Etna wines are interesting and the Mostatos wines (di Noto, di Siracusa, di Pantelleria) make good dessert wines with a strong flavour of Muscat grapes.

Other similar wines are produced in Sardinia, the second largest island in the Mediterranean. Here, too, the traces of ancient civilizations are still apparent. Among the Moscatos and other wines of this island, the greatest one must be Vernaccia. This is made from grapes of the same name, a variety that was imported during the 14th century. Vernaccia is a white wine of 15°; the bouquet is delicate and the taste is warm and pleasantly bitter, reminiscent of almonds. This wine is excellent with lobster and oysters. It is often fortified to become a *vino liqueroso* and then aged in wood for at least two years. Vernaccia is very much a part of life for Sardinians as it is drunk on all important occasions. Sardinia also produces interesting table wines such as Cannonau, a pleasant ruby red wine with a taste which varies from dry to semi-sweet; Monica, a red with a fragrant taste; Nuragus, a dry, balanced white; and Vermentino di Gallura, an excellent dry white with a deep and delicate bouquet. Finally, of course, there are the various Moscatos: di Sorso-Sennori and di Cagliari which are all excellent dessert wines.

Antipasti & Soups

Italians sometimes start their main meal of the day with an *antipasto*, which is a light starter or an appetizer rather than a substantial course.

Salami, cold meats and hams are very much a feature of *antipasti*. Sometimes a selection of different meats is served, but with *prosciutto di Parma* or *San Daniele*, the meat will normally be served on its own or at the most with melon or figs. *Bresàola*, a thinly sliced raw beef, is served with a very simple dressing of olive oil, lemon juice and pepper.

Fish is also served as an *antipasto*, particularly in coastal areas. Anchovies, sardines, whitebait, octopus and squid are served in numerous different ways: cold in an oil-based dressing, or fried and served hot with lemon.

Vegetables and salads make delicious light *antipasti*. Mushrooms, broad (lima) and French beans, courgettes (zucchini), artichokes, tomatoes, peppers, fennel and cauliflower are served raw or lightly cooked and chilled. They are generally tossed in a seasoned dressing of olive oil, garlic, lemon juice or vinegar, and freshly chopped herbs. *Cannellini*, haricot (navy) and *borlotti* beans are often served mixed with tuna fish and a garlic flavoured dressing.

Sometimes hot dishes are served as part of an *antipasto*. Bread is fried or baked with a topping like melted cheese or chicken livers and, in southern Italy individual pizzas, or *pizzette*, are a speciality.

The first course (*primo piatto*) is usually either a soup (*minestra*), or a consommé or clear broth (*brodo*), or a dish of pasta or rice. *Minestre* are usually substantial soups, with pasta or rice added; sometimes these are served as meals in themselves. *Minestrone* (see page 52) is a typical example of this kind of soup. Specific recipes are rarely followed – *minestre* are traditionally made with almost any ingredients that come to hand, including leftover meat and vegetables.

Brodo often have a little pasta, rice, toasted cheese or some croûtons added to them as they are not as substantial as *minestre*. *Zuppa* is another general Italian name for soup and *Zuppa alla pavese* (see page 50) is a well-known soup containing slices of bread topped with raw eggs. Fish soups or stews of the *bouillabaisse* type are usually called *zuppe di pesce*; they tend to be very substantial and are often meals in themselves.

It is customary to serve freshly grated Parmesan cheese with most Italian soups.

PIEMONTE & VALLE D'AOSTA

BAGNA CAÔDA
Anchovy Dip

Metric/Imperial	American
150 ml/¼ pint olive oil	⅔ cup olive oil
3 garlic cloves, peeled and crushed	3 garlic cloves, peeled and crushed
1 × 50 g/2 oz can anchovies, drained and roughly chopped	1 × 2 oz can anchovies, drained and roughly chopped
75 g/3 oz unsalted butter	⅓ cup sweet butter
bowl of sliced raw vegetables (eg. green peppers, carrots, turnip, celery, Jerusalem artichokes)	bowl of sliced raw vegetables (eg. green peppers, carrots, turnip, celery, Jerusalem artichokes)

Heat the oil in a small frying pan (skillet). Add the garlic and anchovies and simmer over low heat for 15 minutes, stirring occasionally. Add the butter and stir until melted.

To serve: stand the frying pan (skillet) over a fondue burner or spirit lamp at the table. Guests then dip the vegetables into the hot sauce.

SERVES 4 to 6

PIEMONTE & VALLE D'AOSTA

FONDUTA
Piedmontese Cheese Fondue

Metric/Imperial	American
300 ml/½ pint warm milk	1¼ cups warm milk
350 g/12 oz fontina cheese★, thinly sliced	¾ lb fontina cheese★, thinly sliced
pinch of salt	pinch of salt
4 egg yolks	4 egg yolks
50 g/2 oz butter, softened	¼ cup butter, softened
TO SERVE:	TO SERVE:
1 truffle or a few button mushrooms, thinly sliced	1 truffle or a few button mushrooms, thinly sliced
few slices toasted bread, cut into triangles	few slices toasted bread, cut into triangles

Set aside a few tablespoons of the milk. Pour the rest of the milk into a large heatproof bowl and stand over a large pan half-filled with gently simmering water. Add the cheese and salt and stir constantly with a wooden spoon until thick and smooth.

Mix together the egg yolks and the reserved warm milk, then stir into the melted mixture. Add the butter gradually, stirring until the fonduta becomes smooth and creamy.

Divide equally between small serving dishes (preferably earthenware). Spread the truffle or mushrooms on top. Serve immediately, with the toast.

SERVES 4 to 6

The history behind Piemonte's most original dish, *Bagna caôda*, is interesting. In the days when there was a heavy tax on salt, the Piedmontese used a lot of anchovies in their cooking – their natural saltiness was an easy means of avoiding tax.

ABOVE: **Fonduta; Bagna caôda**

CROSTINI DI MILZA E FEGATINI

Chicken Livers on Fried Bread

Metric/Imperial	American
225 g/8 oz chicken livers	½ lb chicken livers
vegetable oil for shallow frying	vegetable oil for shallow frying
1 celery stick, minced	1 celery stalk, ground
½ onion, minced	½ onion, ground
4 tablespoons dry white wine	¼ cup dry white wine
salt and freshly ground black pepper	salt and freshly ground black pepper
1 tablespoon minced capers	1 tablespoon ground capers
1–2 tablespoons chicken stock (optional)	1–2 tablespoons chicken stock (optional)
6 slices stale bread, crusts removed, sliced	6 slices stale bread, crusts removed, sliced

Chop the chicken livers finely. Heat 1 tablespoon oil in a heavy pan, add the celery and onion and fry over gentle heat until lightly coloured. Add the chicken livers and fry for a further 5 minutes. Add the wine and continue cooking until it evaporates.

Add salt and pepper to taste, then the capers. Cook for a further 10 minutes, stirring frequently and moistening with a little stock if necessary. Remove from the heat, then purée in an electric blender or work through a sieve (strainer).

Heat the oil in a frying pan (skillet), add the slices of bread and fry until golden brown. Drain thoroughly. Spread thickly with the liver mixture and cut into triangles or fingers. Serve immediately.

SERVES 6

Antipasti & Soups/47

ZUPPA DI VALPELLINE
Cabbage and Cheese Soup

Metric/Imperial	American
1 Savoy cabbage	*1 Savoy cabbage*
12 slices toasted bread	*12 slices toasted bread*
100 g/4 oz bacon rashers, fried	*¼ lb bacon slices, fried*
250 g/9 oz fontina cheese★, sliced	*9 oz fontina cheese★, sliced*
pinch of ground cinnamon	*pinch of ground cinnamon*
freshly ground black pepper	*freshly ground black pepper*
1 litre/1¾ pints meat stock	*4¼ cups meat stock*
25 g/1 oz butter, diced	*2 tablespoons butter, diced*

Cook the cabbage in boiling water for 15 minutes, then drain thoroughly and separate the leaves.

Line the bottom of an ovenproof dish with 4 slices of toast. Cover with half the cabbage, bacon and cheese. Repeat these layers once more, then cover with the remaining 4 slices of toast. Add the cinnamon and pepper to taste to the stock then pour over the toast in the dish.

Bake in a preheated moderate oven (180°C/350°F/Gas Mark 4) for 30 minutes. Remove from the oven, dot the butter over the top, then bake for a further 20 minutes. Serve hot.
SERVES 4 to 6

ACQUACOTTA
Mushroom Savoury

Metric/Imperial	American
7 tablespoons olive oil	*7 tablespoons olive oil*
2 garlic cloves, peeled and sliced	*2 garlic cloves, peeled and sliced*
450 g/1 lb mushrooms, sliced	*1 lb mushrooms, sliced*
225 g/8 oz tomatoes, skinned and chopped	*1 cup skinned and chopped tomatoes*
450 ml/¾ pint light stock	*2 cups light stock*
salt and freshly ground black pepper	*salt and freshly ground black pepper*
6 large slices hot toasted bread, cut into quarters	*6 large slices hot toasted bread, cut into quarters*
65 g/2½ oz Parmesan cheese★, grated	*½–¾ cup grated Parmesan cheese★*
2 eggs, beaten	*2 eggs, beaten*

Heat the oil in a heavy pan, add the garlic and fry gently until browned. Add the mushrooms and cook for 5 minutes, stirring frequently. Add the tomatoes, stock and salt and pepper to taste. Bring to the boil, then lower the heat, cover and simmer gently for 15 minutes.

Divide the toast slices between individual dishes, then sprinkle with about half of the Parmesan. Mix the eggs with the remaining Parmesan and add to the mixture in the pan. Remove from the heat immediately and stir vigorously. Pour over the toast and serve immediately.
SERVES 6

PAPAROT
Spinach Savoury

Metric/Imperial	American
1 kg/2 lb fresh spinach	*2 lb fresh spinach*
150 g/5 oz butter	*⅝ cup butter*
3 garlic cloves, peeled and crushed	*3 garlic cloves, peeled and crushed*
65 g/2½ oz plain flour	*⅔ cup all-purpose flour*
salt and freshly ground black pepper	*salt and freshly ground black pepper*
little cornmeal	*little cornmeal*

Cook the spinach, with just the water clinging to the leaves after washing, until tender. Drain well, then purée in an electric blender or sieve (strain).

Melt the butter in a heavy pan, add the garlic and fry gently until browned. Remove the garlic from the pan, then stir in the plain (all-purpose) flour and cook for 5 minutes, stirring constantly.

Add the spinach and salt and pepper to taste and cook for a further 5 minutes. Stir in a little hot water and bring to the boil, then stir in enough cornmeal to make a fairly solid mixture. Cook gently for 30 minutes, stirring frequently. Serve hot.
SERVES 6

LA CIPOLLATA
Onion Savoury

Metric/Imperial	American
750 g/1¾ lb onions, peeled and sliced	*7 cups peeled and sliced onions*
2 tablespoons olive oil	*2 tablespoons olive oil*
100 g/4 oz bacon, chopped	*½ cup chopped bacon*
few basil leaves, chopped	*few basil leaves, chopped*
salt and freshly ground black pepper	*salt and freshly ground black pepper*
350 g/12 oz tomatoes, skinned and mashed	*1½ cups skinned and mashed tomatoes*
3 eggs, beaten	*3 eggs, beaten*
75 g/3 oz Parmesan cheese★, grated	*¾ cup grated Parmesan cheese★*
4 slices hot toasted bread	*4 slices hot toasted bread*
few basil leaves to garnish	*few basil leaves to garnish*

Put the onions in a bowl, cover with cold water and leave to soak overnight.

Heat the oil in a large heavy pan, add the bacon and fry gently until browned. Drain the onions thoroughly, then add to the pan with the basil and salt and pepper to taste. Cook over low heat for 20 minutes, stirring occasionally.

Add the tomatoes, cover the pan, lower the heat and cook very gently for 10 minutes. Taste and adjust the seasoning. Beat the eggs and Parmesan together, then add to the soup. Remove from the heat immediately and stir vigorously. Put a slice of hot toast in each individual soup bowl, then pour over the hot soup. Serve immediately, garnished with basil.
SERVES 4

Savouries take their place as a first course in an Italian meal, quite the opposite of the British savoury which is traditionally served at the end. Italian savouries are usually made with fresh vegetables, and are invariably substantial. They should therefore be followed by a light main course.

MINESTRA DI RISO E RAPE

Rice and Turnip Soup

Metric/Imperial	American
400 g/14 oz white turnips, peeled and sliced	2¼ cups peeled and sliced white turnips
salt	salt
25 g/1 oz butter	2 tablespoons butter
1 small onion, peeled and chopped	1 small onion, peeled and chopped
75 g/3 oz bacon, chopped	⅓ cup chopped bacon
1.5 litres/2½ pints beef stock	6¼ cups beef stock
freshly ground black pepper	freshly ground black pepper
200 g/7 oz rice	1 cup rice
1 tablespoon chopped parsley	1 tablespoon chopped parsley
50 g/2 oz Parmesan cheese★, grated, to serve	½ cup grated Parmesan cheese★, to serve

Cook the turnips in boiling salted water for 15 minutes until almost tender; drain well.

Melt the butter in a pan, add the turnips and cook gently for 6 to 7 minutes, stirring occasionally. Meanwhile, put the onion and bacon in a separate pan and cook gently, stirring constantly, until lightly browned. Add the stock and salt and pepper to taste and bring to the boil. Add the rice, then lower the heat and simmer for 15 minutes until tender. Stir in the turnips and parsley, then remove from the heat. Serve hot, with Parmesan cheese handed separately.

SERVES 4 to 6

BRODO DI MANZO

Beef Consommé

This beef consommé is used as a basis for many soups, pasta, cheese and vegetables. It is also used as a stock for risottos and sauces.

Metric/Imperial	American
1 kg/2 lb lean beef, in one piece	2 lb lean beef, in one piece
1 onion, peeled	1 onion, peeled
½ stick celery	½ celery stalk
1.75 litres/3 pints water	7½ cups water
salt	salt

Place the beef in a large pan with the onion and celery. Pour in the water and season lightly with salt. Bring to the boil slowly and skim the surface. Cover and cook very gently for 5 to 6 hours; the soup should be just below simmering point.

Strain through a sieve (strainer) lined with muslin (cheese-cloth). Allow to cool, then remove the fat layer from the top. The consommé should be perfectly clear.

Serve hot or use as required for other dishes.

SERVES 4 to 6

ZUPPA ALLA PAVESE

Consommé with Eggs

Metric/Imperial	American
100 g/4 oz butter	½ cup butter
8 small slices bread, crusts removed	8 small slices bread, crusts removed
4 eggs	4 eggs
75 g/3 oz Parmesan cheese★, grated	¾ cup grated Parmesan cheese★
1 litre/1¾ pints Brodo di manzo (see left)	4¼ cups Brodo di manzo (see left)

Melt the butter in a large frying pan (skillet), add the bread and fry until golden brown on both sides.

Put 2 slices of fried bread into each of 4 warmed individual soup bowls, then crack the eggs on top of the bread, taking care not to break the yolks. Sprinkle with the Parmesan. Bring the consommé to the boil, then slowly pour over the eggs. Serve immediately.

SERVES 4

ABOVE: **Minestra di gianchetti; Zuppa alla pavese; Minestra di riso e verze**

MINESTRA DI RISO E VERZE

Cabbage, Rice and Bacon Soup

Metric/Imperial	American
25 g/1 oz butter	2 tablespoons butter
½ onion, chopped	½ onion, chopped
50 g/2 oz streaky bacon, chopped	¼ cup chopped bacon
400 g/14 oz cabbage, shredded	5¼ cups shredded cabbage
1.75 litres/3 pints Brodo di manzo (see opposite)	7½ cups Brodo di manzo (see opposite)
salt and freshly ground black pepper	salt and freshly ground black pepper
200 g/7 oz rice	1 cup rice
1 tablespoon chopped parsley	1 tablespoon chopped parsley
50 g/2 oz Parmesan cheese*, grated, to serve	½ cup grated Parmesan cheese*, to serve

Melt the butter in a large pan, add the onion and bacon and fry gently until lightly coloured. Add the cabbage and fry for 5 minutes, stirring frequently, then stir in the consommé. Bring to the boil then add salt and pepper to taste. Lower the heat, cover the pan and cook gently for 30 minutes.

Stir in the rice and cook for a further 15 minutes or until tender. Add the parsley, then remove from the heat. Serve hot, with Parmesan cheese.

SERVES 4 to 6

MINESTRA MARICONDA

Beef Broth with Parmesan

Metric/Imperial	American
225 g/8 oz bread, crusts removed	½ lb bread, crusts removed
300 ml/½ pint milk	1¼ cups milk
100 g/4 oz butter	½ cup butter
4 eggs, beaten	4 eggs, beaten
150 g/5 oz Parmesan cheese*, grated	1¼ cups grated Parmesan cheese*
pinch of grated nutmeg	pinch of grated nutmeg
salt and freshly ground black pepper	salt and freshly ground black pepper
1.5 litres/2½ pints Brodo di manzo (see opposite)	6¼ cups Brodo di manzo (see opposite)

Crumble the bread into a bowl, add the milk and leave for 30 minutes.

Melt the butter in a small pan. Squeeze the bread as dry as possible, then add to the pan. Cook gently until dry but still soft, stirring constantly. Transfer to a bowl, then add the eggs, 100 g/4 oz/1 cup Parmesan, the nutmeg and salt and pepper to taste. Stir well to mix, cover and leave to stand for 1 hour.

Pour the consommé into a pan and bring to the boil. Stir in the bread mixture gradually then simmer for 5 minutes. Serve hot, with the remaining Parmesan handed separately.

SERVES 4 to 6

It seems the Italians have an irresistible urge to cram their soups full of ingredients – it is even rare to find a clear soup without a little something floating in it. The history behind *Zuppa alla pavese* illustrates this point. The story goes that a Lombardian housewife gave this soup to Francis I after his defeat in the battle of Pavia in 1525. Thinking her plain broth too humble to give a king, and not hearty enough for a tired, hungry and dejected one at that, she quickly broke two eggs into it to make it more substantial.

MINESTRA DI GIANCHETTI

Whitebait Soup

Metric/Imperial	American
1 litre/1¾ pints fish stock	4¼ cups fish stock
350 g/12 oz fresh peas, shelled	2 cups shelled fresh peas
150 g/5 oz vermicelli or capelli d'angelo	5 oz vermicelli or capelli d'angelo
225 g/8 oz whitebait	½ lb whitebait
1 egg, beaten	1 egg, beaten
salt and freshly ground black pepper	salt and freshly ground black pepper

Pour the stock into a large pan and bring to the boil. Add the peas and simmer for 20 minutes. Add the vermicelli and whitebait and cook until almost tender. Stir in the egg and salt and pepper to taste; cook for 1 minute. Serve immediately.

SERVES 4

MINESTRONE ALLA MILANESE

Metric/Imperial	American
2 tablespoons olive oil	2 tablespoons olive oil
100 g/4 oz bacon, chopped	½ cup chopped bacon
1 onion, peeled and chopped	1 onion, peeled and chopped
1 garlic clove, peeled and chopped	1 garlic clove, peeled and chopped
225 g/8 oz tomatoes, skinned and chopped	1 cup skinned and chopped tomatoes
100 g/4 oz dried borlotti or red kidney beans, soaked in cold water overnight	⅓ cup dried borlotti or red kidney beans, soaked in cold water overnight
6 basil leaves, chopped	6 basil leaves, chopped
1 parsley sprig, chopped	1 parsley sprig, chopped
2 litres/3½ pints water	9 cups water
1 carrot, peeled and diced	1 carrot, peeled and diced
1 celery stick, diced	1 celery stalk, diced
275 g/10 oz potatoes, peeled and diced	2 cups diced raw potatoes
225 g/8 oz courgettes, diced	2 large zucchini, diced
225 g/8 oz cabbage, shredded	2¾ cups shredded cabbage
100 g/4 oz fresh peas, shelled	¾ cup shelled fresh peas
salt and freshly ground black pepper	salt and freshly ground black pepper
200 g/7 oz rice	1 cup rice
50 g/2 oz Parmesan cheese★, grated	½ cup grated Parmesan cheese★

Heat the oil in a large saucepan, add the bacon, onion and garlic and sauté for a few minutes. Add the tomatoes, beans, basil, parsley and water. Bring to the boil. Lower the heat, cover and simmer for about 1½ hours, stirring occasionally.

Add the carrot and celery and simmer for a further 30 minutes. Add the remaining ingredients, except the cheese, with salt and pepper to taste. Simmer for 20 minutes or until all the vegetables are tender.

Taste and adjust the seasoning. Leave the soup to stand for 5 minutes, then add the Parmesan. Serve hot.
SERVES 6

JOTA

Bean and Cabbage Soup

Metric/Imperial	American
400 g/14 oz dried haricot beans, soaked in lukewarm water overnight	2 cups dried navy beans, soaked in lukewarm water overnight
100 g/4 oz streaky bacon, chopped	½ cup chopped fatty bacon
2 small heads of cabbage, quartered	2 small heads of cabbage, quartered
2 tablespoons cumin seeds	2 tablespoons cumin seeds
1 bay leaf	1 bay leaf
salt	salt
4 tablespoons olive oil	¼ cup olive oil
2 garlic cloves, peeled and sliced	2 garlic cloves, peeled and sliced
2 tablespoons plain flour	2 tablespoons all-purpose flour
100 g/4 oz cornmeal	1 cup cornmeal

Place the beans and bacon in a saucepan and pour over water to cover. Bring to the boil, cover and cook for 1½ hours, adding more water as necessary.

Meanwhile put the cabbage in a separate pan with the cumin seeds, bay leaf, a little salt and a very little water and cook for 2 to 3 minutes, shaking the pan constantly.

Heat half the oil in another pan, add the garlic and fry until brown. Discard the garlic, then stir the plain (all-purpose) flour into the hot oil in the pan. Cook for 2 minutes, stirring constantly, then add the cabbage and cook for a further 5 minutes.

Transfer the cabbage to the pan containing the beans, add the remaining oil, then the cornmeal a little at a time, stirring well after each addition. Cook gently for 30 minutes, stirring frequently and adding more water or stock if too dry. Taste and add salt if necessary. Serve hot.
SERVES 4 to 6

The famous soup *Jota*, from Friuli-Venezia Giulia, used to be regarded as a poor man's dish. The Triestines even had a saying about it: 'jota jota every day and never polenta and milk'. Nowadays they no longer feel this way about such a nourishing dish – it can be found on the menus of most fashionable restaurants in Trieste.

TRENTINO-ALTO ADIGE

ZUPPA DI ORZO

Barley Soup with Ham

Metric/Imperial	American
25 g/1 oz butter	¼ cup butter
1 onion, peeled and chopped	1 onion, peeled and chopped
1 carrot, peeled and chopped	1 carrot, peeled and chopped
1 celery stick, chopped	1 celery stalk, chopped
100 g/4 oz raw ham or bacon, diced	¼ lb diced raw ham or bacon
250 g/9 oz pearl barley, soaked in cold water for 2 hours	1 cup pearl barley, soaked in cold water for 2 hours
1·5 litres/2½ pints chicken stock	6¼ cups chicken stock
1 bay leaf	1 bay leaf
7 tablespoons single cream	7 tablespoons light cream
40 g/1½ oz Parmesan cheese★ grated	6 tablespoons grated Parmesan cheese★
salt and freshly ground black pepper	salt and freshly ground black pepper

Melt the butter in a large pan, add the onion, carrot and celery and fry gently for 10 minutes. Stir in the ham, barley, stock and bay leaf. Cover and simmer very gently for 1½ hours, stirring frequently. Add the cream, Parmesan and salt and pepper to taste and stir well to combine. Serve hot.
SERVES 4

FRIULI-VENEZIA GIULIA

PAPAZOI

Sweetcorn, Barley and Bean Soup

Metric/Imperial	American
200 g/7 oz dried borlotti or haricot beans	1 cup dried borlotti or navy beans
200 g/7 oz pearl barley	1 cup pearl barley
100 g/4 oz fresh or frozen sweetcorn kernels	¾ cup fresh or frozen kernel corn
2 tablespoons olive oil	2 tablespoons olive oil
100 g/4 oz streaky bacon, finely chopped	½ cup finely chopped fatty bacon
2 garlic cloves, peeled and crushed	2 garlic cloves, peeled and crushed
2 litres/3½ pints light stock	9 cups light stock
225 g/8 oz potatoes, peeled and diced	1½ cups diced raw potatoes
1 tablespoon chopped parsley	1 tablespoon chopped parsley
salt and freshly ground black pepper	salt and freshly ground black pepper

Soak the beans, barley and fresh corn if using, in separate bowls of lukewarm water overnight.

Heat the oil in a large pan, add the bacon and garlic and fry until golden brown. Drain the vegetables and add to the pan with the stock. Bring to the boil, lower the heat and simmer for 45 minutes. Add the potatoes and cook for a further 20 minutes or until the vegetables are tender. Stir in the parsley and salt and pepper to taste. Serve immediately.
SERVES 6 to 8

MINESTRA DI RISO E FAGIOLI

Rice, Bean and Sausage Soup

Metric/Imperial	American
300 g/11 oz dried haricot beans, soaked in lukewarm water overnight	scant 1½ cups dried navy beans, soaked in lukewarm water overnight
4 tablespoons olive oil	¼ cup olive oil
100 g/4 oz streaky bacon, minced	½ cup ground fatty bacon
1 onion, peeled and minced	1 onion, peeled and ground
50 g/2 oz Mortadella★ or Bologna★ sausage, minced	¼ cup ground Mortadella★ or Bologna★ sausage
salt and freshly ground black pepper	salt and freshly ground black pepper
200 g/7 oz rice	1 cup rice

Cook the beans in boiling water for 1½ hours.

Heat the oil in a separate large pan, add the bacon, onion and sausage and fry gently for 10 minutes. Add the beans with their cooking liquid, then add salt and pepper to taste and bring to the boil. (If the soup is too thick, add a little warm water.)

Add the rice to the soup and cook for a further 20 minutes until tender. Serve immediately.

SERVES 4 to 6

RISI E BISI

Rice and Pea Soup

Metric/Imperial	American
25 g/1 oz butter	2 tablespoons butter
50 g/2 oz fatty bacon, minced	¼ cup ground fatty bacon
½ onion, minced	½ onion, ground
225 g/8 oz fresh peas, shelled	1½ cups shelled fresh peas
1 litre/1¾ pints hot chicken stock	4¼ cups hot chicken stock
300 g/11 oz rice	1½ cups rice
50 g/2 oz Parmesan cheese★, grated	½ cup grated Parmesan cheese★
salt and freshly ground black pepper	salt and freshly ground black pepper
1 tablespoon chopped parsley	1 tablespoon chopped parsley

Melt the butter in a large pan, add the bacon and onion and fry gently for 5 minutes until lightly coloured. Add the peas and a few tablespoons of the stock, cover and simmer gently for 20 minutes.

Add the rice and half the remaining stock and bring to the boil again. Lower the heat, cover and simmer for 15 minutes or until the rice is tender.

Add the Parmesan and salt and pepper to taste, then add more stock if necessary – the soup should be fairly thick.

Sprinkle with the parsley, remove from the heat and leave to stand for 1 minute before serving.

SERVES 4

MINESTRA DI STRICHETTI

Soup with Pasta Shapes

Metric/Imperial	American
200 g/7 oz plain flour	1¾ cups all-purpose flour
salt	salt
2 eggs, beaten	2 eggs, beaten
40 g/1½ oz Parmesan cheese★, grated	6 tablespoons grated Parmesan cheese★
1.5 litres/2½ pints well-flavoured beef stock	6¼ cups well-flavored beef stock

Sift the flour with ¼ teaspoon salt onto a work surface and make a well in the centre. Add the eggs and Parmesan, then mix together to a smooth dough.

Flatten the dough with a rolling pin and roll out to a 3 mm/⅛ inch thickness. Cut into 1 cm/½ inch wide strips using a tooth-edged rotary cutter, then cut the strips into pieces 2.5 cm/1 inch long. Pinch each strip in the middle to give a butterfly shape.

Bring the stock to the boil in a large pan, add the butterfly shapes and cook for 6 to 7 minutes. Serve immediately.

SERVES 4

ABOVE: **Preparing Minestra di strichetti**
RIGHT: **Pappa col pomodoro**

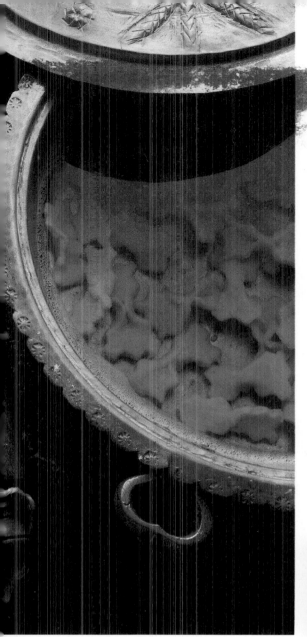

PAPPA COL POMODORO

Tomato Soup with Croûtons

Metric/Imperial	American
4 tablespoons olive oil	¼ cup olive oil
1 onion, peeled and chopped	1 onion, peeled and chopped
3 garlic cloves, peeled and crushed	3 garlic cloves, peeled and crushed
750 g/1¾ lb tomatoes, skinned and chopped	3½ cups skinned and chopped tomatoes
1 litre/1¾ pints chicken stock	4¼ cups chicken stock
salt and freshly ground black pepper	salt and freshly ground black pepper
225 g/8 oz stale bread, crusts removed, diced	8 slices stale bread, crusts removed, diced
few basil leaves, chopped	few basil leaves, chopped

Heat half the oil in a large pan, add the onion and garlic and fry gently for 5 minutes. Add the tomatoes and cook for 5 minutes, then gradually stir in the stock. Add salt and pepper to taste, then simmer for 30 minutes.

Meanwhile, heat the remaining oil in a frying pan (skillet), add the bread cubes and fry, turning, until crisp and golden.

Add the basil and croûtons to the soup and serve immediately.

SERVES 4

The Venetians are purists when it comes to making their famous *Risi e bisi*. They insist the best *Risi e bisi* is only made in the late Spring when the peas are young, fresh and tender. Some Venetians even go to the extreme of insisting the peas come from only one area – the fields along the shores of the lagoon between Choggia and Burano!

GINESTRATA

Chicken Soup

Metric/Imperial	American
4 egg yolks	4 egg yolks
500 ml/18 fl oz chicken stock	2¼ cups chicken stock
300 ml/½ pint dry Marsala wine	1¼ cups dry Marsala wine
pinch of ground cinnamon	pinch of ground cinnamon
75 g/3 oz butter, chopped	⅓ cup butter, chopped
40 g/1½ oz sugar	3 tablespoons sugar
pinch of grated nutmeg	pinch of grated nutmeg

Combine the egg yolks with the stock, Marsala and cinnamon. Pass the liquid through a fine sieve (strainer) into a pan. Cook gently until hot, stirring constantly, then add the pieces of butter and continue stirring until the soup thickens. Pour the soup into warmed individual soup bowls and sprinkle with the sugar and nutmeg. Serve immediately.

SERVES 4

MINESTRA DI CECI

Chick Pea (Garbanzos) Soup

Metric/Imperial	American
450 g/1 lb chick peas	2¼ cups garbanzos
1 teaspoon bicarbonate of soda	1 teaspoon baking soda
50 g/2 oz raw ham or bacon	1 thick slice raw ham or bacon
½ onion, peeled	½ onion, peeled
1 garlic clove, peeled	1 garlic clove, peeled
1 tablespoon chopped parsley	1 tablespoon chopped parsley
pinch of dried marjoram	pinch of dried marjoram
50 g/2 oz butter	¼ cup butter
2 tablespoons olive oil	2 tablespoons olive oil
225 g/8 oz tomatoes, skinned and chopped	1 cup skinned and chopped tomatoes
2 litres/3½ pints water	9 cups water
salt	salt
225 g/8 oz cotechino ★ or other fresh pork sausage, chopped	1 cup chopped cotechino★ or other fresh pork sausage
1 head of chicory, separated into leaves	1 head of endive, separated into leaves
6 slices hot toasted bread	6 slices hot toasted bread
75 g/3 oz pecorino cheese★, grated	¾ cup grated pecorino cheese★
freshly ground black pepper	freshly ground black pepper

Put the chick peas (garbanzos) in a large bowl. Add the soda and cover with cold water. Mix well and leave to soak for 24 hours.

Mince (grind) the ham with the onion and garlic, then place in a large pan with the parsley, marjoram, butter and oil. Cook gently for 6 to 7 minutes, stirring frequently.

Drain the chick peas (garbanzos) and add to the pan with the tomatoes and water. Add salt to taste, bring to the boil, then add the sausage. Cover the pan and simmer gently for 1½ hours.

Add the chicory (endive) and simmer for a further 30 minutes.

Place each slice of toast in an individual soup bowl. Add the cheese to the soup with pepper to taste, then pour over the toast. Serve immediately.

SERVES 6

Thick pulse soups are synonymous with peasant-style cooking, and the regions of Marche and Abruzzi & Molise are noted for their homely *minestre* – soups made thick with vegetables and chick peas (garbanzos).

MINESTRA DI CECI E CASTAGNE

Chestnut Soup with Chick Peas (Garbanzos)

Metric/Imperial	American
400 g/14 oz chick peas	2 cups garbanzos
2.5 litres/4½ pints water	5½ pints water
salt	salt
2 celery sticks, chopped	2 celery stalks, chopped
4 bay leaves	4 bay leaves
7 tablespoons olive oil	7 tablespoons olive oil
450 g/1 lb chestnuts	1 lb chestnuts
4 garlic cloves, peeled and crushed	4 garlic cloves, peeled and crushed
150 g/5 oz salty bacon, chopped	⅝ cup chopped salty bacon
freshly ground black pepper	freshly ground black pepper
4–6 slices hot toasted bread	4–6 slices hot toasted bread

STRACCIATELLA ALLA ROMANA

Chicken Broth

Metric/Imperial	American
3 eggs, beaten	3 eggs, beaten
75 g/3 oz semolina	$\frac{1}{2}$ cup semolina flour
50 g/2 oz Parmesan cheese★, grated	$\frac{1}{2}$ cup grated Parmesan cheese★
1 tablespoon chopped parsley	1 tablespoon chopped parsley
pinch of grated nutmeg	pinch of grated nutmeg
pinch of salt	pinch of salt
1.5 litres/2$\frac{1}{2}$ pints chicken stock	6$\frac{1}{4}$ cups chicken stock

Put the eggs in a bowl with the semolina, Parmesan, parsley, nutmeg and salt. Add a few tablespoons of the stock and stir well to mix.

Pour the remaining stock into a large pan and bring to the boil. Add the semolina mixture, then lower the heat and simmer gently until thick, stirring constantly. Serve immediately.

SERVES 4 to 6

ZUPPA DI TELLINE

Fish Soup

Metric/Imperial	American
750 g/1$\frac{1}{2}$ lb scallops or cockles	1$\frac{1}{2}$ lb scallops or cockles
200 ml/$\frac{1}{3}$ pint water	1 cup water
2 canned anchovy fillets, drained	2 canned anchovy fillets, drained
2 garlic cloves, peeled	2 garlic cloves, peeled
2 tablespoons olive oil	2 tablespoons olive oil
3–4 tablespoons chopped parsley	3–4 tablespoons chopped parsley
350 g/12 oz tomatoes, skinned and sliced	1$\frac{1}{2}$ cups skinned and sliced tomatoes
salt and freshly ground black pepper	salt and freshly ground black pepper
4 slices hot toasted bread	4 slices hot toasted bread

Scrub the scallops or cockles under cold running water, then drain and place in a pan with the water. Cover the pan and cook until the shells open, then remove the fish from the shells and set aside. Sieve (strain) the cooking liquid and reserve.

Mince (grind) the anchovies with the garlic, then place in a large pan with the oil and parsley and cook gently for 5 minutes. Add the tomatoes and salt and pepper to taste, then add the scallops and the reserved cooking liquid making it up to 1 litre/1$\frac{3}{4}$ pints/4$\frac{1}{4}$ cups with water. Bring to the boil and cook for 15 minutes.

Place each slice of toast in an individual soup bowl and pour over the soup. Serve immediately.

SERVES 4

Soak the chick peas (garbanzos) in lukewarm water for 12 hours, then drain. Place in a large pan with the water and $\frac{1}{2}$ teaspoon salt. Add the celery, bay leaves and 2 tablespoons oil. Bring to the boil, then lower the heat and simmer very gently for 1$\frac{1}{2}$ hours until the chick peas are tender and the cooking liquid has reduced about two thirds.

Score the chestnuts on the outside, then cook them in a preheated moderately hot oven (200°C/400°F/Gas Mark 6) for 40 minutes. Remove the shells and skins from the chestnuts, then mash the flesh.

Heat the remaining oil in a large pan, add the garlic and bacon and fry until golden brown. Add the chestnuts and pepper to taste, then cook over gentle heat for 6 to 7 minutes. Remove the bay leaves from the soup, then stir in the chestnut and bacon mixture.

Put the hot toast in the bottom of a soup tureen, then pour over the soup. Leave to stand for 2 to 3 minutes before serving.

SERVES 4 to 6

Minestra di ceci; Zuppa di telline; Stracciatella alla romana

MILLECOSEDDE

Thick Pulse (Legume) Soup

Metric/Imperial	American
100 g/4 oz dried borlotti or red kidney beans	½ cup dried borlotti or red kidney beans
100 g/4 oz dried haricot beans	½ cup dried navy beans
100 g/4 oz chick peas	½ cup garbanzos
100 g/4 oz lentils	½ cup lentils
7 tablespoons olive oil	7 tablespoons olive oil
100 g/4 oz bacon, chopped	½ cup chopped bacon
1 carrot, peeled and chopped	1 carrot, peeled and chopped
1 onion, peeled and chopped	1 onion, peeled and chopped
1 garlic clove, peeled and finely chopped	1 garlic clove, peeled and finely chopped
2 litres/3½ pints light stock	9 cups light stock
½ small cabbage, blanched and shredded	½ small green cabbage, blanched and shredded
225 g/8 oz mushrooms, finely sliced	1½ cups finely sliced mushrooms
salt and freshly ground black pepper	salt and freshly ground black pepper
225 g/8 oz farfalle or other small pasta	½ lb farfalle or other small pasta
100 g/4 oz pecorino cheese★, grated, to serve	1 cup grated pecorino cheese★, to serve

Soak the pulses (legumes) in lukewarm water overnight. Drain and place in a large pan. Cover with water and bring to the boil. Lower the heat, cover the pan and simmer for 1¼ hours.

Heat the oil in a large heavy pan. Add the bacon, carrot, onion and garlic and fry gently for 5 minutes. Add the stock and bring to the boil. Lower the heat, add the cabbage and simmer for 5 minutes.

Drain the pulses (legumes) and add to the pan with the mushrooms and salt and pepper to taste. Stir well, then add the pasta and cook for a further 15 minutes or until the pasta is tender. Sprinkle with the cheese and serve immediately.

SERVES 6 to 8

MINESTRA DI FARRO

Pearl Barley Soup

Metric/Imperial	American
1.5 litres/2½ pints chicken stock	6¼ cups chicken stock
200 g/7 oz pearl barley	1 cup pearl barley
100 g/4 oz pecorino cheese★, diced	⅔ cup diced pecorino cheese★
pinch of dried mint	pinch of dried mint

Bring the stock to the boil in a large pan. Add the barley a little at a time, then lower the heat and simmer for 30 minutes, stirring frequently.

Add the cheese and mint and stir until the cheese is melted. Serve immediately.

SERVES 4

LICURDIA

Onion Soup

Metric/Imperial	American
2 litres/3½ pints chicken stock or water	6¼ cups chicken stock or water
900 g/2 lb small pickling onions, peeled and halved	2 lb baby pickling onions, peeled and halved
25 g/1 oz butter	2 tablespoons butter
pinch of salt	pinch of salt
8 slices hot toasted bread	8 slices hot toasted bread
1 canned red pimento	1 canned red pimiento
75 g/3 oz pecorino cheese★, grated, to serve	¾ cup grated pecorino cheese★, to serve

Pour the stock or water into a large pan, add the onions, butter and the salt, then bring to the boil. Lower the heat, cover the pan and simmer for 1 hour.

Rub the hot toast with the pimento, then put 2 slices in each of 4 individual soup bowls. Pour the boiling soup over the toast, then sprinkle with the cheese. Serve immediately.

SERVES 4 to 6

MINESTRA DI FAVE

Bean and Tomato Soup

Metric/Imperial	American
200 g/7 oz butter beans	1 cup butter beans
4 tablespoons olive oil	¼ cup olive oil
50 g/2 oz streaky bacon, chopped	¼ cup chopped fatty bacon
2 onions, peeled and chopped	2 onions, peeled and chopped
2 celery sticks, chopped	2 celery stalks, chopped
225 g/8 oz tomatoes, skinned and mashed	1 cup skinned and mashed tomatoes
1.5 litres/2½ pints chicken stock or water	6¼ cups chicken stock or water
salt and freshly ground black pepper	salt and freshly ground black pepper
4 slices hot toasted bread	4 slices hot toasted bread
1 tablespoon chopped parsley	1 tablespoon chopped parsley

Soak the beans in lukewarm water overnight.

Heat the oil in a large heavy pan, add the bacon, onions and celery and fry gently for 10 minutes. Drain the beans, then add to the pan with the tomatoes and stock or water. Add salt and pepper to taste, then bring to the boil. Lower the heat, cover the pan and simmer for 1½ hours.

Put a slice of toast in each individual soup bowl. Remove the soup from the heat, stir in the parsley and a little pepper, then pour over the toast. Serve immediately.

SERVES 4

There is an old Calabrian saying about soups that goes: 'soup does seven things: it appeases your hunger, slakes your thirst, fills your stomach, cleans your teeth, makes you sleep, helps you to digest, and puts colour in your cheeks!'

Pasta

The exact origins of pasta making are not known, although records show that it was eaten in Roman times. Some believe that the Italians learnt the art of making pasta from the Chinese, when Marco Polo returned to Italy from the East in the thirteenth century, but there are few Italians who would agree with this theory.

The history of pasta eating in Italy has been the subject of a great debate, but historical records show that the ancient Romans ate pasta as long ago as the 4th or 5th centuries BC, and therefore most people believe that the Etruscans introduced pasta into Italy. The exact nutritional value of commercial pasta varies, but most good quality brands contain as much as 13 per cent protein as well as vitamins, minerals and a small amount of fat. Although pasta is high in carbohydrate, it is usually the sauce served with it that is more fattening than the pasta itself.

The finest commercial pasta is made of durum wheat, mostly imported from Canada. When buying commercial pasta it is wise to read the label on the packet to ensure that this kind of wheat has been used. Durum wheat is one of the hardest varieties of wheat, and when making pasta only the endosperm of the grain kernel is milled into semolina, which is then mixed with water to make the dough. Dried pasta, like spaghetti and other tubular varieties, is more common in southern Italy and abroad than it is in the north of Italy, where the pasta is more likely to be the flat kind, often made with fresh eggs.

Making Pasta

Making pasta at home is not a difficult task, especially if you are used to pastry making, since the skills are similar. It is well worth the effort of mastering the art of pasta making, because the dried varieties, although convenient, cannot compare in flavour to homemade pasta, which is also much lighter in texture. There are no special secrets to pasta making, but once the dough is mixed it should be kneaded thoroughly until very, very smooth, elastic and free from lumps. To prevent the dough from drying out and cracking after kneading and before rolling, it should be wrapped in a cloth wrung out in warm water, then left to rest for about 10 minutes. Rolling and stretching the dough requires the most time, and this is where most cooks cannot spare the patience and energy, for the dough should be so paper-thin that it is almost possible to see through it. It must be dusted frequently with flour throughout this process, as it tends to become sticky with constant handling, and you will need a very large pastry board, table or work surface to allow yourself room to work. (Dividing the dough into two also makes this easier.)

Cutting pasta

The easiest kind of pasta to make at home is the ribbon noodle type known as *tagliatelle* or *fettuccine*, since this can be cut into thin strips simply with a sharp knife. There are various pasta cutting gadgets available from specialist kitchenware shops, the most common ones being noodle machines with which the dough can be rolled and cut by the simple turning of a handle. There are also round and square ravioli cutters, and ravioli trays which have wells with sharp edges – the dough is rolled over the tray with a rolling pin and the shapes are cut out automatically. After cutting the dough, it should be left for about 10 minutes to dry out before cooking.

PASTA ALL'UOVO

Plain Egg Pasta

Metric/Imperial	American
225 g/8 oz plain flour	2 cups all-purpose flour
2 large eggs	2 eggs
2 teaspoons oil	2 teaspoons oil
½ teaspoon salt	½ teaspoon salt
a little water	a little water

Sift the flour onto a work surface and make a well in the centre. Put the eggs, oil and salt into the well and mix together with the fingertips. Gradually draw the flour into the egg mixture and knead together, adding a little water if the dough seems dry. Dust the work surface with flour and knead the dough firmly until smooth and elastic. Wrap in cling film (plastic wrap) and set aside for about 1 hour.

Roll out the dough on a lightly floured surface, first in one direction and then the other, until it is paper-thin. Dust lightly with flour and leave to rest for 10 to 20 minutes to allow the pasta to dry slightly. It is then ready to be cut into the required shapes.

After cutting the dough leave it for about 10 minutes to dry out before cooking.

MAKES ABOUT 350 g/12 OZ PASTA

Pasta verde

Pasta verde is *pasta all'uovo* coloured green with spinach. It is an attractive pale green colour flecked with darker green. Use the basic recipe above and add 50 g/2 oz/¼ cup cooked spinach (squeezed very dry and either sieved (strained) or chopped very finely) with the eggs. Follow the recipe as above, remembering that this pasta is stickier than plain pasta and it will be necessary to flour the work surface more frequently.

MAKES ABOUT 400 g/14 OZ PASTA

Cannelloni: Cut the pasta into rectangles, about 7.5 × 10 cm/3 × 4 inches.

Lasagne: Either cut into strips, about 1 cm/½ inch wide, or into rectangles 7.5 × 13 cm/3 × 5 inches.

Taliarini, tagliatelle or fettuccine: Roll the sheet of pasta loosely into a Swiss (jelly) roll shape, and with a sharp knife cut across into even strips 3 mm/⅛ inch wide for *taliarini*, 5 mm/¼ inch for *tagliatelle* or *fettuccine*. Shake out the strips lightly so that they unroll, and leave to dry.

Cooking pasta

Homemade pasta is very simple and quick to cook – more so than the dried varieties. Italians like their pasta *al dente* – tender without being soft and sticky: it should have a little resistance to the bite to be absolutely perfect. Cooking time varies according to the size and shape; small homemade pasta can be cooked in as little as 2 to 5 minutes, whereas larger shapes can take up to 6 or 7 minutes. Dried pasta takes a little longer than this, from 6 to 15 minutes. Tubular pasta tends to cook faster than the flat varieties, but even this depends on thickness, and if using commercial pasta it is always advisable to consult the manufacturer's cooking times for best results.

Allow 450 g/1 lb uncooked pasta for 4 to 6 servings and at least 2.25–3.5 litres/4–6 pints (U.S. 5–7 pints) water. Bring the water to the boil in a large tall pan, then stir in 15 ml/1 tablespoon salt. Add the pasta to the water gradually (long spaghetti has to be gently eased into the pan), then cook for the required time, keeping the water at a constant rolling boil and stirring occasionally with a wooden pasta 'fork' or spoon to keep the pasta separate. When the pasta is *al dente*, drain and serve immediatly on hot plates or dishes. Pasta should always be served immediately, unless it is the lasagne type which is to be baked.

Serving Pasta

Italians serve their pasta in numerous ways, depending on the occasion and the region, although it is almost always served after the *antipasto* and before the main course. One of the simplest ways to serve it is with butter and grated cheese, although the Neapolitans are fond of it with a tomato sauce, and other regions prefer it with a *ragù* of meat or offal (variety meats). There are numerous types of filled pasta such as *ravioli*, *tortellini* and *cannelloni*. Very small pasta shapes are added to soups.

Pasta comes in the most bewildering number of different shapes and sizes, not to mention the number of different names for these, many of which are purely regional or peculiar to a certain manufacturer. The following list includes all the common pasta shapes and those used in recipes in this book. Many of these shapes are interchangeable, such as *tagliatelle* and *fettuccine* or *cannelloni* and *manicotti*, so it is not worth going to the ends of the earth searching for exactly the right one. Choose whichever can be obtained easily or appeals to you, bearing in mind the recipe.

Types of Pasta

Annellini: Sometimes known as *anelli*, these very small ring shapes are used in soups.
Bigoli: Kind of spaghetti.
Cannelloni: These large tubular shapes are stuffed with a variety of ingredients. Flat lasagne-type pasta can also be used for baked cannelloni. The

stuffing is spread on the flat pasta, which is then rolled around it.
Capelli d'Angelo: A long extremely thin pasta of the *vermicelli* type that derives its name from the fact that it is as fine as 'angel's hair'. It is often sold coiled into 'nest' shapes (*capelli d'angelo a nidi*). Other names are *capellini* and *capel Venere*.
Cappelletti: These small round pasta are shaped like little hats. Fresh *cappelletti* are stuffed and served like ravioli. Also sold as *pagliacci*.
Chitarra: A kind of spaghetti made on a special guitar-shaped frame which makes them square rather than tubular. Sometimes also called *spaghetti alla chitarra*.
Conchiglie: A shell-shaped pasta; *conchigliette* are very small shell-shapes for use in soups.
Farfalle: This pasta is in the shape of bows or butterflies. *Farfallette* are small *farfalle*.
Fedelini: A thin kind of spaghetti. Also known as *spaghettini*.
Fettuccine: A flat ribbon noodle usually sold coiled into 'nest' shapes as *fettuccine a nidi*. Egg *fettuccine* and *fettuccine verde* are also common. *Fettuccine* are the Roman equivalent of *tagliatelle*.
Fusilli: Spiral-shaped pasta which look like small hollow coils or springs. Available both long and short. Similar types are known as *spirale ricciolo*, but these are not hollow.
Lasagne: Flat sheets of pasta used for baking in layers with meat and cheese and sauces, according to individual recipes. Can also be rolled around stuffings to make baked cannelloni. Available in different widths and sizes, sometimes ridged or with a crimped edge. *Lasagne verde* are common.
Linguine: Very thin, narrow ribbon noodle.
Macaroni: Italian *maccheroni* is usually long like spaghetti but much thicker and hollow. Short-cut or 'elbow' macaroni is very common outside Italy. Short *maccheroni* is also available in many different forms in Italy, see *Rigatoni*.
Manicotti: Large tubular pasta which is stuffed like *cannelloni*. Also called *tuffoloni*.
Mezza Zita: A tubular pasta, slightly thicker than macaroni. *Zita* is thicker than *mezza zita*.
Orecchiette: Small ear-shaped pasta.
Paglia e fieno: Flat ribbon noodles, the same as *tagliatelle*, but sold coiled up. Egg and spinach noodles are both available.
Pappardelle: Very wide ribbon noodles.
Penne: Short tubular pasta like short macaroni, but with angled rather than straight ends. *Penne rigate* are ridged, *pennine* are a thinner variety.
Ravioli: Filled pasta shapes, either square or round. Fillings vary enormously from one region to another, but fresh ravioli in Italy bears little or no resemblance to the canned varieties common abroad. Other forms of pasta that are stuffed and served like *ravioli* are *agnolotti*, *crolini*, *cappelletti* and *tortellini*. These shapes are usually served with butter and cheese, with a sauce or *ragù*, or in a clear soup. They are seldom served smothered in the

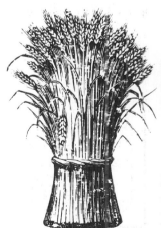

thick tomato sauce with which so many non-Italians associate them.

Rigatoni: A kind of ridged short macaroni, of which there are many different varieties.

Rotelle: Wheel-shaped small pasta, often used in soups.

Spaghetti: The most common form of pasta outside Italy. The name derives from the Italian word *spago* meaning 'string'. The thickness of *spaghetti* varies slightly from one region to another, and it is simply a matter of availability and personal taste which one you choose.

Tagliatelle: The most common form of flat ribbon noodle. Eaten more in the north of Italy than the south. Plain *tagliatelle*, egg *tagliatelle* and *tagliatelle verde* are all available, both loose and *a nidi* – 'in nests'.

Tortelli/Tortellini: Small stuffed pasta made by folding circles of dough over a stuffing, then coiling the pasta round into small circles. They are served like ravioli.

Trenette: Narrow, ribbon pasta, very similar to *linguine*.

Vermicelli: Neapolitan name for spaghetti. There are many kinds, some are available *a nidi* – 'in nests'.

Zita/Zitone: See *Mezza Zita*

There are numerous other small pasta for use in soups such as *risoni, stelline, ditalini, quadretti, tripolini* and *canestrine*.

KEY

1	Tortellini	16	Ditalini
2	Semini di melo	17	Fusilli
3	Orecchiette	18	Rotelle
4	Farfallette	19	Fettuccine verde
5	Lumache	20	Penne rigate
6	Capelli d'Angelo	21	Stelline
7	Penne	22	Farfalle
8	Pappardelle	23	Ravioli
9	Fedelini	24	Rigatoni
10	Spaghetti	25	Cannelloni
11	Fettuccine	26	Manicotti
12	Tagliatelle	27	Maccheroni
13	Annellini	28	Mezza zita
14	Conchiglie	29	Zita
15	Cappelletti	30	Lasagne

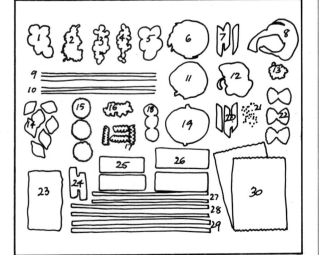

PIEMONTE & VALLE D'AOSTA

FETTUCCINE ALL'ALBESE

Ribbon Noodles with Parmesan and Butter

Metric/Imperial	American
400 g/14 oz fettuccine	14 oz fettuccine
salt	salt
75 g/3 oz Parmesan cheese★, grated	¾ cup grated Parmesan cheese★
65 g/2½ oz butter, softened	5 tablespoons softened butter
pinch of grated nutmeg	pinch of grated nutmeg
freshly ground black pepper	freshly ground black pepper
1 truffle d'Alba or a few button mushrooms, thinly sliced	1 truffle d'Alba or a few button mushrooms, thinly sliced

Cook the fettuccine in plenty of boiling salted water until *al dente*. Drain thoroughly, then pile in a warmed serving dish. Add the Parmesan, butter, nutmeg and salt and pepper to taste and fold gently to mix. Top with the truffle or mushrooms and serve immediately, with a well-flavoured meat ragù if preferred.

SERVES 4 to 6

LIGURIA

TRENETTE COL PESTO ALLA GENOVESE

Narrow Ribbon Pasta with Basil

Metric/Imperial	American
50 g/2 oz basil leaves, chopped	1½ cups chopped fresh basil leaves
pinch of sea salt	pinch of sea salt
3 garlic cloves, peeled and chopped	3 garlic cloves, peeled and chopped
6 tablespoons olive oil	6 tablespoons olive oil
25 g/1 oz pine kernels, lightly toasted and chopped	¼ cup pine kernels, lightly toasted and chopped
40 g/1½ oz pecorino cheese★, grated	6 tablespoons grated pecorino cheese★
65 g/2½ oz Parmesan cheese★, grated	⅔ cup grated Parmesan cheese★
575 g/1¼ lb trenette	1¼ lb trenette
salt	salt

Crush the basil with the sea salt, garlic and half the oil, using a pestle and mortar. Add the remaining oil, the pine kernels and grated cheeses. Stir well to mix.

Cook the trenette in plenty of boiling salted water until *al dente*. Drain thoroughly, reserving 1 tablespoon of the cooking water and mixing it with the basil mixture. Pile the pasta in a warmed serving dish and pour over the sauce. Serve immediately.

SERVES 6

RAVIOLI GENOVESE

Metric/Imperial	American
FILLING:	FILLING:
25 g/1 oz butter	2 tablespoons butter
3 tablespoons olive oil	3 tablespoons olive oil
1 onion, peeled and finely chopped	1 onion, peeled and finely chopped
1 celery stick, finely chopped	1 celery stalk, finely chopped
1 small carrot, peeled and finely chopped	1 small carrot, peeled and finely chopped
$\frac{1}{2}$ bay leaf	$\frac{1}{2}$ bay leaf
1 clove	1 clove
225 g/8 oz piece stewing beef	$\frac{1}{2}$ lb piece stewing beef
salt and freshly ground black pepper	salt and freshly ground black pepper
3–4 tablespoons white wine	3–4 tablespoons white wine
1 tablespoon tomato purée	1 tablespoon tomato paste
75 g/3 oz Parmesan cheese★, grated	$\frac{3}{4}$ cup grated Parmesan cheese★
2 eggs, beaten	2 eggs, beaten
pinch of grated nutmeg	pinch of grated nutmeg
175 g/6 oz fresh breadcrumbs (approximately)	3 cups fresh bread crumbs (approximately)
PASTA:	PASTA:
450 g/1 lb pasta all'uovo (see page 60: $1\frac{1}{2} \times$ quantity)	1 lb pasta all'uovo (see page 60: $1\frac{1}{2} \times$ quantity)
TO FINISH:	TO FINISH:
1.5 litres/$2\frac{1}{2}$ pints beef stock	$6\frac{1}{4}$ cups beef stock
50 g/2 oz Parmesan cheese★, grated	$\frac{1}{4}$ cup grated Parmesan cheese★

To make the filling: heat the butter and oil in a heavy pan, add the onion and fry gently until golden. Add the celery, carrot, bay leaf and clove and cook gently for 5 minutes. Add the beef and salt and pepper to taste and fry until golden brown on all sides. Add the wine, boil until it evaporates, then add the tomato purée (paste) dissolved in a little warm water. Cover the pan and simmer for 2 hours.

Meanwhile make the pasta and leave to stand for 1 hour.

Remove the meat from the pan and mince (grind) it into a bowl. Remove the clove and bay leaf from the cooking liquor, then add the liquor to the meat with the Parmesan, 1 beaten egg and the nutmeg. Stir in enough breadcrumbs to bind the mixture.

Divide the dough in half and roll each piece into a paper-thin sheet. Put heaped teaspoonfuls of the filling at regular intervals, about 5 cm/2 inches apart on one piece of dough. Brush the other sheet of dough with the remaining beaten egg and place loosely over the filling. Press the pasta between the filling firmly to seal. Cut around the balls of filling with a rotary cutter, then place the ravioli on a cloth sprinkled with flour.

Bring the stock to the boil in a large pan. Add the ravioli and cook for 5 minutes or until they rise to the surface. Transfer to a warmed serving dish with a slotted spoon. Add the Parmesan and fold gently to mix. Serve immediately.

SERVES 6

COLZETTI ALLA POLCEVERASCA

Pasta Shapes with Butter and Marjoram

If pine kernels are not available, use chopped walnuts instead.

Metric/Imperial	American
PASTA:	PASTA:
350 g/12 oz pasta all'uovo (see page 60)	$\frac{3}{4}$ lb pasta all'uovo (see page 60)
TO SERVE:	TO SERVE:
75 g/3 oz butter	6 tablespoons butter
1 tablespoon chopped pine kernels	1 tablespoon chopped pine kernels
1 tablespoon chopped marjoram	1 tablespoon chopped marjoram
75 g/3 oz Parmesan cheese★, grated	$\frac{3}{4}$ cup grated Parmesan cheese★

Make the pasta and leave to stand for 1 hour.

Knead the dough well, then divide into small balls about the size of walnuts. Flatten the balls of dough with the fingertips dipped in flour, then form each one into a figure-of-eight shape. Place the shapes on a cloth sprinkled with flour and leave to dry in a cool place for 1 hour.

Cook the pasta shapes in plenty of boiling salted water for 5 minutes or until they rise to the surface. Remove from the pan with a slotted spoon as soon as they are cooked and pile into a warmed serving dish; keep hot.

Melt the butter in a small pan, add the pine kernels and marjoram and heat, stirring, for 1 minute, then pour over the colzetti. Sprinkle with the Parmesan and serve immediately.

SERVES 4

During the 'pasta war' in the Italian press in the 1930s, journalists, cooks, restaurant owners and even doctors attacked each other over the subject of pasta. One poet even went as far as to say that pasta was 'an obsolete heavy food, inducing scepticism, sloth and pessimism'.

PIZZOCCHERI

Tagliatelle with Cabbage and Cheese

Metric/Imperial	American
PASTA:	PASTA:
300 g/11 oz buckwheat flour	2¾ cups buckwheat flour
150 g/5 oz plain flour	1¼ cups all-purpose flour
3 eggs, beaten	3 eggs, beaten
7 tablespoons milk	7 tablespoons milk
salt	salt
TO SERVE:	TO SERVE:
400 g/14 oz potatoes, peeled and diced	2⅓ cups diced raw potatoes
450 g/1 lb cabbage	1 lb cabbage
175 g/6 oz butter	¾ cup butter
2 garlic cloves, peeled	2 garlic cloves, peeled
2 sage stalks	2 sage stalks
225 g/8 oz bitto or pecorino cheese★, diced	1 cup diced bitto or pecorino cheese★
freshly ground black pepper	freshly ground black pepper

To make the pasta: sift both the flours onto a work surface and make a well in the centre. Add the eggs, milk, a little lukewarm water and a pinch of salt. Mix together to make a smooth dough, then leave to stand for 10 minutes.

Roll out the dough to a paper-thin sheet. Cut into tagliatelle strips, about 5 cm/2 inches long and 1 cm/½ inch wide.

Cook the potatoes and cabbage in a large pan of boiling salted water for 15 minutes. Add the tagliatelle, boil for 5 minutes or until *al dente*, then drain.

Melt the butter in a small pan, add the garlic and sage and fry until the garlic is browned. Remove the garlic and sage from the butter. Pile the tagliatelle mixture in a warmed serving dish. Pour the butter over the top, then add the cheese and sprinkle liberally with pepper. Serve immediately.

SERVES 6

PASTA E FASIOI

Tagliatelle and Broad (Lima) Bean Soup

Metric/Imperial	American
300 g/11 oz broad beans, shelled	1½ cups shelled lima beans
1.2 litres/2 pints water	5 cups water
salt	salt
7 tablespoons olive oil	7 tablespoons olive oil
½ onion, chopped	½ onion, chopped
2 garlic cloves, peeled and crushed	2 garlic cloves, peeled and crushed
1 tablespoon chopped parsley	1 tablespoon chopped parsley
200 g/7 oz tagliatelle, broken up	2 cups broken tagliatelle
freshly ground black pepper	freshly ground black pepper

Put the beans in a large pan with the water, a little salt, the oil, onion, garlic and parsley. Bring to the boil, lower the heat and simmer for 20 minutes until the beans are tender.

Remove half the beans, mash them and return to the liquid. Add the tagliatelle and salt and pepper to taste, then cook for a further 5 to 10 minutes until *al dente*. Serve hot, sprinkled with pepper.

SERVES 4

CASONSEI

Ravioli from Lombardy

Metric/Imperial	American
PASTA:	PASTA:
350 g/12 oz pasta all'uovo (see page 60)	¾ lb pasta all'uovo (see page 60)
FILLING:	FILLING:
25 g/1 oz butter	2 tablespoons butter
1 garlic clove, peeled and crushed	1 garlic clove, peeled and crushed
1 tablespoon chopped parsley	1 tablespoon chopped parsley
225 g/8 oz minced beef	1 cup ground beef
25 g/1 oz fresh breadcrumbs	½ cup fresh bread crumbs
25 g/1 oz Parmesan cheese★, grated	¼ cup grated Parmesan cheese★
1 egg, beaten	1 egg, beaten
1 egg yolk	1 egg yolk
pinch of grated nutmeg	pinch of grated nutmeg
salt and freshly ground black pepper	salt and freshly ground black pepper
TO SERVE:	TO SERVE:
1.5 litres/2½ pints chicken stock or water	6¼ cups chicken stock or water
100 g/4 oz butter, melted	½ cup butter, melted
100 g/4 oz Parmesan cheese★, grated	1 cup grated Parmesan cheese★

Make the pasta and leave to stand for 1 hour.

Meanwhile, make the filling: melt the butter in a heavy pan, add the garlic and parsley and fry gently until lightly browned. Add the beef and cook gently, stirring, for 10 minutes. Remove from the heat and leave to cool, then add the remaining filling ingredients and mix thoroughly.

Roll out the dough to a paper-thin sheet. Cut into rectangular shapes, about 15 × 7.5 cm/6 × 3 inches. Divide the filling between the rectangles, placing it in the centre of each one. Fold the longer sides over the filling and press the edges together to seal. Bend gently into a horseshoe shape, with the sealed edge on the inside of the curve.

Bring the stock or salted water to the boil in a large saucepan. Add the casonsei and cook for about 5 minutes or until they rise to the surface. Remove from the pan with a slotted spoon and pile into a warmed serving dish. Top with the melted butter and Parmesan. Serve immediately.

SERVES 4

ABOVE: **Rotolo ripieno; Pasta e fasioi**

ROTOLO RIPIENO

Pasta Roulade

Metric/Imperial

FILLING:

40 g/1½ oz butter

575 g/1¼ lb calf's liver,
chopped

150 g/5 oz pork loin,
chopped

225 g/8 oz salsiccia a metro★,
chopped

900 g/2 lb fresh spinach

50 g/2 oz mushrooms,
chopped

150 g/5 oz Parmesan
cheese★, grated

salt and freshly ground
black pepper

PASTA:

300 g/11 oz plain flour

pinch of salt

3 eggs, beaten

TO FINISH:

25 g/1 oz Parmesan
cheese★, grated

65 g/2½ oz butter, melted

American

FILLING:

3 tablespoons butter

2½ cups chopped veal liver

⅔ cup chopped pork loin

1 cup chopped salsiccia a
metro★

2 lb fresh spinach

½ cup chopped mushrooms

1¼ cups grated Parmesan
cheese★

salt and freshly ground
black pepper

PASTA:

2¾ cups all-purpose flour

pinch of salt

3 eggs, beaten

TO FINISH:

¼ cup grated Parmesan
cheese★

5 tablespoons butter,
melted

To make the filling: melt the butter in a heavy pan, add the liver, pork and sausage and fry gently for 8 minutes. Cook the spinach in a separate pan, with just the water clinging to the leaves after washing, until tender. Drain thoroughly. Drain the meat, then mince (grind) it with the spinach. Add the mushrooms, Parmesan and salt and pepper to taste. Mix well.

To make the pasta: sift the flour and salt onto a work surface and make a well in the centre. Add the eggs and mix to a smooth dough.

Flatten the dough with a rolling pin and roll out to a rectangular sheet, about 3 mm/⅛ inch thick. Spread the filling over the dough, leaving a 3 cm/1¼ inch border around the edges. Roll up the dough as for a Swiss (jelly) roll. Wrap in a piece of muslin (cheesecloth) and secure the ends with thin string.

Place the roll in a long, narrow flameproof casserole and cover with lightly salted cold water. Bring to the boil, lower the heat and simmer for 20 minutes. Remove the casserole from the heat, and leave the roll to cool in the water.

Remove the muslin (cheesecloth) and cut the roulade into 2 cm/¾ inch thick slices. Place the slices in a buttered ovenproof dish. Sprinkle with the Parmesan and butter. Place under a preheated hot grill (broiler) for 5 minutes, then serve immediately.

SERVES 6

CAPPELLETTI DI MAGRO

Ravioli with Cheese Filling

In Emilia-Romagna and most of the nothern regions of Italy, pasta is usually made at home. Eggs are nearly always included in the dough and the finished pasta is served with a substantial filling or sauce. The dishes on these and the following two pages are typical of the area.

Metric/Imperial

PASTA:
400 g/14 oz plain flour
salt
4 eggs, beaten
FILLING:
225 g/8 oz ricotta cheese★
100 g/4 oz Bel Paese
    cheese★, grated
50 g/2 oz Parmesan
    cheese★, grated
2 eggs, beaten
pinch of grated nutmeg
TO SERVE:
1.5 litres/2½ pints stock or
    water
100 g/4 oz butter, melted
75 g/3 oz Parmesan
    cheese★, grated

American

PASTA:
3½ cups all-purpose flour
salt
4 eggs, beaten
FILLING:
1 cup ricotta cheese★
½ cup grated Bel Paese
    cheese★
½ cup grated Parmesan
    cheese★
2 eggs, beaten
pinch of grated nutmeg
TO SERVE:
6¼ cups stock or water
½ cup butter, melted
¾ cup grated Parmesan
    cheese★

To make the pasta: sift the flour and a pinch of salt onto a work surface and make a well in the centre. Add the eggs and mix to a smooth dough. Shape into a ball, wrap in a damp cloth and leave to stand for about 30 minutes.

Meanwhile, make the filling: put the ricotta and Bel Paese in a bowl and beat well. Add the Parmesan, eggs, a pinch of salt and the nutmeg and beat thoroughly.

Roll out the dough to a paper-thin sheet. Cut into 4 cm/1¾ inch squares with a tooth-edged rotary cutter. Put a little filling in the centre of each square, then fold the dough over the filling to make triangles. Turn the corners of the triangles upwards.

Bring the stock or salted water to the boil in a large pan. Add the ravioli and cook for 5 minutes or until they rise to the surface. Remove from the pan with a slotted spoon and pile into a warmed serving dish. Sprinkle the melted butter and Parmesan over the top and serve immediately.

SERVES 4

ABOVE: **Preparing Cappelleti di magro and Gnocco fritto**

GARGANELLI DI LUGO

Macaroni with Meat and Vegetable Ragù

Metric/Imperial	American
PASTA:	PASTA:
400 g/14 oz plain flour	3½ cups all-purpose flour
pinch of salt	pinch of salt
4 eggs, beaten	4 eggs, beaten
25 g/1 oz Parmesan cheese★, grated	¼ cup grated Parmesan cheese★
pinch of grated nutmeg	pinch of grated nutmeg
RAGÙ:	RAGÙ:
25 g/1 oz mushrooms	¼ cup mushrooms
1 onion, peeled	1 onion, peeled
1 carrot, peeled	1 carrot, peeled
1 celery stick	1 celery stalk
50 g/2 oz raw ham or bacon	1 thick slice raw ham or bacon
65 g/2½ oz butter	
4 tablespoons olive oil	5 tablespoons butter
¼ cup grated Parmesan	¼ cup olive oil
¼ pint/150 ml beef stock	⅔ cup beef stock
75 g/3 oz minced beef	⅓ cup ground beef
75 g/3 oz minced pork	⅓ cup ground pork
7 tablespoons red wine	7 tablespoons red wine
400 g/14 oz tomatoes, skinned and mashed	1¾ cups skinned and mashed tomatoes
salt and freshly ground black pepper	salt and freshly ground black pepper
100 g/4 oz frozen peas	1 cup frozen peas
75 g/3 oz Parmesan cheese★, grated, to serve	¾ cup grated Parmesan cheese★, to serve

To make the pasta: sift the flour and salt onto a work surface, then make a well in the centre. Add the eggs, Parmesan and nutmeg and mix to a smooth dough. Leave to stand for 20 minutes.

Flatten the dough with a rolling pin and roll into a sheet that is not too thin. Cut into 2 cm/¾ inch squares. Roll each square, corner to corner, round the handle of a wooden spoon to form macaroni.

To make the ragù: mince (grind) the mushrooms with the onion, carrot, celery and ham or bacon. Heat 50 g/2 oz/¼ cup butter and the oil in a heavy pan, add the minced (ground) mixture and simmer for 10 minutes, adding the stock gradually during cooking.

Add the minced (ground) meats and cook over a high heat for 5 minutes. Stir in the wine, cover and simmer very gently for 15 minutes.

Add the tomatoes, a little more stock and salt and pepper to taste. Cover again and cook for a further 30 minutes, adding more stock if necessary.

Melt the remaining butter in a separate pan, add the peas and cook for 5 minutes. Stir into the ragù and cook for a further 5 minutes.

Cook the macaroni in plenty of boiling salted water until al dente. Drain thoroughly and pile into a warmed serving dish. Top with the ragù and Parmesan. Serve immediately.
SERVES 4

GNOCCO FRITTO

Fried Pasta Shapes

Metric/Imperial	American
350 g/12 oz plain flour	3 cups all-purpose flour
pinch of salt	pinch of salt
40 g/1½ oz lard	3 tablespoons shortening
vegetable oil for shallow-frying	vegetable oil for shallow-frying

Sift the flour and salt onto a work surface and make a well in the centre. Add the lard (shortening) and mix together with enough lukewarm water to give a smooth dough. Knead well until no longer sticky, adding a little extra flour if necessary. Flatten the dough with a rolling pin and roll out to a thin sheet. Cut into rectangular shapes, about 7.5 × 3 cm/3 × 1½ inches and prick all over with a fork.

Shallow-fry the rectangles a few at a time in hot oil until golden brown. Drain on absorbent kitchen paper while frying the remainder. Serve hot with an assortment of sausages.
SERVES 4

CANNELLONI PIACENTINI

Cannelloni Piacenza Style

Metric/Imperial

PASTA:
200 g/7 oz plain flour
salt
2 eggs, beaten
2 egg yolks
50 g/2 oz butter, melted
300 ml/½ pint milk
    (approximately)
FILLING:
900 g/2 lb fresh spinach,
    cooked, well drained and
    chopped
1 tablespoon chopped
    parsley
150 g/5 oz ricotta cheese★
100 g/4 oz mascarpone
    cheese★
65 g/2½ oz Parmesan
    cheese★, grated
1 egg, beaten
1 egg yolk
pinch of grated nutmeg
TO FINISH:
50 g/2 oz Parmesan
    cheese★, grated
75 g/3 oz butter, melted

American

PASTA:
1¾ cups all-purpose flour
salt
2 eggs, beaten
2 egg yolks
¼ cup butter, melted
1¼ cups milk
    (approximately)
FILLING:
2 lb fresh spinach, cooked,
    well drained and chopped
1 tablespoon chopped
    parsley
⅔ cup ricotta cheese★
½ cup mascarpone cheese★
⅔ cup grated Parmesan
    cheese★
1 egg, beaten
1 egg yolk
pinch of grated nutmeg
TO FINISH:
½ cup grated Parmesan
    cheese★
⅓ cup butter, melted

To make the pasta: sift the flour and a pinch of salt into a bowl. Add the eggs, egg yolks and 1 tablespoon melted butter, then stir in the milk gradually, adding enough to give a semi-liquid batter. Continue stirring for a further 10 minutes.

Heat 1 tablespoon of the remaining butter in a small frying pan (skillet). Pour in just enough batter to cover the bottom, tilting the pan to spread evenly. Fry until golden on both sides. Remove from the pan and repeat with the remaining batter, adding more butter to the pan as necessary. Trim the fritters to a rectangular shape.

To make the filling: put the spinach, parsley and ricotta in a bowl and beat well. Add the mascarpone, Parmesan, egg, egg yolk, nutmeg and a pinch of salt. Stir well. Divide the filling between the pasta rectangles, placing it in the centre of each one. Fold the edges over the filling, to form a parcel shape.

Arrange the cannelloni in a single layer in a buttered ovenproof dish. Sprinkle with the Parmesan and the butter and bake in a preheated moderately hot oven (200°C/400°F/Gas Mark 6) for 20 minutes until golden brown. Serve hot.

SERVES 4

BELOW: **Cannelloni piacentini; Lasagne alla bolognese**

CRESCENTINE
Tuscan Deep-Fried Pasta

Metric/Imperial	American
½ teaspoon dried yeast	½ teaspoon active dry yeast
¼ teaspoon sugar	¼ teaspoon sugar
450 g/1 lb plain flour	4 cups all-purpose flour
salt	salt
25 g/1 oz butter	2 tablespoons butter
150 ml/¼ pint lukewarm stock	⅔ cup lukewarm stock
vegetable oil for deep-frying	vegetable oil for deep-frying
freshly ground black pepper	freshly ground black pepper

Dissolve the yeast and sugar in a little water; set aside for 10 minutes. Sift the flour and a little salt onto a work surface. Stir in the yeast, then add the butter and enough stock to make a soft dough. Knead well, then roll out to a fairly thick sheet.

Fold the 4 corners of the dough inwards to the centre, then flatten with the rolling pin. Fold and flatten again at least 5 more times. Roll the dough out to a sheet, about 5 mm/¼ inch thick, and cut into small rectangles.

Deep-fry the shapes, a few at a time, in hot oil until golden brown and puffed up. Drain on absorbent kitchen paper while frying the remainder. Sprinkle with salt and pepper and serve hot.
SERVES 6

In the north of Italy, cannelloni is most frequently made at home by wrapping rectangular pieces of dough around a filling. Southern Italians are more likely to use packets of ready-made tubes when making cannelloni.

LASAGNE ALLA BOLOGNESE

Metric/Imperial	American
225 g/8 oz green or plain lasagne	½ lb green or plain lasagne
RAGÙ:	RAGÙ:
15 g/½ oz butter	1 tablespoon butter
1 onion, peeled and finely chopped	1 onion, peeled and finely chopped
1 small carrot, peeled and finely chopped	1 small carrot, peeled and finely chopped
1 celery stick, finely chopped	1 celery stalk, finely chopped
3 rashers bacon, finely chopped	3 bacon slices, finely chopped
350 g/12 oz finely minced beef	1½ cups finely ground beef
100 g/4 oz chicken livers, finely minced	¼ lb chicken livers, finely chopped
4 tablespoons dry white wine	4 tablespoons dry white wine
300 ml/½ pint beef stock	1¼ cups beef stock
1 tablespoon tomato purée	1 tablespoon tomato paste
grated nutmeg	grated nutmeg
salt and freshly ground black pepper	salt and freshly ground black pepper
BÉCHAMEL SAUCE:	BÉCHAMEL SAUCE:
40 g/1½ oz butter	3 tablespoons butter
40 g/1½ oz plain flour	⅓ cup all-purpose flour
600 ml/1 pint warm milk	2½ cups warm milk
4 tablespoons double cream	¼ cup heavy cream
grated nutmeg	grated nutmeg
50 g/2 oz Parmesan cheese* grated	½ cup grated Parmesan cheese*

To make the ragù: melt the butter in a large shallow pan. Add the vegetables and bacon and fry gently, stirring, for about 10 minutes until golden. Add the beef and fry, stirring, until evenly browned. Add the chicken livers and cook, stirring, for 1 to 2 minutes, then add the wine, stock, tomato purée (paste), nutmeg and salt and pepper to taste. Bring to the boil, cover and simmer gently for 1 hour, stirring occasionally.

Cook the lasagne in a large pan of boiling salted water until al dente, stirring occasionally to prevent the pasta sticking. Immediately add cold water to the pan to prevent further cooking, drain and lay the strips side by side on a clean tea towel.

To make the Béchamel sauce: melt the butter in a pan, stir in the flour and cook for 1 minute. Take off the heat and stir in the milk and cream. Return to the heat and cook, stirring, until smooth. Season with salt and nutmeg to taste. Put a layer of lasagne in the bottom of a buttered ovenproof dish. Cover with a layer of ragù, then a layer of béchamel and sprinkle with a little Parmesan. Continue these layers, finishing with a thick layer of Béchamel sauce and a good sprinkling of Parmesan. Bake in a preheated moderately hot oven (200°C/400°F/Gas Mark 6) for 30 minutes, or until golden on top. Serve immediately.
SERVES 6

It is not uncommon to find truffles in Italian recipes, and both the black and white varieties are used. They are mostly found in northern Italy, in the regions of Piemonte, Emilia-Romagna, Tuscany and Umbria. White truffles are thought to be the greater delicacy of the two, and the best of these are found in the Langhe area of Piemonte during the winter months. The black truffles suggested in *Spaghetti alla nursina* grow prolifically in the Norcia area of Umbria, where even the pigs can be seen feeding on them!

PAPPARDELLE CON LA LEPRE

Tagliatelle with Marinated Hare

This dish makes an excellent main course.

Metric/Imperial	American
1 hare, cleaned and cut into small pieces	*1 hare, cleaned and cut into small pieces*
500 ml/18 fl oz red wine	*2¼ cups red wine*
1 celery stick, chopped	*1 celery stalk, chopped*
1 onion, peeled and sliced	*1 onion, peeled and sliced*
1 bay leaf	*1 bay leaf*
few black peppercorns	*few black peppercorns*
75 g/3 oz belly pork	*3 oz fatty pork slices*
1 carrot, peeled	*1 carrot, peeled*
4 tablespoons olive oil	*¼ cup olive oil*
salt and freshly ground black pepper	*salt and freshly ground black pepper*
7 tablespoons beef stock	*7 tablespoons beef stock*
400 g/14 oz tagliatelle	*14 oz tagliatelle*
75 g/3 oz Parmesan cheese★, grated	*¾ cup grated Parmesan cheese★*
50 g/2 oz butter, softened	*¼ cup softened butter*

Put the hare in a bowl, with the wine, celery, half the onion, the bay leaf and peppercorns. Leave to marinate for 3 to 4 hours, stirring from time to time.

Mince (grind) the pork with the remaining onion and the carrot. Heat the oil in a large heavy pan, add the minced (ground) mixture and fry gently for 5 minutes. Drain the hare, reserving the marinade, then add to the pan with salt and pepper to taste. Fry until browned on all sides, then add a little of the reserved marinade and the stock. Cover and cook for 1½ hours until the hare is tender, stirring occasionally and adding more marinade and stock as necessary during cooking. Transfer the pieces of hare to a warmed serving dish. Strain the cooking juices and keep hot.

Cook the tagliatelle in boiling salted water until *al dente*, then drain thoroughly. Pile the tagliatelle in a warmed serving dish and moisten with a little of the cooking liquor from the hare. Add the Parmesan and butter and fold gently to mix. Serve immediately, with the hare in a separate dish.

SERVES 4

SPAGHETTI ALLA NURSINA

Spaghetti with Truffles or Mushrooms

Metric/Imperial	American
6 tablespoons olive oil	*6 tablespoons olive oil*
1 black truffle, or 50 g/2 oz morels or field mushrooms, sliced	*1 sliced black truffle, or ½ cup sliced morels or field mushrooms*
1 garlic clove, peeled and crushed	*1 garlic clove, peeled and crushed*
2 canned anchovies, drained and chopped	*2 canned anchovies, drained and chopped*
400 g/14 oz spaghetti	*14 oz spaghetti*
salt	*salt*

Heat the oil in a heavy pan, add the truffle or mushrooms, and cook gently for 5 minutes. Remove from the heat and add the garlic and anchovies. Return to the heat and cook very gently for 5 minutes, stirring constantly. Remove from the heat and set aside.

Cook the spaghetti in plenty of boiling salted water until *al dente*. Drain thoroughly, then pile in a warmed serving dish. Pour over the sauce, fold gently to mix and serve immediately.

SERVES 4

VINCISGRASSI
Lasagne with Ragù

Metric/Imperial	American
RAGÙ:	RAGÙ:
3–4 tablespoons olive oil	3–4 tablespoons olive oil
50 g/2 oz butter	¼ cup butter
1 onion, peeled and chopped	1 onion, peeled and chopped
350 g/12 oz minced beef	1½ cups ground beef
100 g/4 oz raw ham or bacon, diced	½ cup diced raw ham or bacon
4 tablespoons white wine	¼ cup white wine
4 tomatoes, skinned and chopped	4 tomatoes, skinned and chopped
pinch of grated nutmeg	pinch of grated nutmeg
salt and freshly ground black pepper	salt and freshly ground black pepper
350 g/12 oz calf's sweetbreads	¾ lb veal sweetbreads
PASTA:	PASTA:
400 g/14 oz plain flour	3½ cups all-purpose flour
pinch of salt	pinch of salt
150 g/5 oz semolina	scant 1 cup semolina flour
4 eggs, beaten	4 eggs, beaten
50 g/2 oz lard	¼ cup shortening
3–4 tablespoons white wine	3–4 tablespoons white wine
TO FINISH:	TO FINISH:
100 g/4 oz Parmesan cheese★, grated	1 cup grated Parmesan cheese★
50–75 g/2–3 oz mozzarella cheese★	2–3 oz mozzarella cheese★
50 g/2 oz butter, melted	¼ cup butter, melted

To make the ragù: heat the oil and butter in a heavy pan, add the onion and fry gently for 5 minutes until golden. Add the beef and ham and cook, stirring, over moderate heat for 10 minutes. Add the wine, tomatoes, nutmeg and salt and pepper to taste, then lower the heat and simmer for 1 hour.

Meanwhile, cook the sweetbreads in boiling water for 10 minutes, then drain and cut into cubes. Add to the ragù and cook for 5 minutes.

To make the pasta: sift the flour and salt onto a work surface, stir in the semolina and make a well in the centre. Add the eggs, lard (shortening) and wine and mix to a smooth dough. Shape into a ball, wrap in a damp cloth and leave to stand for about 30 minutes.

Flatten the dough with a rolling pin and roll into a thin sheet. Cut into lasagne strips, about 10 cm/4 inches long. Cook the lasagne in plenty of boiling salted water for 6 to 7 minutes until al dente; drain thoroughly.

Put a layer of lasagne in the bottom of a buttered deep ovenproof dish. Cover with a layer of sauce, then sprinkle with Parmesan and top with a few slices of mozzarella. Continue these layers until all the ingredients are used, finishing with a layer of cheese. Sprinkle with the melted butter. Bake in a preheated moderately hot oven (200°C/400°F/Gas Mark 6) for 20 minutes. Serve immediately.
SERVES 6

ABOVE: **Vincisgrassi**
LEFT: **Pappardelle con la lepre**

SPAGHETTINI AL RANCETTO
Vermicelli in Tomato and Marjoram Sauce

Metric/Imperial	American
4 tablespoons olive oil	¼ cup olive oil
1 onion, peeled and sliced	1 onion, peeled and sliced
150 g/5 oz bacon, diced	⅝ cup diced bacon
225 g/8 oz tomatoes, skinned and chopped	1 cup skinned and chopped tomatoes
1 tablespoon chopped marjoram	1 tablespoon chopped marjoram
salt and freshly ground black pepper	salt and freshly ground black pepper
400 g/14 oz vermicelli	14 oz vermicelli
50 g/2 oz pecorino cheese★, grated	½ cup grated pecorino cheese★

Heat the oil in a heavy pan, add the onion and bacon and fry gently for 5 minutes, stirring frequently. Add the tomatoes and cook for 10 minutes, then add the marjoram and salt and pepper to taste; keep warm.

Cook the vermicelli in plenty of boiling salted water until al dente. Drain thoroughly, then pile in a warmed serving dish. Pour the sauce over the top, add the pecorino, then fold gently to mix. Serve immediately.
SERVES 4

MACCHERONI ALLA PESARESE

Zitone Pesaro Style

Metric/Imperial	American
175 g/6 oz turkey breast meat	6 oz turkey breast meat
2 chicken livers	2 chicken livers
100 g/4 oz ham	¼ lb ham
50 g/2 oz mushrooms	½ cup mushrooms
100 g/4 oz butter	½ cup butter
1 small onion, peeled and chopped	1 small onion, peeled and chopped
7 tablespoons dry white wine	7 tablespoons dry white wine
pinch of grated nutmeg	pinch of grated nutmeg
salt and freshly ground black pepper	salt and freshly ground black pepper
7 tablespoons cream	7 tablespoons cream
300 g/11 oz zitone	11 oz zitone
75 g/3 oz gruyère cheese, grated	¾ cup grated gruyère cheese

Mince (grind) the turkey, chicken livers, ham and mushrooms. Melt 2 tablespoons butter in a heavy pan, add the onion and fry gently until golden. Stir in the minced (ground) mixture and cook, stirring, for 10 minutes.

Add the wine and simmer gently until it has evaporated by half, then add the nutmeg and salt and pepper to taste. Transfer to a bowl, add a little of the cream and stir well, to give a smooth, creamy filling.

Cook the zitone in plenty of boiling salted water until *al dente*. Drain thoroughly, then stuff with the filling.

Arrange the stuffed zitone in two layers in a buttered baking dish, covering each layer with the cream and gruyère. Dot the remaining butter over the top. Bake in a preheated moderately hot oven (200°C/400°F/Gas Mark 6) for 15 minutes. Serve hot.

SERVES 4

SPAGHETTI CACIO E PEPE

Spaghetti with Pecorino Cheese

Metric/Imperial	American
400 g/14 oz spaghetti	14 oz spaghetti
salt	salt
100 g/4 oz pecorino cheese★, grated	1 cup grated pecorino cheese★
freshly ground black pepper	freshly ground black pepper

Cook the spaghetti in plenty of boiling salted water until *al dente*. Drain thoroughly, reserving 2 to 3 tablespoons of the cooking water. Place in a warmed serving dish, add the reserved liquid, pecorino and plenty of pepper. Toss well to mix and serve immediately.

SERVES 4

SPAGHETTI ALL'AMATRICIANA

Spaghetti with Tomato and Bacon Ragù

Metric/Imperial	American
1 tablespoon olive oil	1 tablespoon olive oil
100 g/4 oz lean bacon, diced	½ cup diced lean bacon
350 g/12 oz tomatoes, skinned and chopped	1½ cups skinned and chopped tomatoes
1 canned pimento	1 canned pimiento
400 g/14 oz spaghetti	14 oz spaghetti
salt	salt
50 g/2 oz pecorino or Parmesan cheese★, grated	½ cup grated pecorino or Parmesan cheese★

Heat the oil in a heavy pan, add the bacon and fry gently for 5 minutes until golden. Add the tomatoes and pimento and continue cooking over moderate heat for 10 minutes, stirring occasionally.

Meanwhile, cook the spaghetti in plenty of boiling salted water until *al dente*, then drain thoroughly. Remove the pimento from the ragù. Pile the spaghetti in a warmed serving dish, pour over the ragù and sprinkle with the cheese. Fold gently to mix and serve immediately.

SERVES 4

ABOVE: **Maccheroni alla pesarese; Spaghetti alla ciociàra; Spaghetti alla carbonara**

SPAGHETTI ALLA CARBONARA

Spaghetti with Egg and Bacon

Metric/Imperial	American
25 g/1 oz butter	2 tablespoons butter
100 g/4 oz bacon, diced	½ cup diced bacon
1 garlic clove, peeled	1 garlic clove, peeled
400 g/14 oz spaghetti	14 oz spaghetti
salt and freshly ground black pepper	salt and freshly ground black pepper
3 eggs, beaten	3 eggs, beaten
40 g/1½ oz Parmesan cheese★, grated	6 tablespoons grated Parmesan cheese★
40 g/1½ oz pecorino cheese★, grated	6 tablespoons grated pecorino cheese★

Melt the butter in a heavy pan, add the bacon and garlic, fry gently until browned, then remove the garlic from the pan.

Cook the spaghetti in plenty of boiling salted water until *al dente*. Drain thoroughly and add to the bacon. Stir well, then remove from the heat. Add the eggs, a pinch of pepper, half the Parmesan and half the pecorino. Toss until the eggs turn creamy yellow, then add the remaining cheeses. Toss again and serve immediately.

SERVES 4

SPAGHETTI ALLA CIOCIÀRA

Spaghetti with Olives

Metric/Imperial	American
150 ml/¼ pint olive oil	⅔ cup olive oil
1 yellow or green pepper, cored, seeded and sliced	1 yellow or green pepper, cored, seeded and sliced
3 tomatoes, skinned and chopped	3 tomatoes, skinned and chopped
salt and freshly ground black pepper	salt and freshly ground black pepper
100 g/4 oz black olives, halved and stoned	¾ cup pitted ripe olives
400 g/14 oz spaghetti	14 oz spaghetti
65 g/2½ oz pecorino or Parmesan cheese★, grated	⅝ cup grated pecorino or Parmesan cheese★

Heat the oil in a heavy pan, add the pepper, tomatoes and salt and pepper to taste. Cover and simmer gently for 20 minutes, stirring occasionally. Add the olives and cook for 5 minutes.

Meanwhile, cook the spaghetti in plenty of boiling salted water until *al dente*. Drain thoroughly and add to the sauce. Fold gently to mix, then pile into a warmed serving dish and sprinkle with the cheese. Serve immediately.

SERVES 4

The Romans are particularly fond of spaghetti. These recipes from Lazio illustrate how easy it is to serve spaghetti in more interesting ways than the ubiquitous *Spaghetti Bolognese*.

Pasta is most often boiled, or boiled then baked. Deep-frying is another excellent method of cooking pasta which is perhaps less well known outside Italy. It is particularly suitable for the stuffed ravioli type of pasta. In recipes like these the pasta becomes more like a crisp batter.

FETTUCCINE ABRUZZESI
Ribbon Noodles with Herbs and Bacon

Metric/Imperial	American
3 tablespoons olive oil	3 tablespoons olive oil
100 g/4 oz fatty bacon or belly pork, chopped	½ cup chopped fatty bacon or pork
1 onion, peeled and chopped	1 onion, peeled and chopped
150 ml/¼ pint chicken stock	⅔ cup chicken stock
1 tablespoon chopped parsley	1 tablespoon chopped parsley
4 basil leaves, chopped	4 basil leaves, chopped
salt and freshly ground black pepper	salt and freshly ground black pepper
400 g/14 oz fettuccine	14 oz fettuccine
65 g/2½ oz pecorino cheese★, grated	⅔ cup grated pecorino cheese★

Heat the oil in a heavy pan, add the bacon and onion and fry gently for 5 minutes. Add the stock, parsley, basil and salt and pepper to taste. Cook gently, stirring occasionally, until reduced and slightly thickened.

Meanwhile, cook the noodles in boiling salted water until *al dente*. Drain thoroughly and pile into a warmed serving dish. Add the sauce and pecorino and fold gently to mix. Serve immediately.

SERVES 4

PANZAROTTI ALLA ROMANA
Fried Ravioli

Metric/Imperial	American
DOUGH:	DOUGH:
300 g/11 oz plain flour	2¾ cups all-purpose flour
salt	salt
50 g/2 oz butter, diced	¼ cup butter, diced
2 egg yolks	2 egg yolks
FILLING:	FILLING:
100 g/4 oz gruyère cheese, diced	½ cup diced gruyère cheese
75 g/3 oz cooked ham, minced	⅓ cup ground cooked ham
40 g/1½ oz Parmesan cheese★, grated	⅓ cup grated Parmesan cheese★
1 egg, beaten	1 egg, beaten
1 tablespoon chopped parsley	1 tablespoon chopped parsley
freshly ground black pepper	freshly ground black pepper
TO FINISH:	TO FINISH:
1 egg white, lightly whisked vegetable oil for deep-frying	1 egg white, lightly whisked vegetable oil for deep-frying

To make the dough: sift the flour and a pinch of salt onto a work surface and make a well in the centre. Add the butter and egg yolks and work to a smooth dough, adding a little lukewarm water if necessary.

To make the filling: put the gruyère in a bowl with the ham, Parmesan, egg, parsley and salt and pepper to taste. Stir well until thoroughly combined.

Flatten the dough with a rolling pin and roll out to a sheet, about 5 mm/¼ inch thick. Cut into 12.5 cm/5 inch circles. Divide the filling between the circles, placing it in the centre of each one. Brush the edges of the circles with a little egg white, then fold the dough over the filling to enclose it completely.

Deep-fry the ravioli a few at a time in hot oil until golden brown. Drain on absorbent kitchen paper while frying the remainder. Serve hot.

SERVES 6

SPAGHETTI AGLIO, OLIO E PEPERONCINO
Spaghetti with Garlic and Pimento

Metric/Imperial	American
400 g/14 oz spaghetti	14 oz spaghetti
salt	salt
3–4 tablespoons olive oil	3–4 tablespoons olive oil
2 garlic cloves, peeled	2 garlic cloves, peeled
1 canned pimento, sliced	1 canned pimiento, sliced
1 tablespoon chopped parsley	1 tablespoon chopped parsley

Cook the spaghetti in plenty of boiling salted water until *al dente*. Meanwhile, heat the oil in a heavy pan, add the garlic and pimento and fry gently until the garlic is well browned.

Drain the spaghetti thoroughly and pile into a warmed serving dish. Discard the garlic and pimento from the oil, then pour over the spaghetti. Stir in the parsley and serve immediately.

SERVES 4

CALZONI DI RICOTTA ALLA MOLISANA

Ravioli with Ricotta and Provolone

Metric/Imperial	American
DOUGH:	DOUGH:
400 g/14 oz plain flour	3½ cups all-purpose flour
salt	salt
100 g/4 oz lard, diced	½ cup shortening, diced
2 eggs, beaten	2 eggs, beaten
juice of 1 lemon	juice of 1 lemon
FILLING:	FILLING:
250 g/9 oz ricotta cheese★	1 cup ricotta cheese★, firmly packed
100 g/4 oz ham, diced	½ cup diced ham
100 g/4 oz provolone cheese★, diced	½ cup diced provolone cheese★
2 egg yolks	2 egg yolks
freshly ground black pepper	freshly ground black pepper
TO FINISH:	TO FINISH:
1 egg white, lightly whisked	1 egg white, lightly whisked
vegetable oil for deep-frying	vegetable oil for deep-frying

To make the dough: sift the flour and a pinch of salt onto a work surface and make a well in the centre. Add the lard (shortening), eggs and lemon juice, then work all the ingredients together to make a smooth dough.

To make the filling: press the ricotta through a sieve (strainer) into a bowl. Add the ham, provolone, egg yolks and salt and pepper to taste. Mix well until thoroughly combined.

Flatten the dough with a rolling pin and roll out into a fairly thin sheet. Cut out 4 circles, each one about 20 cm/8 inches in diameter. Divide the filling between the circles, placing it in the centre of each one. Brush the edges of the circles with a little egg white, then fold the dough over the filling to enclose it completely.

Deep-fry the ravioli one at a time in hot oil until golden brown. Drain on absorbent kitchen paper while frying the remainder. Serve hot.

SERVES 4

ABOVE: **Fettuccine abruzzesi; Panzarotti alla romana**
LEFT: **Calzoni di ricotta alla molisana**

PASTA E CECI ALLA NAPOLETANA

Noodles with Chick Peas (Garbanzos)

Metric/Imperial	American
200 g/7 oz chick peas	1 cup garbanzos
1 litre/1¾ pints water	4¼ cups water
7 tablespoons olive oil	7 tablespoons olive oil
4 tomatoes, skinned and chopped	4 tomatoes, skinned and chopped
2 garlic cloves, peeled and crushed	2 garlic cloves, peeled and crushed
200 g/7 oz wholemeal or green fettuccine	7 oz wholemeal or green fettuccine
1 tablespoon chopped parsley	1 tablespoon chopped parsley
6 basil leaves, chopped	6 basil leaves, chopped
salt and freshly ground black pepper	salt and freshly ground black pepper

Soak the chick peas (garbanzos) in lukewarm water overnight. Drain and place in a large pan with the water, 3 tablespoons oil, the tomatoes and half the garlic. Bring to the boil, lower the heat, cover and simmer for 1 hour.

Add the fettuccine and cook for a further 15 minutes. Add the parsley, basil, remaining garlic and oil, and salt and pepper to taste. Serve immediately.

SERVES 4

SPAGHETTI ALLA PUTTANESCA

Spaghetti with Anchovies and Olives

Metric/Imperial	American
7 tablespoons olive oil	7 tablespoons olive oil
1 garlic clove, peeled and sliced	1 garlic clove, peeled and sliced
1 red pepper, cored, seeded and sliced	1 red pepper, cored, seeded and sliced
100 g/4 oz canned anchovies, drained and pounded	¼ lb canned anchovies, drained and pounded
400 g/14 oz tomatoes, skinned and chopped	1¾ cups skinned and chopped tomatoes
100 g/4 oz black olives, halved and stoned	¾ cup pitted ripe olives
1 tablespoon capers	1 tablespoon capers
400 g/14 oz spaghetti	14 oz spaghetti
salt	salt

Heat the oil in a heavy pan, add the garlic and red pepper and fry gently for 6 to 7 minutes until the garlic is well browned. Add the anchovies and cook, stirring until thoroughly blended.

Add the tomatoes, olives and capers and stir well. Cook gently for about 20 minutes, stirring occasionally.

Meanwhile, cook the spaghetti in plenty of boiling salted water until *al dente*. Drain thoroughly and pile into a warmed serving dish. Pour the sauce over the top and serve immediately.

SERVES 4

SPAGHETTI ALLA NAPOLETANA

Spaghetti with Tomato and Basil Sauce

Metric/Imperial	American
7 tablespoons olive oil	7 tablespoons olive oil
1 onion, peeled and chopped	1 onion, peeled and chopped
750 g/1¾ lb ripe tomatoes, chopped	3½ cups chopped tomatoes
1 tablespoon chopped basil	1 tablespoon chopped basil
salt and freshly ground black pepper	salt and freshly ground black pepper
400 g/14 oz spaghetti	14 oz spaghetti

Heat the oil in a heavy pan, add the onion and fry gently for 5 minutes. Add the tomatoes, basil and salt and pepper to taste. Cook gently for 30 minutes.

Meanwhile, cook the spaghetti in plenty of boiling salted water until *al dente*. Drain thoroughly and pile into a warmed serving dish. Pour the sauce over the top and serve immediately.

SERVES 4

SPAGHETTI ALLE VONGOLE

Spaghetti with Clams

Fresh mussels may be used instead of clams in the sauce for this recipe.

Metric/Imperial	American
1 kg/2 lb fresh clams, scrubbed	2 lb fresh clams, scrubbed
7 tablespoons water	7 tablespoons water
7 tablespoons olive oil	7 tablespoons olive oil
1 garlic clove, peeled and sliced	1 garlic clove, peeled and sliced
400 g/14 oz tomatoes, skinned and mashed	1¾ cups skinned and mashed tomatoes
400 g/14 oz spaghetti	14 oz spaghetti
salt and freshly ground black pepper	salt and freshly ground black pepper
1 tablespoon chopped parsley	1 tablespoon chopped parsley

Put the clams in a large pan with the water. Cook until the shells open, then remove the clams from their shells. Strain the cooking liquid and reserve.

Heat the oil in a heavy pan, add the garlic and fry gently for 5 minutes. Remove the garlic, then add the tomatoes and the reserved cooking liquid to the pan. Stir and simmer for 20 minutes.

Meanwhile, cook the spaghetti in plenty of boiling salted water until *al dente*. Drain thoroughly. Add the clams and parsley to the tomato sauce and heat through for 1 minute. Pile the spaghetti in a warmed serving dish, add the sauce and a pinch of pepper and fold gently to mix. Serve immediately.

SERVES 4

The majority of commercially made pasta comes from the city of Naples in Campania. According to the experts, the water in the city is exactly the right kind to make perfect pasta. The combination of hard wheat and water makes it unnecessary to include the eggs in commercial pasta (eggs are needed when making pasta at home as a binding agent), but many manufacturers include eggs because of popular demand.

PASTA COL CAVOLFIORE

Pasta with Cauliflower

Metric/Imperial	American
2 litres/3½ pints water	9 cups water
salt	salt
675 g/1½ lb cauliflower, divided into florets	1½ lb cauliflower, divided into florets
400 g/14 oz mezze zite or macaroni	14 oz mezze zite or macaroni
7 tablespoons olive oil	7 tablespoons olive oil
25 g/1 oz stale breadcrumbs	1 slice stale bread, crumbled
freshly ground black pepper	freshly ground black pepper

Bring the water and a little salt to the boil in a large pan, add the cauliflower and cook for 3 minutes. Add the pasta and cook for a further 12 minutes or until *al dente*.

Drain the cauliflower and pasta and pile into a warmed serving dish; keep hot. Heat the oil in a small pan, add the breadcrumbs and fry over brisk heat until well browned. Sprinkle over the cauliflower and pasta, add pepper to taste and fold gently to mix. Serve immediately.

SERVES 4

RIGATONI ALLA PASTORA

Rigatoni with Cheese and Sausage

Metric/Imperial	American
225 g/8 oz salsiccia a metro★, skinned and chopped	1 cup skinned and chopped salsiccia a metro★
500 ml/18 fl oz water	2¼ cups water
225 g/8 oz ricotta cheese★	1 cup ricotta cheese★
salt and freshly ground black pepper	salt and freshly ground black pepper
400 g/14 oz rigatoni	14 oz rigatoni
75 g/3 oz pecorino cheese★, grated	¾ cup grated pecorino cheese★

Put the sausage and water in a large pan, cover and boil until the sausage is tender and the fat rises to the surface. Skim off the fat and reserve. Drain the sausage.

Put the ricotta cheese in a bowl and beat well to soften. Add the fat from the sausage, with salt and pepper to taste; stir well.

Cook the rigatoni in plenty of boiling salted water until *al dente*. Drain thoroughly.

Add the rigatoni, sausage and pecorino to the ricotta mixture and fold gently to mix. Serve immediately.

SERVES 4

ABOVE: **Pasta col cavolfiore; Rigatoni alla pastora; Sagne chine**

SAGNE CHINE

Baked Lasagne in Rich Ragù

Metric/Imperial	American
PASTA:	PASTA:
400 g/14 oz coarse bran (durum wheat) flour	3½ cups coarse bran (durum wheat) flour
½ teaspoon salt	½ teaspoon salt
FILLING:	FILLING:
4 artichoke hearts	4 artichoke hearts
salt	salt
100 g/4 oz mushrooms	1 cup mushrooms
225 g/8 oz minced pork	1 cup ground pork
1 egg yolk	1 egg yolk
freshly ground black pepper	freshly ground black pepper
plain flour for coating	all-purpose flour for coating
25 g/1 oz lard or butter	2 tablespoons lard or butter
1 onion, peeled and chopped	1 onion, peeled and chopped
150 g/5 oz shelled peas	1 cup shelled peas
1 bay leaf	1 bay leaf
4 hard-boiled eggs, sliced	4 hard-cooked eggs, sliced
150 g/5 oz mozzarella cheese*, sliced	5 oz mozzarella cheese*, sliced
65 g/2½ oz pecorino cheese*, grated	⅔ cup grated pecorino cheese*
4 tablespoons chicken stock	¼ cup chicken stock

To make the pasta: stir the flour with the salt, then mix in enough lukewarm water to form a fairly hard dough. Flatten the dough with a rolling pin and roll into a fairly thin sheet. Cut the dough into 9 cm/3½ inch squares.

To make the filling: cook the artichoke hearts in boiling salted water for 15 minutes, then drain and slice into small sections. Parboil the mushrooms for 5 minutes, then drain and slice. Put the pork in a bowl with the egg yolk and salt and pepper to taste; mix well. Shape this mixture into small balls, about the size of walnuts, then coat with flour.

Melt the lard or butter in a heavy pan, add the meatballs and fry over moderate heat for 15 minutes, shaking the pan constantly. Remove from the pan with a slotted spoon and drain on absorbent kitchen paper. Add the onion and peas to the pan and cook gently for 5 minutes. Add the artichokes, mushrooms, bay leaf and a few tablespoons water to moisten. Simmer for a further 10 minutes.

Arrange the ingredients in layers in a buttered deep ovenproof dish, alternating the pasta, egg and mozzarella slices, meatballs and vegetables. Sprinkle each layer with a little pecorino.

Pour the stock over the top layer. Bake in a preheated moderately hot oven (200°C/400°F/Gas Mark 6) for 15 minutes. Serve hot.

SERVES 4

ABOVE: **Pasta col broccolo; Rigatoni al forno; Pasta 'ncaciata**

RIGATONI AL FORNO

Baked Rigatoni

Metric/Imperial

1 thick slice stale bread
150 g/5 oz minced beef
75 g/3 oz pecorino cheese★, grated
1 egg, beaten
1 tablespoon chopped parsley
1 garlic clove, peeled and crushed
salt and freshly ground black pepper
4 tablespoons olive oil
150 g/5 oz sopressata sausage★, diced
200 ml/⅓ pint red wine
400 g/14 oz tomatoes, skinned and chopped
300 g/11 oz rigatoni
3 hard-boiled eggs, sliced
100 g/4 oz provola cheese★, sliced

American

1 thick slice stale bread
⅔ cup ground beef
¾ cup grated pecorino cheese★
1 egg, beaten
1 tablespoon chopped parsley
1 garlic clove, peeled and crushed
salt and freshly ground black pepper
¼ cup olive oil
⅔ cup diced sopressata sausage★
1 cup red wine
1¾ cups skinned and chopped tomatoes
11 oz rigatoni
3 hard-cooked eggs, sliced
¼ lb provola cheese★, sliced

Soak the bread in lukewarm water, then squeeze dry. Combine with the beef, one third of the pecorino, the egg, parsley, garlic and salt and pepper to taste. Stir well to mix, then shape into small balls, about the size of walnuts.

Heat the oil in a pan, add the sausage and meatballs and cook over moderate heat for 10 minutes. Add the wine and simmer until it has evaporated, then add the tomatoes and salt and pepper to taste. Lower the heat and simmer for 40 minutes.

Meanwhile, cook the rigatoni in plenty of boiling salted water until *al dente*. Drain thoroughly.

Line the bottom of a buttered deep ovenproof dish with a layer of sauce, cover with a layer of rigatoni, then sprinkle with pecorino. Cover with a layer of sliced egg, then a layer of provola. Continue with these layers until all the ingredients are used, finishing with a layer of sauce and a sprinkling of pecorino. Bake in a preheated moderately hot oven (200°C/400°F/Gas Mark 6) for 15 minutes. Serve hot.
SERVES 4

Cook the broccoli in boiling salted water for 15 minutes. Drain thoroughly.

Heat half the oil in a heavy pan, add the onion and fry gently for 5 minutes. Add the tomatoes and salt and pepper to taste, cover the pan and simmer for 30 minutes.

Heat the remaining oil in a separate pan, add the garlic and fry gently until browned. Add the anchovies and cook, stirring, until broken down. Add to the sauce with the raisins, broccoli and pine kernels. Cook for a further 5 minutes, stirring frequently. Meanwhile, cook the macaroni in boiling salted water until al dente. Drain thoroughly and pile into a warmed serving dish. Pour over the sauce, then add the basil and pecorino and fold gently to mix. Serve immediately.

SERVES 4

PASTA 'NCACIATA

Tagliatelle with Ragù

Metric/Imperial	American
7 tablespoons olive oil	7 tablespoons olive oil
1 onion, peeled and chopped	1 onion, peeled and chopped
1 carrot, peeled and chopped	1 carrot, peeled and chopped
1 celery stick, chopped	1 celery stalk, chopped
1 garlic clove, peeled and thinly sliced	1 garlic clove, peeled and thinly sliced
800 g/1¾ lb tomatoes, skinned and mashed	3½ cups skinned and mashed tomatoes
225 g/8 oz minced veal	1 cup ground veal
100 g/4 oz chicken livers, minced	½ cup ground chicken livers
salt and freshly ground black pepper	salt and freshly ground black pepper
450 g/1 lb tagliatelle, broken into pieces	4 cups broken tagliatelle
2 hard-boiled eggs, sliced	2 hard-cooked eggs, sliced
100 g/4 oz mozzarella cheese★, cut into strips	¼ lb mozzarella cheese★, cut into strips
25 g/1 oz pecorino cheese★, grated	¼ cup grated pecorino cheese★

Heat the oil in a heavy pan, add the onion, carrot, celery and garlic and fry gently for 6 to 7 minutes. Add the tomatoes, veal, chicken livers and salt and pepper to taste. Cover the pan and simmer for 30 minutes.

Cook the tagliatelle in plenty of boiling salted water until al dente. Drain thoroughly, then spread a layer of tagliatelle in the bottom of a buttered ovenproof dish. Sprinkle with the ragù, then cover with a layer of egg slices and strips of mozzarella. Continue with these layers until all the ingredients are used, then sprinkle the pecorino on top. Bake in a preheated moderate oven (180°C/350°F/Gas Mark 4) for 20 minutes until golden brown. Serve immediately.

SERVES 6

The islands of Italy follow the southern style of cooking. Pasta is common fare, but both the Sicilians and the Sardinians have their own pasta dishes which are unique to each island.

PASTA COL BROCCOLO

Macaroni with Broccoli

Metric/Imperial	American
350 g/12 oz broccoli	¾ lb broccoli
salt	salt
4 tablespoons olive oil	¼ cup olive oil
1 onion, peeled and sliced	1 onion, peeled and sliced
450 g/1 lb tomatoes, skinned and mashed	2 cups skinned and mashed tomatoes
freshly ground black pepper	freshly ground black pepper
1 garlic clove, peeled and crushed	1 garlic clove, peeled and crushed
6 canned anchovies, drained and soaked in milk	6 canned anchovies, drained and soaked in milk
40 g/1½ oz seedless raisins, soaked in lukewarm water for 15 minutes	4½ tablespoons seedless raisins soaked in lukewarm water for 15 minutes
40 g/1½ oz pine kernels	4½ tablespoons pine kernels
350 g/12 oz macaroni	¾ lb macaroni
4 basil leaves, chopped	4 basil leaves, chopped
75 g/3 oz pecorino cheese★, grated	¾ cup grated pecorino cheese★

VERMICELLI ALLA SIRACUSANA

Vermicelli Syracuse Style

Metric/Imperial	American
1 green pepper	1 green pepper
7 tablespoons olive oil	7 tablespoons olive oil
2 garlic cloves, peeled	2 garlic cloves, peeled
1 aubergine, diced	1 eggplant, diced
400 g/14 oz tomatoes, skinned and mashed	1¾ cups skinned and mashed tomatoes
1 tablespoon capers	1 tablespoon capers
8 black olives, halved and stoned	8 ripe olives, halved and pitted
1 tablespoon chopped basil	1 tablespoon chopped basil
4 canned anchovies, drained and soaked in milk	4 canned anchovies, drained and soaked in milk
freshly ground black pepper	freshly ground black pepper
400 g/14 oz vermicelli	14 oz vermicelli
75 g/3 oz pecorino cheese★, grated	¾ cup grated pecorino cheese★

Grill (broil) the pepper under a preheated medium grill (broiler), turning frequently, until charred. Peel off the skin. Cut the pepper in half, remove the core and seeds and slice the flesh.

Heat the oil in a heavy pan, add the garlic and fry gently until browned. Discard the garlic. Add the aubergine (eggplant) and tomatoes and simmer for 10 minutes. Add the pepper, capers, olives, basil, anchovies and pepper to taste. Simmer for a further 10 minutes, stirring frequently.

Meanwhile cook the vermicelli in plenty of boiling salted water until *al dente*. Drain thoroughly and pile into a warmed serving dish. Pour over the sauce, sprinkle with pecorino and fold gently to mix. Serve immediately.

SERVES 4

MACCHERONI AL POMODORO

Macaroni in Tomato Sauce

This recipe gives instructions for making macaroni from fresh pasta; commerical dried pasta can alternatively be used.

Metric/Imperial	American
PASTA:	PASTA:
400 g/14 oz plain flour	3½ cups all-purpose flour
salt	salt
4 eggs, beaten	4 eggs, beaten
1 tablespoon olive oil	1 tablespoon olive oil
TOMATO SAUCE:	TOMATO SAUCE:
7 tablespoons olive oil	7 tablespoons olive oil
2 garlic cloves, peeled and crushed	2 garlic cloves, peeled and crushed
800 g/1¾ lb tomatoes, skinned and mashed	3½ cups skinned and mashed tomatoes
freshly ground black pepper	freshly ground black pepper
1 tablespoon chopped parsley	1 tablespoon chopped parsley

To make the pasta: sift the flour and a pinch of salt onto a work surface, then make a well in the centre. Add the eggs and oil and mix together to a smooth dough.

Flatten the dough with a rolling pin and roll into a paper-thin sheet. Fold the dough over on itself several times, then cut it into fairly long slices. Cut these slices into strips about 6 to 7 cm/2½ inches long. Wind the strips tightly around a large knitting needle (pin) to make small cylindrical shapes. Place the macaroni in a single layer on a cloth sprinkled with flour, then leave to dry for 1 hour.

Meanwhile, make the sauce: heat the oil in a heavy pan, add the garlic and fry gently for 5 minutes. Add the tomatoes and salt and pepper to taste. Bring to the boil, lower the heat and simmer for 30 minutes.

Meanwhile cook the macaroni in plenty of boiling salted water until *al dente*. Drain thoroughly and pile into a warmed serving dish. Pour over the sauce, sprinkle with the parsley and serve immediately.

SERVES 4

ABOVE: **Vermicelli alla siracusana; Culingiones; Maccheroni al pomodoro**

CULINGIONES
Ravioli with Ragù

Metric/Imperial	American
PASTA:	PASTA:
450 g/1 lb pasta all'uovo (see page 60: 1½ × quantity)	1 lb pasta all'uovo (see page 60 : 1½ × quantity)
FILLING:	FILLING:
300 g/11 oz pecorino cheese★, grated	2¾ cups grated pecorino cheese★
400 g/14 oz fresh spinach, cooked, well drained and chopped	2 cups chopped cooked spinach, well drained
2 eggs, beaten	2 eggs, beaten
pinch of saffron powder	pinch of saffron powder
salt and freshly ground black pepper	salt and freshly ground black pepper
RAGÙ:	RAGÙ:
3 tablespoons olive oil	3 tablespoons olive oil
1 onion, peeled and chopped	1 onion, peeled and chopped
100 g/4 oz fatty bacon or belly pork, chopped	½ cup chopped fatty bacon or pork slices
225 g/8 oz minced veal	1 cup ground veal
1 tablespoon chopped parsley	1 tablespoon chopped parsley
6 basil leaves, chopped	6 basil leaves, chopped
575 g/1¼ lb tomatoes, skinned and mashed	2½ cups skinned and mashed tomatoes
75 g/3 oz pecorino cheese★, grated, to serve	¾ cup grated pecorino cheese★, to serve

Make the pasta and leave to stand for about 1 hour.

Meanwhile make the filling: put the cheese, spinach, half the beaten egg, and the saffron in a bowl. Season with salt and pepper to taste and mix thoroughly.

Flatten the dough with a rolling pin and roll out to a paper-thin sheet. Put heaped teaspoonfuls of the filling over one half of the dough at regular intervals, about 5 cm/2 inches apart.

Brush the other half of the dough with the remaining egg and place loosely over the filling. Press the pasta between the filling firmly to seal. Cut between the filling to make small squares of ravioli, using a tooth-edged rotary cutter. Place the squares in a single layer on a cloth sprinkled with flour, and leave to dry for about 1 hour.

Meanwhile make the ragù: heat the oil in a heavy pan, add the onion and bacon and fry gently for 5 minutes. Add the veal, parsley and basil and cook for 10 minutes. Add the tomatoes and salt and pepper to taste. Simmer for 1 hour, adding a little warm water if the sauce is too thick.

Cook the ravioli in plenty of boiling salted water for 5 minutes or until they rise to the surface. Remove from the pan with a slotted spoon and pile into a warmed serving dish. Pour over the ragù and sprinkle with the pecorino. Serve immediately.

SERVES 4

Rice, Polenta, Gnocchi

The rice fields of the Po Valley are reminiscent of the paddy fields of the East, for the Italians use the river for irrigation in exactly the same way as the Chinese, making Vercelli in Piemonte the greatest rice-producing area in Italy. Piedmontese rice has long been regarded as the best quality. Not surprisingly, Italians in the north are bigger rice eaters than those in central and southern Italy who eat more pasta.

Rice is not eaten as a vegetable accompaniment in Italy, but as a first course (*primo piatto*). The one exception to this is the famous saffron-coloured *Risotto alla milanese* (see page 88), which is the traditional accompaniment to *Ossibuchi alla milanese* (see page 128).

A risotto should have a creamy consistency, the rice should be moist (*all'onda*), and the grains of rice should be separate and *al dente*. This perfect end result is achieved by cooking gently and adding the liquid to the rice gradually during cooking, waiting for it to be absorbed by the rice before adding more. Frequent stirring is also essential to avoid sticking. Unlike rice dishes in other countries, a risotto is always made with short-grain rice which is very absorbent. Long-grain, Patna or short-grain pudding rice are not suitable. The best types of rice to use are *arborio*, *superfino* or *avorio*; all of these can be purchased at Italian specialist shops. *Avorio* is ideal for the novice risotto maker as it is pre-fluffed. *Carnaroli* is said to be the best of all the rices, but it is unusual to find it outside Italy.

There is more to risotto than rice, however, as quite apart from a well-flavoured homemade stock, a risotto can have other ingredients added such as vegetables, chicken livers, meat and Parmesan cheese, making it almost a meal in itself. Even leftover risotto is made into a dish in its own right, usually in the form of a fried 'cake', which is served turned out of the frying pan (skillet) and cut into portions. Risotto can also be used to make croquettes (*suppli*) and rissoles (*arancini*).

Rice for plain boiling (*fino*) is available in most good supermarkets and delicatessens outside Italy labelled 'Italian rice'.

Polenta is another staple foodstuff of northern Italy; it is rarely eaten in the regions south of Rome. A basic *polenta* is made with *polenta* or maize flour and salted water. Maize flour is known as *granturco* in Italy, and it is available here in specialist and health food shops. The varieties available are very coarse, medium coarse and fine; the coarser the flour is, the more yellow in colour. Whatever the type of flour used, *polenta* is invariably made in a special large copper pan called a *paiolo*. The method is always the same – the flour is added gradually to a pan of hot water and the mixture is stirred constantly throughout the cooking time with a long wooden stick to prevent lumps forming.

Plain boiled *polenta* can be rather bland, so it is often served with a strong-flavoured sauce or with grated cheese. Some of the best *polenta* dishes are those that have been cooked twice; the *polenta* is left to cool, then fried or grilled (broiled) and served with a sauce. Cold *polenta*, cut into slices or chunks, is eaten as bread in some parts of northern Italy.

Gnocchi are also eaten as a first course (*primo piatto*). They are little 'dumplings' most often made of potatoes or flour, or a mixture of the two; sometimes this can be combined with meat, cheese or spinach (*gnocchi verde*). The shapes of gnocchi also vary, from perfect spheres to elongated cylinders. Some of them are stamped into rounds with small cutters, then baked in layers in the oven.

A type of gnocchi called *Canderli* (see page 89) which comes from the region of Trentino-Alto Adige is made with bread. Gnocchi are usually served with a sauce of some kind – tomato sauce or a simple mixture of butter and grated Parmesan cheese are common. Very small gnocchi are sometimes added to *brodo*, and are even used in goulash-type casseroles and stews, particularly in north-eastern regions.

LIGURIA

FARINATA

Chick Pea (Garbanzos) Bake

Metric/Imperial	American
1.5 litres/2½ pints water	6¼ cups water
450 g/1 lb chick pea flour	4 cups garbanzos flour
salt	salt
6–8 tablespoons olive oil	6–8 tablespoons olive oil
freshly ground black pepper	freshly ground black pepper

Pour the water into a large heavy pan, then gradually stir in the flour. Add salt to taste. Cook over gentle heat for 1 hour, stirring frequently and skimming the surface with a slotted spoon occasionally; the mixture should be smooth and quite thick.

Pour the mixture into an oiled roasting pan and level the surface. Sprinkle the oil over the surface. Bake in a preheated moderately hot oven (200°C/400°F/Gas Mark 6) for 30 minutes until golden brown.

Sprinkle liberally with pepper and serve immediately.
SERVES 6

POLENTA CÔNCIA

Polenta with Fontina

Metric/Imperial	American
2 litres/3½ pints water	9 cups water
300 g/11 oz polenta (yellow maize flour)	1⅔ cups polenta (yellow maize flour)
salt and freshly ground black pepper	salt and freshly ground black pepper
225 g/8 oz fontina cheese★, diced	1½ cups diced fontina cheese★
50 g/2 oz Parmesan cheese★, grated	½ cup grated Parmesan cheese★
150 g/5 oz butter, melted	⅔ cup butter, melted

Bring the water to the boil in a large pan, add the flour gradually, then add salt and pepper to taste and stir well to mix. Add the fontina and cook very gently for 45 minutes, stirring frequently.

Pour the polenta into a shallow dish and sprinkle with the Parmesan and a little pepper. Pour the melted butter over the top and serve immediately.

SERVES 4 TO 6

RISO ALLA NOVARESE

Rice Novara Style

Metric/Imperial	American
50 g/2 oz butter	¼ cup butter
275 g/10 oz brown or white rice	1⅓ cups brown or white rice
750 ml/1¼ pints water	3 cups water
salt	salt
4 canned anchovies, drained and roughly chopped	4 canned anchovies, drained and roughly chopped
1 garlic clove, peeled and chopped	1 garlic clove, peeled and chopped
1 tablespoon chopped parsley	1 tablespoon chopped parsley
juice of 1 lemon	juice of 1 lemon
7 tablespoons olive oil	7 tablespoons olive oil
1 truffle or a few button mushrooms, thinly sliced	1 truffle or a few button mushrooms, thinly sliced

Melt the butter in a flameproof casserole, add the rice and stir over moderate heat for 2 to 3 minutes. Add the water and a little salt and bring to the boil.

Cover the casserole and transfer to a preheated moderate oven (180°C/350°F/Gas Mark 4). Bake for 20 minutes, without stirring, until the rice has absorbed the liquid.

Meanwhile, pound the anchovies, garlic and parsley to a paste, using a mortar and pestle. Add the lemon juice and oil gradually, stirring until evenly blended.

To serve: fold the anchovy mixture gently into the rice. Spread the truffle or mushrooms over the top. Serve immediately.

SERVES 4

LEFT: Farinata; Riso alla novarese

RISOTTO ALLA MILANESE

This is the traditional accompaniment to Ossibuchi alla milanese (see page 128).

Metric/Imperial	American
150 g/5 oz butter	⅔ cup butter
½ onion, chopped	½ onion, chopped
salt and freshly ground black pepper	salt and freshly ground black pepper
7 tablespoons dry white wine	7 tablespoons dry white wine
1 litre/1¾ pints hot beef stock	4¼ cups hot beef stock
400 g/14 oz rice	2 cups rice
¼ teaspoon saffron powder	¼ teaspoon saffron powder
100 g/4 oz Parmesan cheese★, grated	1 cup grated Parmesan cheese★
4 tablespoons cream	¼ cup cream

Melt half the butter in a large heavy pan, add the onion and a little pepper and fry gently until golden. Add the wine and 7 tablespoons of the stock. Boil until reduced by half.

Add the rice and cook for 5 minutes, stirring constantly, then add the saffron and salt and pepper to taste. Continue cooking for 20 minutes, stirring in the hot stock a cup at a time as the liquid is absorbed, until the rice is tender.

Remove from the heat, stir in the remaining butter, the Parmesan and cream and leave to stand for 1 minute. Serve hot.

SERVES 4 TO 6

RISOTTO ALLA VALTELLINESE

Risotto with Cabbage and Beans

Metric/Imperial	American
200 g/7 oz broad beans, fresh or frozen	1 cup lima beans, fresh or frozen
1 medium cabbage, shredded	1 medium cabbage, shredded
300 g/11 oz rice	1½ cups rice
salt	salt
75 g/3 oz butter	⅓ cup butter
few sage leaves, chopped	few sage leaves, chopped
50 g/2 oz Parmesan cheese★, grated	½ cup grated Parmesan cheese★
freshly ground black pepper	freshly ground black pepper

Parboil the broad (lima) beans, if fresh, for 2 to 3 minutes, then drain. Put the cabbage, rice and a little salt in a large heavy pan with plenty of water and simmer for 10 minutes. Add the beans and cook for a further 10 minutes.

Drain the rice and vegetables and spoon into a warmed serving dish. Melt the butter in a small pan with the sage, then pour over the rice. Add the Parmesan and a little pepper and fold gently to mix. Serve immediately.

SERVES 4 TO 6

RISOTTO ARROSTO

Baked Risotto

Metric/Imperial	American
100 g/4 oz butter	½ cup butter
½ onion, chopped	½ onion, chopped
225 g/8 oz salsiccia a metro★, chopped	1 cup chopped salsiccia a metro★
150 g/5 oz shelled peas	scant 1 cup shelled peas
2 artichoke hearts, chopped	2 artichoke hearts, chopped
25 g/1 oz mushrooms, chopped	¼ cup chopped mushrooms
400 ml/⅔ pint beef stock	2 cups beef stock
salt and freshly ground black pepper	salt and freshly ground black pepper
400 g/14 oz rice	2 cups rice
1 litre/1¾ pints water	4¼ cups water
75 g/3 oz Parmesan cheese★, grated	¾ cup grated Parmesan cheese★

Melt 3 tablespoons butter in a large flameproof casserole, add the onion and fry gently until golden. Stir in the sausage and fry, stirring, for 3 minutes. Add the peas, artichoke hearts, mushrooms, stock and salt and pepper to taste. Cook gently for 20 minutes.

Meanwhile, put the rice and water in a separate pan, add salt to taste and boil for 5 minutes. Drain, then add to the vegetable mixture with the Parmesan and remaining butter.

Bake in a preheated moderately hot oven (200°C/400°F/Gas Mark 6) for 20 minutes until a golden-brown crust forms on the top of the rice. Serve immediately.

SERVES 4 TO 6

Strangolapreti, literally translated, means 'strangled priests'. These little spinach-flavoured dumplings seem to have created confusion over the exact meaning of their name. Some Italians tell the story of priests being strangled to death by these dumplings because of the heaviness of the mixture, whereas others say the priests were so delighted by their taste that they literally choked to death with the sheer pleasure of tasting them!

STRANGOLAPRETI

Spinach Dumplings

Metric/Imperial	American
225 g/8 oz dry crumbly bread, diced	½ lb dry crumbly bread, diced
150 ml/¼ pint boiling water	⅔ cup boiling water
225 g/8 oz fresh spinach, cooked, well drained and chopped	1 cup chopped cooked spinach, well drained
3 eggs, beaten	3 eggs, beaten
150 g/5 oz plain flour	1¼ cups all-purpose flour
pinch of grated nutmeg	pinch of grated nutmeg
salt and freshly ground black pepper	salt and freshly ground black pepper
TO SERVE:	TO SERVE:
50 g/2 oz butter	¼ cup butter
few sage leaves, chopped	few sage leaves, chopped
75 g/3 oz Parmesan cheese*, grated	¾ cup grated Parmesan cheese*

Put the bread in a shallow bowl and pour over the boiling water. Cover with a saucer or plate, put a weight on top and leave to stand overnight.

Drain the bread, then squeeze it as dry as possible. Mix the bread with the spinach, eggs, flour, nutmeg and salt and pepper to taste.

Drop the mixture a spoonful at a time into a large pan of boiling salted water and boil for 5 minutes or until the dumplings rise to the surface.

Meanwhile, melt the butter with the sage in a separate pan. Remove the dumplings from the pan with a slotted spoon and place in a warmed serving dish.

Serve immediately, with the melted butter and Parmesan cheese.
SERVES 4 TO 6

CANDERLI

Dumplings with Salami and Bacon

Metric/Imperial	American
350 g/12 oz dry crumbly bread, diced	¾ lb dry crumbly bread, diced
150 ml/¼ pint milk	⅔ cup milk
2 tablespoons olive oil	2 tablespoons olive oil
100 g/4 oz smoked bacon, chopped	½ cup chopped smoked bacon
50 g/2 oz salami, chopped	¼ cup chopped salami
50 g/2 oz plain flour	½ cup all-purpose flour
1 tablespoon chopped parsley	1 tablespoon chopped parsley
1 egg, beaten	1 egg, beaten
1 egg yolk	1 egg yolk
salt	salt
1.5 litres/2½ pints beef stock	6¼ cups beef stock
Tomato sauce (see page 84), to serve	Tomato sauce (see page 84), to serve

Put the bread in a bowl, pour over the milk and leave to soften for about 1½ hours.

Heat the oil in a small pan, add the bacon and salami and fry gently for 5 minutes. Remove from the pan with a slotted spoon and transfer to a bowl. Squeeze the bread as dry as possible, then add to the bowl with the flour, parsley, egg, egg yolk and salt to taste. Mix until thoroughly combined, then shape the mixture into dumplings, the size of walnuts.

Bring the stock to the boil in a large pan. Add the dumplings a few at a time and simmer until they rise to the surface. Remove from the pan with a slotted spoon and place in a warmed serving dish. Serve hot, with tomato sauce.
SERVES 4 TO 6

ABOVE: **Canderli; Risotto alla valtellinese; Strangolapreti**

Canderli are believed to be German in origin, as are many dishes from the northern regions of Italy. They are a type of gnocchi made with bread rather than the usual potatoes or flour.
Canderli are purely local to Trentino-Alto Adige, and it is unlikely they will be found in other Italian regions.

GNOCCHI DELLA CARNIA

Potato Dumplings with Parmesan

Metric/Imperial	American
900 g/2 lb potatoes	2 lb potatoes
salt	salt
225 g/8 oz plain flour	2 cups all-purpose flour
100 g/4 oz Parmesan cheese★, grated	1 cup grated Parmesan cheese★
2 eggs, beaten	2 eggs, beaten
75 g/3 oz sugar	6 tablespoons sugar
pinch of grated nutmeg	pinch of grated nutmeg
50 g/2 oz butter, melted	$\frac{1}{4}$ cup butter, melted
pinch of ground cinnamon	pinch of ground cinnamon

Cook the potatoes in boiling salted water until tender, then peel and mash. Blend in the flour, half the cheese, the eggs, 2 tablespoons sugar, the nutmeg and a pinch of salt. Shape the mixture into large round dumplings.

Drop the dumplings a few at a time into a large pan of boiling salted water and boil for 15 minutes. Remove from the pan with a slotted spoon and pile into a warmed serving dish. Sprinkle over the butter, remaining cheese and sugar, and the cinnamon. Serve immediately.

SERVES 6

RISOTTO ALLA SBIRAGLIA

Chicken Risotto

Metric/Imperial	American
1 × 1 kg/2–2$\frac{1}{2}$ lb oven-ready chicken	1 × 2–2$\frac{1}{2}$ lb oven-ready chicken
2 litres/3$\frac{1}{2}$ pints water	9 cups water
2 celery sticks	2 celery stalks
2 onions, peeled	2 onions, peeled
2 carrots, peeled	2 carrots, peeled
salt and freshly ground black pepper	salt and freshly ground black pepper
3–4 tablespoons olive oil	3–4 tablespoons olive oil
7 tablespoons white wine	7 tablespoons white wine
350 g/12 oz tomatoes, skinned and mashed	1$\frac{1}{2}$ cups skinned and mashed tomatoes
450 g/1 lb rice	2$\frac{1}{4}$ cups rice
75 g/3 oz butter, softened	$\frac{1}{3}$ cup softened butter
75 g/3 oz Parmesan cheese★, grated	$\frac{3}{4}$ cup grated Parmesan cheese★

Remove the bones from the chicken and place them in a large pan with the water. Add 1 celery stick (stalk), 1 onion and 1 carrot and season liberally with salt and pepper. Bring to the boil, lower the heat, cover and simmer for 1$\frac{1}{2}$ hours. Strain the stock and keep hot.

Meanwhile, dice the chicken meat, removing all skin. Finely chop the remaining vegetables. Heat the oil in a large heavy pan, add the vegetables and fry gently until lightly coloured. Add the chicken and fry for a further 5 minutes, stirring constantly, then add the wine and boil until it evaporates.

Add the tomatoes and salt and pepper to taste. Cover and cook gently for 20 minutes, adding a little of the chicken stock if the mixture becomes dry.

Stir in the rice, then add 200 ml/$\frac{1}{3}$ pint/1 cup chicken stock. Cook for 20 to 25 minutes until the rice is just tender, adding a little more stock to moisten, as necessary.

Remove from the heat, add the butter and Parmesan and fold gently to mix. Serve immediately.

SERVES 6

RISOTTO DI SCAMPI

Risotto with Scampi

If fresh scampi is unobtainable, frozen, thawed, scampi may be used instead. Omit the first stage of precooking the scampi in seasoned water and use a fish stock or light chicken stock as the cooking liquor for the risotto.

Metric/Imperial	American
450 g/1 lb fresh scampi	1 lb fresh scampi
1 litre/1$\frac{3}{4}$ pints water	4$\frac{1}{4}$ cups water
1 bay leaf, chopped	1 bay leaf, chopped
2 garlic cloves, peeled and chopped	2 garlic cloves, peeled and chopped
salt	salt
3 tablespoons olive oil	3 tablespoons olive oil
75 g/3 oz butter, softened	$\frac{1}{3}$ cup softened butter
1 onion, peeled and chopped	1 onion, peeled and chopped
400 g/14 oz rice	2 cups rice
3–4 tablespoons white wine	3–4 tablespoons white wine
freshly ground black pepper	freshly ground black pepper

Wash the scampi and put them in a pan with the water, bay leaf, garlic and a pinch of salt. Bring to the boil and cook for 5 minutes. Remove the scampi from the water with a slotted spoon and peel off the shells. Return the shells to the water and boil for a further 5 minutes, then strain and keep the stock hot.

Meanwhile, dice the scampi. Heat the oil and 2 tablespoons butter in a large heavy pan, add the onion and fry gently until golden. Stir in the rice, then add the wine. Cook gently for 15 minutes, stirring frequently. Add the stock a little at a time to moisten as necessary during cooking.

Add the scampi, remaining butter and salt and pepper to taste, then cook for a further 5 to 10 minutes until the rice is just tender. Remove from the heat, leave to stand for 1 minute, then serve.

SERVES 4 TO 6

BELOW: **Risotto alla sbiraglia; Risotto di scampi**

RISOTTO ALLA FIORENTINA

Risotto with Meat

Metric/Imperial	American
2 tablespoons olive oil	2 tablespoons olive oil
65 g/2½ oz butter, softened	5 tablespoons softened butter
1 onion, peeled and sliced	1 onion, peeled and sliced
225 g/8 oz minced beef	1 cup ground beef
100 g/4 oz kidneys, sliced	½ cup sliced kidneys
1 chicken liver, sliced	1 chicken liver, sliced
400 g/14 oz tomatoes, skinned and mashed	1¾ cups skinned and mashed tomatoes
salt and freshly ground black pepper	salt and freshly ground black pepper
400 g/14 oz rice	2 cups rice
1 litre/1¾ pints hot beef stock	4¼ cups hot beef stock
75 g/3 oz Parmesan cheese★, grated	¾ cup grated Parmesan cheese★

Heat the oil and half the butter in a large heavy pan, add the onion and fry gently for 5 minutes until golden. Add the beef, kidneys and chicken liver, increase the heat and fry until browned, stirring constantly. Add the tomatoes and salt and pepper to taste, lower the heat and cook gently for 30 minutes.

Stir in the rice, then add half the stock. Cook for 20 minutes, stirring frequently and adding the remaining stock to moisten as necessary. Remove from the heat, stir in the remaining butter and the Parmesan and fold gently to mix. Leave to stand for 2 minutes, then serve.
SERVES 4 TO 6

RISOTTO ALLA PARMIGIANA

Risotto with Parmesan

Metric/Imperial	American
100 g/4 oz butter, softened	½ cup softened butter
½ onion, peeled and chopped	½ onion, peeled and chopped
freshly ground black pepper	freshly ground black pepper
3–4 tablespoons white wine	3–4 tablespoons white wine
400 g/14 oz rice	2 cups rice
1 litre/1¾ pints hot beef stock	4¼ cups hot beef stock
100 g/4 oz Parmesan cheese★, grated	1 cup grated Parmesan cheese★

Melt half the butter in a heavy pan, add the onion and fry gently until soft. Add pepper to taste, then the wine and boil until it evaporates.

Add the rice and cook stirring, for 2 to 3 minutes so that it absorbs the mixture. Cook gently for 20 to 25 minutes until the rice is just tender, stirring frequently and adding the hot stock a little at a time to moisten.

Remove from the heat, add the remaining butter and the Parmesan and fold gently to serve.
SERVES 4 TO 6

The northern Italians eat rice dishes and risottos to the same extent as the Italians in the south eat pasta. Every Italian cook has a favourite method of cooking risotto, sometimes serving it as a simple rice dish with grated Parmesan cheese as its only accompaniment, other times turning it into a substantial meal in itself by adding chicken, meat, offal (variety meats), fish or vegetables.

SUPPLÌ DI RISO

Risotto Croquettes with Veal Ragù

Metric/Imperial	American
500 ml/18 fl oz water	2¼ cups water
90 g/3½ oz butter	⅓ cup plus 1 tablespoon butter
4 tomatoes, skinned and chopped	4 tomatoes, skinned and chopped
salt	salt
250 g/9 oz rice	1¼ cups rice
2 eggs, beaten	2 eggs, beaten
50 g/2 oz Parmesan cheese★, grated	½ cup grated Parmesan cheese★
½ onion, chopped	½ onion, chopped
50 g/2 oz minced veal	¼ cup ground veal
50 g/2 oz veal sweetbreads, diced (optional)	¼ cup diced veal sweetbreads (optional)
2 chicken livers, diced	2 chicken livers, diced
25 g/1 oz raw ham or bacon, minced	2 tablespoons ground raw ham or bacon
25 g/1 oz button mushrooms, diced	¼ cup diced button mushrooms
1 tablespoon tomato purée	1 tablespoon tomato paste
freshly ground black pepper	freshly ground black pepper
100 g/4 oz provatura or mozzarella cheese★, diced	½ cup diced provatura or mozzarella cheese★
dried breadcrumbs for coating	dried bread crumbs for coating
vegetable oil for deep-frying	vegetable oil for deep-frying

Pour the water into a large pan, add one third of the butter, the tomatoes and salt to taste. Bring to the boil and add the rice. Lower the heat and simmer for 20 minutes or until the rice is just tender, stirring occasionally.

Remove from the heat and stir in the eggs and Parmesan. Transfer the mixture to a large board, level the surface and leave to cool.

Melt the remaining butter in a small pan, add the onion, veal, sweetbreads if using, chicken livers, ham and mushrooms. Simmer for 5 minutes, then add the tomato purée (paste) diluted with a little warm water. Add salt and pepper to taste, then cover and simmer for 20 minutes, stirring occasionally.

Form the rice into croquette shapes, the size of small oranges, then make a hollow in each one. Spoon a little ragù mixture in each hollow together with a few pieces of provatura or mozzarella, then cover the hollow with a little rice and press firmly to seal.

Roll the croquettes in breadcrumbs. Deep-fry, a few at a time, in hot oil until golden brown. Drain on absorbent kitchen paper while frying the remainder. Serve hot, accompanied by any remaining filling.
SERVES 4 TO 6

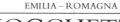

GNOCCHETTI DI RICOTTA

Cheese-Flavoured Gnocchi

Metric/Imperial	American
350 g/12 oz ricotta cheese★	1½ cups ricotta cheese★
150 g/5 oz plain flour	1¼ cups all-purpose flour
150 g/5 oz Parmesan cheese★, grated	1¼ cups grated Parmesan cheese★
2 eggs, beaten	2 eggs, beaten
2 egg yolks	2 egg yolks
pinch of grated nutmeg	pinch of grated nutmeg
salt	salt
100 g/4 oz butter, melted	½ cup butter, melted

Put the ricotta in a bowl with the flour, half the Parmesan, the eggs and egg yolks, nutmeg and a pinch of salt. Blend together to form a smooth dough, then knead well. Shape the dough into two long thin sticks, using floured hands, then cut into short pieces about 2 cm/¾ inch long. Leave to stand for 30 minutes.

Cook the gnocchi in boiling unsalted water for 3 minutes. Remove from the pan with a slotted spoon and pile into a warmed serving dish. Top with the melted butter and the remaining Parmesan cheese. Serve immediately.
SERVES 4

GNOCCHI DI SEMOLINO

Metric/Imperial	American
600 ml/1 pint milk	2½ cups milk
3 egg yolks	3 egg yolks
250 g/9 oz semolina	1½ cups semolina flour
100 g/4 oz butter	½ cup butter
pinch of grated nutmeg	pinch of grated nutmeg
salt and freshly ground black pepper	salt and freshly ground black pepper
100 g/4 oz Parmesan cheese★, grated	1 cup grated Parmesan cheese★

Bring the milk to just below boiling point in a large pan. Mix 3 tablespoons of the hot milk with the egg yolks and set aside.

Add the semolina to the milk in the pan gradually, stirring constantly, then add half the butter, the nutmeg and salt and pepper to taste. Bring to the boil and cook, stirring, until a fairly thick paste is obtained.

Remove the pan from the heat and mix in one third of the Parmesan. Add the egg yolk and milk mixture a little at a time, beating constantly to obtain a smooth paste. Spoon the mixture into a large shallow dish, so it is about 1 cm/½ inch thick. Leave to cool.

Cut the semolina into circles, about 4 cm/1½ inches in diameter, and arrange in a buttered ovenproof dish, overlapping them slightly. Sprinkle with the remaining Parmesan. Melt the remaining butter and sprinkle over the top. Bake in a preheated moderately hot oven (200°C/400°F, Gas Mark 6) for 15 minutes. Serve hot.
SERVES 4

Supplì di riso are often given the nickname of *supplì al telefono* – 'croquettes on the telephone'. This is because the mozzarella cheese in the middle of the croquettes melts and stretches when they are cooked. When the croquettes are bitten into, the cheese resembles telephone 'wires'.

ARANCINI DI RISO

Chicken Liver and Rice Rissoles

Metric/Imperial	American
400 g/14 oz rice	2 cups rice
salt	salt
3 tablespoons olive oil	3 tablespoons olive oil
1 onion, peeled and minced	1 onion, peeled and ground
2 celery sticks, grated	2 celery stalks, grated
400 g/14 oz tomatoes, skinned and chopped	1¾ cups skinned and chopped tomatoes
freshly ground black pepper	freshly ground black pepper
75 g/3 oz butter	6 tablespoons butter
100 g/4 oz shelled peas	¾ cup shelled peas
100 g/4 oz chicken livers, chopped	½ cup chopped chicken livers
6–8 tablespoons chicken stock	6–8 tablespoons chicken stock
1 tablespoon chopped parsley	1 tablespoon chopped parsley
100 g/4 oz dried breadcrumbs for coating	1 cup dried bread crumbs for coating
vegetable oil for deep-frying	vegetable oil for deep-frying

Cook the rice in plenty of boiling salted water for 20 minutes or until tender. Drain and leave to cool.

Heat the olive oil in a pan, add the onion and celery and fry over gentle heat for 5 minutes. Add the tomatoes and salt and pepper to taste, and cook gently for 30 minutes, stirring occasionally. Allow to cool.

Meanwhile, melt one third of the butter in a small pan, add the peas and cook gently until tender. Add salt and pepper to taste.

Melt another third of the butter in a separate pan, add the chicken livers and stock and simmer for a few minutes until they are tender. Remove from the heat and stir in the parsley.

Combine the cold rice with the remaining butter and the tomato mixture. Form into rissole shapes, then make a hollow in each one. Spoon a few peas and a little of the liver mixture into each hollow. Cover the hollow with a little rice and press firmly to seal.

Roll the rissoles in breadcrumbs. Deep-fry, a few at a time, in hot oil until golden brown. Drain on absorbent kitchen paper while frying the remainder. Serve hot.

SERVES 6

ABOVE: **Supplì di riso; Gnocchi de semolino; Gnocchetti di ricotta**

Pizzas, Pies & Savoury Doughs

It is believed that pizzas were originally invented by the Neapolitans to use up leftover bread dough. The classic recipe for this delicious food is the *Pizza Napoletana* (see page 98). In Italy, pizzas are made fresh to order in *pizzerie*, special bakeries equipped with brick ovens that reach exceptionally high temperatures so that the dough is 'set' almost immediately on entering the oven.

Pizzas can very easily be baked at home in conventional ovens, and many Italian housewives regularly make their own. There is no special secret to success, since the base is usually an ordinary bread dough made with yeast, and the choice of toppings is endless and can be varied according to the ingredients which happen to be to hand. Plain (all purpose) flour is used for the dough and either dried or fresh (compressed) yeast, whichever is more convenient. Be sure to knead the dough very thoroughly until springy, smooth and elastic (10 to 15 minutes should be long enough) before rolling and stretching it out to the required shape and thickness. Pizzas do not necessarily have to be round; some are large ovals, some are square (see *Chizze*, page 97), and others known as *pizzette* are baked as individual circles about the diameter of the top rim of a teacup – these are often served as an *antipasto*.

The thickness of the dough is quite important, since dough that has been rolled too thin will be hard and brittle, but if the dough is too thick, the pizza will be yeasty and indigestible. Roll the dough out to a thickness between 5 mm–1 cm/$\frac{1}{4}$–$\frac{1}{2}$ inch, and try to keep the edges slightly thicker than the middle to prevent the topping from running off the dough during baking. Some cooks place a plain flan ring around the dough on the baking (cookie) sheet to help contain the pizza as it rises and cooks.

The filling should then be spread to within 1 cm/$\frac{1}{2}$ inch of the edge and the remaining ingredients placed on top. Always preheat the oven before putting the pizza in, and serve straight from the oven.

There are many variations of the classic pizza throughout southern Italy and in parts of the north. *Pizza Campofranco* (see page 98) is made with a yeast pastry rather than a bread dough and has a double crust, with a filling in the middle. Pies of this kind are quite common, so too are individual pastries like the traditional pizza bread *Calzone alla pugliese* (see page 100). Savoury doughs are quite often fried in Italy. The dough is usually stamped into rounds and deep-fried to make individual pizzas.

ABOVE: **Sardenaira**

TORTA SUL TESTO
Fried Pizza Dough

This recipe is used as a basis for the other pizzas. The quantities given below yield 450 g/1 lb dough. If a recipe requires less, reduce the quantities accordingly.

Metric/Imperial	American
15 g/$\frac{1}{2}$ oz dried yeast	2 packages (4 teaspoons)
120 ml/4 fl oz warm water	active dry yeast
450 g/1 lb plain flour	$\frac{1}{2}$ cup warm water
salt	4 cups all-purpose flour
3 tablespoons olive oil	salt
	3 tablespoons olive oil

Dissolve the yeast in the water. Sift the flour and a little salt onto a working surface. Stir in the yeast liquid, then add the oil and enough lukewarm water to make a smooth dough. Cover with oiled plastic wrap and leave to rise in a warm place for 30 minutes.

Flatten the dough with a rolling pin, then divide in half. Roll each piece out into a circle, about 1 cm/$\frac{1}{2}$ inch thick. Heat a large iron griddle or frying pan (skillet). When it is very hot, add one of the dough circles and cook, without additional fat, turning and pricking the dough with a fork, until crisp and golden. Repeat with the remaining dough. Serve in place of bread.
SERVES 4

FITASCETTA
Onion Pizza

Metric/Imperial	American
75 g/3 oz butter	$\frac{1}{3}$ cup butter
750 g/1$\frac{1}{2}$ lb onions, peeled and finely sliced	6 cups finely sliced onions
salt	salt
450 g/1 lb pizza dough (see left)	1 lb pizza dough (see left)
1 tablespoon caster sugar	1 tablespoon sugar

Melt the butter in a large frying pan (skillet), add the onions and fry gently for 30 minutes, stirring frequently. Remove from the heat, then add salt to taste.

Knead the dough until smooth and elastic, then flatten with a rolling pin and roll out to a 25 cm/10 inch circle, 1 cm/$\frac{1}{2}$ inch thick. Place the circle on an oiled baking (cookie) sheet. Spread the onions over the dough, then sprinkle with the sugar. Leave to rise in a warm place for 20 minutes. Bake in a preheated moderately hot oven (200°C/400°F/Gas Mark 6) for 30 to 35 minutes. Serve hot.
SERVES 6 TO 8

SARDENAIRA

Tomato and Anchovy Pizza

Metric/Imperial	American
7 tablespoons olive oil	7 tablespoons olive oil
450 g/1 lb onions, peeled and sliced	4 cups sliced onions
salt and freshly ground black pepper	salt and freshly ground black pepper
450 g/1 lb tomatoes, chopped	2 cups chopped tomatoes
450 g/1 lb pizza dough (see opposite)	1 lb pizza dough (see opposite)
100 g/4 oz canned anchovy fillets, drained and cut in half lengthways	4 oz canned anchovy fillets, drained and cut in half lengthways
100 g/4 oz black olives, halved and stoned	1 cup ripe olives, halved and pitted
few garlic cloves, peeled and slivered	few garlic cloves, peeled and slivered
1 tablespoon chopped basil	1 tablespoon chopped basil

Heat 3 tablespoons oil in a heavy pan, add the onions and fry gently for 10 minutes. Add salt and pepper to taste, then remove from the heat.

Place the tomatoes in a saucepan. Add salt and pepper to taste and simmer for 10 to 15 minutes until reduced to a pulp; strain.

Knead the dough until smooth and elastic, then flatten with a rolling pin and roll out to a 25 cm/10 inch circle, 1 cm/½ inch thick. Place the circle in a shallow baking tin to fit. Leave to rise in a warm place for 20 minutes.

Spread the onions and tomato pulp over the dough. Arrange the anchovy fillets and olive halves on top. Add slivers of garlic according to taste, then sprinkle with the basil and remaining oil. Bake in a preheated moderately hot oven (200°C/400°F/Gas Mark 6) for 35 to 40 minutes. Serve hot.

SERVES 6 TO 8

Pizza bakers in Naples are often cooks, artists and actors all in one. They can be seen through the windows of *pizzerie* pulling, stretching and kneading the pizza dough, then spreading and sprinkling the topping over with a flourish. The pizza tray is then pushed into the oven on a special long-handled shovel and the pizza baker starts his show all over again.

ERBAZZONE REGGIANO

Spinach Quiche

Metric/Imperial	American
DOUGH:	DOUGH:
300 g/11 oz plain flour	2¾ cups all-purpose flour
½ teaspoon salt	½ teaspoon salt
65 g/2½ oz butter	¼ cup plus 1 tablespoon butter
1 tablespoon vegetable oil	1 tablespoon vegetable oil
FILLING:	FILLING:
1 kg/2 lb fresh spinach, cooked	2 lb fresh spinach, cooked
4 tablespoons olive oil	¼ cup olive oil
50 g/2 oz smoked bacon, chopped	¼ cup diced smoked bacon
1 tablespoon chopped parsley	1 tablespoon chopped parsley
1 garlic clove, peeled and crushed	1 garlic clove, peeled and crushed
1 egg, beaten	1 egg, beaten
50 g/2 oz Parmesan cheese★, grated	½ cup grated Parmesan cheese★
25 g/1 oz butter, melted	2 tablespoons melted butter

To make the dough: sift the flour and salt into a bowl. Rub in the butter until the mixture resembles bread-crumbs. Knead in the oil. Mix together, adding enough lukewarm water to give a smooth dough. Leave to stand in a cool place while making the filling.

To make the filling: Drain the spinach thoroughly and purée in an electric blender or press through a sieve (strainer). Heat the oil in a pan, add the bacon and fry for 2 minutes. Stir in the spinach and cook gently for 10 minutes. Add the parsley and garlic and cook for 2 minutes. Remove from the heat and stir in the egg, Parmesan, and salt to taste. Leave to cool.

Flatten two-thirds of the dough with a rolling pin and roll out into a thin sheet. Brush a 25 cm/10 inch quiche or flan dish liberally with melted butter, then line with the sheet of dough. Spoon the spinach filling into the dish. Dampen the edges of the dough.

Roll out the remaining dough to make a lid. Place over the filling and pinch the edges together to seal. Prick the centre of the dough with a fork and brush with the remaining melted butter. Bake in a preheated moderately hot oven (200°C/400°F/Gas Mark 6) for 45 to 50 minutes. Serve hot or cold.
SERVES 6

The Italian word *pizza* means simply 'pie', and although the classic Neapolitan-style pizzas are not conventional pies in the strict sense of the word, there are some versions of pizza which are pies with double crusts. Sometimes they are baked in large tins then sliced for serving, as in the recipe *Erbazzone Reggiano*, other times they are made into individual pies and deep-fried, like *Chizze*. This type of pizza is most often referred to as *pizza alla casalinga* (homemade pizza), because it is more likely to be cooked at home or in a private restaurant than in a *pizzerie*. It is rarely seen outside Italy.

PIZZA AL FORMAGGIO

Cheese Pizza

Metric/Imperial	American
20 g/¾ oz fresh yeast	¾ cake compressed yeast
120 ml/4 fl oz warm water	½ cup warm water
350 g/12 oz plain flour	3 cups all-purpose flour
½ teaspoon salt	½ teaspoon salt
90 g/3½ oz Parmesan cheese★	3½ oz Parmesan cheese★
90 g/3½ oz gruyère cheese	3½ oz gruyère cheese
40 g/1½ oz pecorino cheese★	1½ oz pecorino cheese★
2 eggs, beaten	2 eggs, beaten

Dissolve the yeast in 4 tablespoons of the water. Sift 100 g/4 oz/1 cup of the flour with the salt into a bowl. Make a well in centre and knead to a soft, smooth dough. Place in a large bowl, sprinkle with a little of the remaining flour and cut a cross shape on the top. Cover with a clean cloth and leave to rise in a warm place for 15 minutes.

Meanwhile, grate 50 g/2 oz of the Parmesan and half the gruyère into a bowl. Cut the remaining cheese into cubes. Add to the grated cheeses, with the eggs. Mix well, then stir in the remaining flour. Gradually mix in the remaining water. Add the ball of dough to the cheese mixture and knead thoroughly until the dough is no longer sticky. Return to the bowl, cover again and leave to rise for 1½ hours or until doubled in bulk.

Flatten the dough with a rolling pin and roll out to a 20 cm/8 inch circle. Place the circle on an oiled baking (cookie) sheet and leave to rise in a warm place for 40 minutes. Bake in a preheated moderately hot oven (200°C/400°F/Gas Mark 6) for 20 to 25 minutes. Serve hot.

SERVES 4

LEFT: **Erbazzone reggiano;**
BELOW: **Preparing Chizze**

CHIZZE

Spinach and Ricotta Pizza Squares

Metric/Imperial	American
50 g/2 oz cooked spinach	¼ cup cooked spinach
50 g/2 oz ricotta cheese★	¼ cup ricotta cheese★
75 g/3 oz Parmesan cheese★, grated	¾ cup grated Parmesan cheese★
450 g/1 lb pizza dough (see page 94)	1 lb pizza dough (see page 94)
1 egg white, lightly whisked	1 egg white, lightly whisked
vegetable oil for deep-frying	vegetable oil for deep-frying

Drain the spinach thoroughly and purée in an electric blender or press through a sieve (strainer). Mix with the ricotta and Parmesan. Flatten the dough with a rolling pin and roll out to 5 mm/¼ inch thickness. With a tooth-edged rotary cutter, cut the dough into 5 cm/2 inch squares.

Put 1 teaspoon of the spinach mixture in the centre of half of the squares. Brush the edges of these squares with the whisked egg white, then cover with the remaining squares of dough, pressing the edges together firmly to seal.

Deep-fry the squares, a few at a time, in hot oil until golden brown. Drain on absorbent kitchen paper. Repeat with the remainder. Serve hot.

SERVES 6

CIACCI DI RICOTTA

Ricotta Griddle Cakes

Metric/Imperial	American
15 g/½ oz fresh yeast	½ cake compressed yeast
500 ml/18 fl oz milk	2¼ cups milk
400 g/14 oz ricotta cheese★	1¾ cups ricotta cheese★
75 g/3 oz plain flour	¾ cup all-purpose flour
salt	salt
25 g/1 oz lard	2 tablespoons lard

Dissolve the yeast in 3 tablespoons of the milk. Put the ricotta in a bowl and gradually add the remaining milk, stirring constantly. Stir in enough flour to give a smooth paste. Mix in the yeast and salt to taste.

Heat a griddle pan or heavy frying pan (skillet), then add a small piece of lard. When melted, pour in 2 tablespoonfuls of the griddle cake mixture and fry until golden brown on both sides, turning once. Remove from the pan and keep hot while frying the remaining mixture. Serve hot with assorted cold meats.

SERVES 4

RIGHT: **Pizza Campofranco; Pizza Napoletana; Focaccia salata**

PIZZA CAMPOFRANCO
Ham and Cheese Pizza Pie

Metric/Imperial	American
DOUGH:	DOUGH:
25 g/1 oz fresh yeast	1 cake compressed yeast
4–5 tablespoons lukewarm milk	4–5 tablespoons lukewarm milk
300 g/11 oz plain flour	2¾ cups all-purpose flour
½ teaspoon salt	½ teaspoon salt
25 g/1 oz sugar	2 tablespoons sugar
150 g/5 oz butter, diced	⅔ cup butter, diced
2 eggs, beaten	2 eggs, beaten
FILLING:	FILLING:
2 tablespoons olive oil	2 tablespoons olive oil
2 ripe tomatoes, skinned, seeded and chopped	2 ripe tomatoes, skinned, seeded and chopped
freshly ground black pepper	freshly ground black pepper
6 basil leaves, finely chopped	6 basil leaves, finely chopped
175 g/6 oz mozzarella cheese★, sliced	6 oz mozzarella cheese★, sliced
150 g/5 oz raw smoked or cooked ham, cut into thin strips	⅔ cup shredded raw smoked or cooked ham
50 g/2 oz pecorino cheese★, grated	½ cup grated pecorino cheese★
TO FINISH:	TO FINISH:
beaten egg to glaze	beaten egg to glaze
basil leaves to garnish	basil leaves to garnish

To make the dough: dissolve the yeast in the milk. Sift the flour and salt onto a work surface. Stir in the sugar and make a well in the centre. Add the butter, eggs and the dissolved yeast and work the ingredients together to give a smooth dough. Knead well until pliable, then shape into a ball.

Put the dough in a bowl sprinkled with flour, cover with a clean cloth and leave to rise at room temperature for 2 hours or until doubled in bulk.

Meanwhile, make the filling: heat the oil in a pan, add the tomatoes and cook over moderate heat for 5 minutes. Add salt and pepper to taste, then remove from the heat.

Knead the dough for 5 minutes, then break off two-thirds and flatten with a rolling pin. Roll out to a thin circle and use to line an oiled 23 cm/9 inch loose-bottomed cake tin (springform pan). Spread the tomatoes on top of the dough, then sprinkle with the basil. Cover with half the mozzarella and the ham, then top with the remaining mozzarella and the pecorino cheese.

Flatten the remaining dough and roll out to a circle to fit the top of the pizza. Place the circle over the filling, then press the edges firmly together to seal. Leave in a warm place to rise for 30 to 40 minutes. Brush the top with beaten egg. Bake in a preheated moderately hot oven (200°C/400°F/Gas Mark 6) for 15 minutes, then lower the temperature to (190°C/375°F/Gas Mark 5) and bake for a further 20 minutes. Serve immediately, garnished with basil.
SERVES 8

PIZZA NAPOLETANA
Pizza with Mozzarella, Tomatoes and Anchovies

Metric/Imperial	American
4 tablespoons olive oil	4 tablespoons olive oil
350 g/12 oz tomatoes, chopped	1½ cups chopped tomatoes
salt and freshly ground black pepper	salt and freshly ground black pepper
450 g/1 lb pizza dough (see page 94)	1 lb pizza dough (see page 94)
175 g/6 oz mozzarella cheese★, sliced	6 oz mozzarella cheese★, sliced
8 canned anchovy fillets, drained and cut in half lengthways	8 canned anchovy fillets, drained and cut in half lengthways
2 teaspoons chopped basil or oregano	2 teaspoons chopped basil or oregano

Heat half the oil in a pan, add the tomatoes and cook over moderate heat for 5 minutes. Season with salt and pepper to taste and remove from the heat.

Knead the dough until smooth and elastic, then flatten with a rolling pin and roll out to a 25 cm/10 inch circle.

Place the circle on an oiled baking (cookie) sheet. Spread the tomato pulp over the dough, leaving a 1 cm/½ inch margin around the edge. Place the cheese slices on the tomatoes. Arrange the anchovy fillets in a lattice pattern on top. Sprinkle with the basil or oregano, the remaining oil and salt and pepper to taste. Leave to rise in a warm place for 20 minutes.

Bake in a preheated moderately hot oven (200°C/400°F/Gas Mark 6) for 25 minutes. Serve hot.
SERVES 4

FOCACCIA SALATA
Tomato and Herb Pizza

Metric/Imperial	American
225 g/½ lb pizza dough (see page 94)	½ lb pizza dough (see page 94)
3 tomatoes, skinned and chopped	3 tomatoes, skinned and chopped
2 garlic cloves, peeled and slivered	2 garlic cloves, peeled and slivered
1 tablespoon chopped marjoram	1 tablespoon chopped marjoram
2 tablespoons olive oil	2 tablespoons olive oil
salt and freshly ground black pepper	salt and freshly ground black pepper

Knead the dough until smooth and elastic, then flatten with a rolling pin and roll out to a 25 cm/10 inch circle. Place the circle on an oiled baking (cookie) sheet. Make little grooves with the fingertips at regular intervals in the dough, then fill the grooves with the tomatoes and garlic. Sprinkle with the marjoram, oil and salt and pepper to taste. Leave in a warm place to rise for 20 minutes. Bake in a preheated moderately hot oven (200°C/400°F/Gas Mark 6) for 25 minutes. Serve hot or cold.
SERVES 4

Pizza Napoletana is the pizza best known outside Italy, mainly because it was the emigré Neapolitans who first opened *pizzerie* in England and the United States and introduced the world to their colourful cheese and tomato topped dough. Tomatoes are an essential ingredient for *Pizza Napoletana*, but sometimes when fresh tomatoes are not available in winter, the Neapolitans make *salsa pizzaiola*, a sauce topping made with canned tomatoes. Mozzarella cheese has exactly the right melting qualities for pizza toppings, and is another vital ingredient for *pizza Napoletana*; if it is difficult to obtain, Bel Paese or gruyère can be used instead.

FOCACCIA DI PATATE
Potato Bread

Metric/Imperial	American
275 g/10 oz potatoes	10 oz potatoes
25 g/1 oz fresh yeast	1 cake compressed yeast
450 ml/¾ pint warm water	2 cups warm water
900 g/2 lb plain flour	8 cups all-purpose flour
2 teaspoons salt	2 teaspoons salt
1 tablespoon olive oil	1 tablespoon olive oil

Cook the potatoes in their skins in boiling water until tender. Drain, peel and mash them. Dissolve the yeast in 4 tablespoons of the water.

Spread the mashed potato on a work surface, then sprinkle with the flour, the dissolved yeast and salt. Mix together with enough warm water to give a smooth dough; knead well.

Place the dough on an oiled baking (cookie) sheet, flatten with a rolling pin and form into a 25 cm/10 inch circle with the hands. Place in a baking tin to fit. Cover with a clean cloth and leave to rise at room temperature for 1½ hours.

Sprinkle with the oil and bake in a preheated moderately hot oven (200°C/400°F/Gas Mark 6) for 40 minutes or until golden brown. Leave to cool before serving.

SERVES 8

PANZEROTTI
Mozzarella Pasties

Metric/Imperial	American
5 tomatoes, skinned and chopped	5 tomatoes, skinned and chopped
salt and freshly ground black pepper	salt and freshly ground black pepper
450 g/1 lb pizza dough (see page 94)	1 lb pizza dough (see page 94)
175 g/6 oz mozzarella cheese★, sliced	6 oz mozzarella cheese★, sliced
1 egg white, lightly whisked	1 egg white, lightly whisked
vegetable oil for deep-frying	vegetable oil for deep-frying

Press the tomatoes through a sieve (strainer) or work in an electric blender, then sieve (strain) to remove the seeds. Put the tomato flesh in a pan with salt and pepper to taste and cook gently for 10 minutes or until reduced to a thick pulp.

Flatten the dough with a rolling pin and roll out to about 5 mm/¼ inch thickness. Cut the dough into circles about 10 cm/4 inches in diameter.

Spread the tomato mixture over one half of each circle of dough, then top with a slice of mozzarella and sprinkle with a little salt and pepper. Brush the edges with egg white. Fold the dough over the filling to make half-moon shapes, pressing the edges firmly to seal.

Deep-fry, a few at a time, in hot oil until golden brown, then drain on absorbent kitchen paper while frying the remainder. Serve hot.

SERVES 4 TO 6

CALZONE ALLA PUGLIESE
Onion Pasties

Metric/Imperial	American
100 g/4 oz seedless raisins	⅔ cup seedless raisins
4 tablespoons olive oil	4 tablespoons olive oil
575 g/1¼ lb onions, peeled and sliced	5 cups sliced onions
150 g/5 oz black olives, stoned and finely chopped	1 cup pitted ripe olives, finely chopped
5 canned anchovy fillets, drained and finely chopped	5 canned anchovy fillets, drained and finely chopped
4 tomatoes, skinned and chopped	4 tomatoes, skinned and chopped
freshly ground black pepper	freshly ground black pepper
50 g/2 oz Parmesan cheese★, grated	½ cup grated Parmesan cheese★
50 g/2 oz pecorino cheese★, grated	½ cup grated pecorino cheese★
450 g/1 lb pizza dough (see page 94)	1 lb pizza dough (see page 94)

BELOW: **Panzerotti; Pitta**

A *focaccia*, like any other pizza, comes in many different forms. The most common *focaccia* is one from Genoa in Liguria, although it is not as well known outside Italy as, for instance, the Neapolitan pizza. The Genoese *focaccia* is a basic pizza dough that is served as a bread and is particularly good with cheese. The *focaccia* from Apulia & Basilicata on this page is a potato version; there are other versions like the one on the preceding page, which has a topping of tomatoes and herbs.

Soak the raisins in lukewarm water for 15 minutes. Meanwhile, heat 2 tablespoons oil in a pan, add the onions and fry over gentle heat for 5 minutes. Add the olives, anchovies and tomatoes. Drain the raisins and dry thoroughly, then add to the onion mixture with pepper to taste. Cook for a further 15 minutes, then remove from the heat, stir in the grated cheeses and leave to cool.

Divide the dough in two, making one piece slightly larger than the other. Flatten the larger piece of dough and roll out to fit an oiled 23 cm/9 inch springform (pan) or loose-bottomed cake tin. Line the base and sides of the tin (pan) with two thirds of the dough. Spread the filling on top.

Flatten the remaining dough and roll out to make a lid. Place over the filling and press the edges together to seal. Leave to rise in a warm place for 30 minutes. Sprinkle with the remaining oil. Bake in a preheated moderately hot oven (200°C/400°F/Gas Mark 6) for 15 minutes, then lower the temperature to (190°C/375°F/Gas Mark 5) and bake for a further 25 minutes. Serve hot.

SERVES 6 TO 8

PITTA
Egg, Cheese and Ham Pie

Metric/Imperial	American
DOUGH:	DOUGH:
25 g/1 oz fresh yeast	1 cake compressed yeast
6 tablespoons warm water	6 tablespoons warm water
300 g/11 oz plain flour	2¾ cups all-purpose flour
salt	salt
2 eggs, beaten	2 eggs, beaten
20 g/¾ oz lard, melted	1½ tablespoons lard, melted
1 tablespoon vegetable oil	1 tablespoon vegetable oil
FILLING:	FILLING:
100 g/4 oz caciocavallo cheese★, sliced	¼ lb caciocavallo cheese★, sliced
2 hard-boiled eggs, sliced	2 hard-cooked eggs, sliced
200 g/7 oz ricotta cheese★	scant cup ricotta cheese★
100 g/4 oz cured ham or cooked bacon, sliced	¼ lb cured ham or cooked bacon, sliced
freshly ground black pepper	freshly ground black pepper
oil for brushing	oil for brushing

To make the dough: dissolve the yeast in 4 tablespoons of the water. Sift half the flour and a pinch of salt onto a work surface, then make a well in the centre. Add the dissolved yeast and mix together with the remaining water to give a smooth dough. Shape into a ball and leave to rise at room temperature for 1 hour.

Sift the remaining flour onto the work surface and work it into the risen dough with the eggs, lard and oil. Knead until smooth and pliable.

Flatten two thirds of the dough with a rolling pin and roll out to a circle. Use to line an oiled 23 cm/9 inch cake tin (springform pan). Arrange the caciocavallo, egg slices, ricotta and ham in layers in the tin (pan), sprinkling each layer with salt and pepper to taste.

Flatten the remaining dough and roll out to make a lid for the pie. Place the circle over the filling, fold the edges inwards, pressing together firmly to seal. Leave in a warm place to rise for 30 to 40 minutes.

Brush the top with oil. Bake in a preheated moderately hot oven (200°C/400°F/Gas Mark 6) for 30 minutes. Serve hot or cold.

SERVES 6

Pizzas, Pies & Savoury Doughs/101

Egg & Cheese Dishes

Eggs are important in the Italian kitchen, both as an ingredient in cooking, and as cooked dishes in their own right. Eggs are used to give more substance to soups as in *Zuppa alla pavese* (see page 50) and to give more body to sauces. They are also used for binding mixtures like stuffings for ravioli and cannelloni. *Frittelle* (crêpes) made with eggs are popular, so too are *frittate* (omelets). These are more like Spanish omelets, with all kinds of different ingredients incorporated into the basic mixture. Eggs are also used in Italian cakes and desserts; perhaps the most famous of these is *Zabaione* (see page 186), which is made from egg yolks.

Cheese is used in countless Italian dishes, as so many of the Italian cheeses have good melting properties. The different types of cheeses have already been described (see pages 32–5). The most common Italian cooking cheeses which are available in this country are *mozzarella*, Parmesan and *ricotta*. *Mozzarella* is a southern cheese most frequently used for its unique melting properties

on pizzas. It is also deep-fried, as in *Mozzarella in carrozza* (see page 105), which literally translated means 'mozzarella in a carriage', and is a kind of deep-fried cheese sandwich. *Provatura fritta* (see page 105) is a famous Roman dish of deep-fried cheese; these days it is usually made with *mozzarella*, *provatura* cheese is almost impossible to obtain, even in Italy. *Crostini* is another Roman cheese speciality – *mozzarella* baked on bread, then garnished with anchovies.

Ricotta, the Italian soft curd cheese, is often used in cheese croquettes and in stuffings for *frittelle* (crêpes). It is probably used as much in sweet dishes as it is in savoury ones, mainly because its rather bland flavour lends itself to such strong spices as nutmeg, cloves and cinnamon, and to liqueurs and candied fruits. It is often used in this way as a filling for pies and pastries. Parmesan is a perfect cooking cheese as its flavour marries well with many different ingredients. It should ideally always be bought in the piece and freshly grated at the time of using.

FRITTATA ALL 'ARETINA

Omelet in Tomato and Herb Sauce

Metric/Imperial	American
6 eggs	6 eggs
1 tablespoon plain flour	1 tablespoon all-purpose flour
65 g/2½ oz dried breadcrumbs	⅔ cup dried bread crumbs
salt and freshly ground black pepper	salt and freshly ground black pepper
4 tablespoons olive oil	¼ cup olive oil
1 onion, peeled and chopped	1 onion, peeled and chopped
1 celery stick, chopped	1 celery stalk, chopped
1 bunch parsley, chopped	1 bunch parsley, chopped
3 basil leaves, chopped	3 basil leaves, chopped
350 g/12 oz tomatoes, skinned and chopped	1½ cups skinned and chopped tomatoes

Put the eggs in a bowl with the flour, breadcrumbs and salt and pepper to taste. Beat well to mix.

Heat the oil in a frying pan (skillet). Pour in the mixture and tilt the pan so that the mixture covers the base. Fry the omelet on both sides until set, shaking the pan frequently to prevent the mixture from sticking. Remove from the pan and leave to cool slightly, then cut into slices.

Add the onion, celery and herbs to the pan with a little more oil if necessary; fry gently for 5 minutes. Add the tomatoes and cook gently for 10 minutes, then return the slices of omelet to the pan and heat through for 5 minutes. Serve immediately.

SERVES 4

FRITTATA CON ERBA TARGONE

Tarragon Omelet

Metric/Imperial	American
1 small bunch tarragon	1 small bunch tarragon
6 eggs	6 eggs
2 tablespoons cream	2 tablespoons cream
salt and freshly ground black pepper	salt and freshly ground black pepper
50 g/2 oz butter	¼ cup butter
tarragon leaves to garnish	tarragon leaves to garnish

Discard the stems from the tarragon and chop the leaves. Put the eggs in a bowl with the cream, tarragon and salt and pepper to taste. Beat well to mix.

Melt the butter in a frying pan (skillet). Pour in the mixture and tilt the pan so that the mixture covers the base. Fry the omelet on both sides until set, shaking the pan frequently to prevent the mixture from sticking. Serve immediately, garnished with tarragon.

SERVES 4

ABOVE: **Frittata di carciofi**

FRITTATA DI CARCIOFI

Artichoke Omelet

Metric/Imperial	American
3 globe artichokes	3 globe artichokes
plain flour for coating	all-purpose flour for coating
4 tablespoons olive oil	4 tablespoons olive oil
salt and freshly ground black pepper	salt and freshly ground black pepper
50 g/2 oz butter	¼ cup butter
6 eggs, beaten	6 eggs, beaten

Wash the artichokes, discard the hard outer leaves, then cut off and discard two-thirds of the tops with a sharp knife. Cut the artichokes in half, remove the choke then cut into slivers and coat with flour. Heat the oil in a frying pan (skillet) and fry the artichokes until well browned. Drain on absorbent kitchen paper and sprinkle with salt and pepper.

Melt the butter in a frying pan (skillet), add the artichokes, then pour in the beaten eggs and sprinkle with more salt and pepper. Tilt the pan so that the mixture covers the base. Cook on both sides until set, shaking the pan frequently to prevent the omelet from sticking. Serve immediately.

SERVES 4

FRITTATA ALLA BOLOGNESE

Omelet with Parmesan

Metric/Imperial	American
6 eggs, separated	6 eggs, separated
25 g/1 oz plain flour	¼ cup all-purpose flour
3–4 tablespoons water	3–4 tablespoons water
150 g/5 oz Parmesan cheese★, grated	1¼ cups grated Parmesan cheese★
1 tablespoon chopped parsley	1 tablespoon chopped parsley
salt and freshly ground black pepper	salt and freshly ground black pepper
50 g/2 oz butter	¼ cup butter

Put the egg yolks in a bowl with the flour and beat well with a wooden spoon until smooth. Stir in the water, then add the Parmesan, parsley and salt and pepper to taste; beat well.

Beat the egg whites until stiff and carefully fold into the omelet mixture. Melt the butter in a large frying pan (skillet), pour in the mixture and tilt the pan so that the mixture covers the base.

Fry on both sides until the omelet is set, shaking the pan frequently to prevent sticking. Serve immediately.

SERVES 4

The Italian *frittata* is best described as an omelet, yet it is nothing like the light fluffy French *omelette* which is folded over during cooking. The Italians make *frittate* rather like a cross between a pancake (crêpe) and an omelet: they cook them until set on both sides in the frying pan (skillet) like a pancake mixture. They are rarely served plain, but are full of ingredients, especially vegetables and herbs, cheese and sometimes meat or leftovers. They are always served flat on the plate and eaten cut into slices or wedges. *Frittate* are often eaten cold, in which case they are an excellent idea for picnics in summer.

Truffles are a highly-prized fungus which grow underground in the root systems of certain trees. They are gathered with the help of specially trained dogs who have a keen sense of smell. The dogs sniff out the truffles, which are then carefully removed from the ground by the truffle hunter with a special tool.

FRITTATA DI TARTUFI

Omelet with Truffles or Mushrooms

Black truffles are used in Italy, but if these are unavailable or prohibitively expensive, mushrooms make an acceptable alternative.

Metric/Imperial	American
6 eggs	*6 eggs*
4 tablespoons cream	*¼ cup cream*
salt and freshly ground	*salt and freshly ground*
black pepper	*black pepper*
100 g/4 oz black truffles or	*¼ lb black truffles or*
mushrooms, chopped	*mushrooms, chopped*
40 g/1½ oz butter	*3 tablespoons butter*
juice of ½ lemon	*juice of ½ lemon*
parsley sprig to garnish	*parsley sprig to garnish*

Put the eggs in a bowl with the cream and salt and pepper to taste. Beat well, then stir in the truffles or mushrooms.

Melt the butter in a frying pan (skillet). Pour in the mixture and tilt the pan so that the mixture covers the base. Fry on both sides until set, shaking the pan frequently to prevent the omelet from sticking. Remove from the heat and sprinkle with the lemon juice. Serve immediately, garnished with parsley.

SERVES 4

FRITTATA AL BASILICO

Omelet with Basil and Cheese

Metric/Imperial	American
6 eggs	*6 eggs*
50 g/2 oz pecorino cheese★,	*½ cup grated pecorino*
grated	*cheese★*
50 g/2 oz coarsely chopped	*1½ cups coarsely chopped*
basil	*basil*
salt and freshly ground	*salt and freshly ground*
black pepper	*black pepper*
50 g/2 oz butter	*¼ cup butter*

Put all the ingredients, except the butter, in a bowl and beat well.

Melt the butter in a frying pan (skillet). Pour in the mixture and tilt the pan so that the mixture covers the base. Fry on both sides until set, shaking the pan frequently to prevent the omelet from sticking. Serve immediately.

SERVES 4

PROVATURA FRITTA
Fried Cheese Cubes

Metric/Imperial
400 g/14 oz provatura or
    mozzarella cheese★, cut
    into 3.5 cm/1½ inch cubes
plain flour for coating
1–2 eggs, beaten
dried breadcrumbs for
    coating
vegetable oil for deep-frying
sage or basil leaves to
    garnish

American
14 oz provatura or
    mozzarella cheese★, cut
    into 1½ inch cubes
all-purpose flour for coating
1–2 eggs, beaten
dried bread crumbs for
    coating
vegetable oil for deep-frying
sage or basil leaves to
    garnish

Coat the cheese lightly in flour, dip into the beaten
eggs, then coat with breadcrumbs. Dip again into the
beaten eggs and coat with a second layer of
breadcrumbs.

Deep-fry the cubes, a few at a time, in the hot oil
until golden brown. Drain on absorbent kitchen paper
while frying the remainder. Serve hot, garnished with
sage or basil.

SERVES 4

BELOW: **Frittata di tartufi;
Frittata al basilico;
Provatura fritta**

MOZZARELLA IN CAROZZA
Deep-Fried Cheese Sandwiches

Metric/Imperial
4 thick slices mozzarella
    cheese★
8 slices of bread, crusts
    removed
1–2 tablespoons plain flour
2 eggs, beaten
pinch of salt
vegetable oil for shallow
    frying

American
4 thick slices mozzarella
    cheese★
8 slices of bread, crusts
    removed
1–2 tablespoons all-purpose
    flour
2 eggs, beaten
pinch of salt
vegetable oil for shallow
    frying

Trim the mozzarella slices to fit the bread. Sandwich
each slice of cheese between 2 slices of bread, pressing
firmly. Sprinkle the inside edges with a little flour and
cold water and press together firmly to seal.

Put the eggs and salt in a large shallow dish. Add the
sandwiches and turn to coat evenly. Leave to stand for
20 minutes.

Pour the oil into a frying pan (skillet) to a depth of
1 cm/½ inch. Place over moderate heat. Fry the sandwiches in the hot oil until golden brown on both
sides, then drain on absorbent kitchen paper. Serve hot.

SERVES 4

Fish & Shellfish

With an extensive coastline, well-stocked lakes, rivers and streams, it is hardly surprising that Italy regards fish as one of her staple foodstuffs. In general the Italians treat their fish simply, avoiding the rich and heavy types of sauces with wine and cream, of which the French are so fond. The Italians prefer to concentrate more on the fish itself.

Simple methods like grilling (broiling), barbecuing, baking and marinating are the most popular ways of cooking fish. Small fry such as fresh anchovies and sardines are usually served simply deep-fried with a garnish of lemon. Even the fish stews and soups are the simple kind, with little more than a basic tomato sauce flavoured with onions, garlic and herbs, in which to cook the fish.

The variety of seafood obtainable in Italy is infinite and many types are unique to that part of the Mediterranean. Amongst the most popular dishes are *baccalà* (salt fish), eels and various hearty fish soups.

Baccalà in Italy is white fish – usually cod – that has been salted and dried. It is sometimes also called *stoccafisso* by Italians and this can be misleading as stockfish is an unsalted dried fish. Before using *baccalà* it must be soaked in several changes of cold water to remove excess saltiness. The length of soaking time will vary according to whether the *baccalà* has been soaked before buying and if so, how long. The Venetian *Baccalà mantecato* (see page 109) is probably the most famous of all *baccalà* dishes. It is like the French *brandade de morue*, a kind of creamed paste or spread, made by pounding the *baccalà* to break it down, then mixing it with olive oil, garlic and seasonings to taste. It is served with pieces of fried bread or *polenta*, which diners use to scoop up the fish.

Eels are also common throughout Italy and can be cooked in many different ways. The Italians particularly like to spit roast, bake or stew them, or serve them casseroled, sometimes in a simple tomato sauce or with wine. Marinated eels are a popular Christmas dish.

In the south, where the local population relies more heavily on fish than in the more fertile northern regions, each fishing village has its own version of the substantial fish soup which is similar to the French *bouillabaisse*. There is the famous *burrida* from Genoa, the *brodetto* of Abbruzzi, Marche and Campania, the *cassola* from Sicily, or the *zuppa di pesce* from Apulia. Each region is justifiably proud of its own version, with its particular varieties of fish and flavouring ingredients.

ABOVE: **Datteri di mare in sughetto; Gamberetto all'erba; Friscieü di gianchetti**

FRISCIEÜ DI GIANCHETTI

Whitebait Fritters

Metric/Imperial	American
200 g/7 oz plain flour	1¾ cups all-purpose flour
salt and freshly ground black pepper	salt and freshly ground black pepper
300 ml/½ pint lukewarm water (approximately)	1¼ cups lukewarm water (approximately)
450 g/1 lb whitebait	1 lb whitebait
vegetable oil for deep-frying	vegetable oil for deep-frying
4 lemon wedges, to serve	4 lemon wedges, to serve

Sift the flour with a pinch of salt and pepper into a bowl. Add enough lukewarm water to obtain a thick coating batter, beating vigorously until smooth. Add the whitebait to the batter and stir until thoroughly coated.

Heat the oil in a deep-fryer. Add the whitebait, a few at a time, and deep-fry until golden brown and crisp. Drain on absorbent kitchen paper and keep hot while frying the remainder. Serve hot with lemon wedges.

SERVES 4

FRIULI-VENEZIA GIULIA

GAMBERETTO ALL'ERBA

Shrimps with Herbs

Metric/Imperial	American
4 tablespoons olive oil	¼ cup olive oil
4 garlic cloves, peeled	4 garlic cloves, peeled
575 g/1¼ lb cooked shelled shrimps	1¼ lb cooked shelled shrimp
5 basil leaves, finely chopped	5 basil leaves, finely chopped
5 marjoram leaves, finely chopped	5 marjoram leaves, finely chopped
3–4 parsley sprigs, finely chopped	3–4 parsley sprigs, finely chopped
pinch of paprika pepper	pinch of paprika pepper
pinch of salt	pinch of salt
3–4 tablespoons dry white wine	3–4 tablespoons dry white wine
marjoram sprigs to garnish	marjoram sprigs to garnish

Heat the oil in a flameproof casserole, add the garlic and fry gently until browned. Remove the garlic, then add the shrimps, herbs, paprika, salt and wine and cook gently until the shrimps are heated through.

Serve immediately, garnished with marjoram.

SERVES 4 TO 6

Mix the oil, lemon juice and onion together and season liberally with salt and pepper. Place the fish in a shallow dish, pour over the marinade and leave to marinate for 1 hour, turning from time to time.

Drain the fish thoroughly and dry on absorbent kitchen paper. Coat with flour. Dip in the beaten eggs, then coat with breadcrumbs, pressing them firmly into the fish.

Melt the butter in a frying pan (skillet), add the fish and fry gently until golden brown on both sides and cooked through. Transfer to a warmed serving platter and pour over the cooking juices. Serve immediately.
SERVES 4

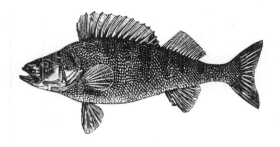

DATTERI DI MARE IN SUGHETTO

Mussels on Croûtons

Metric/Imperial	American
1.5 kg/3 lb mussels	3 lb mussels
150 ml/¼ pint olive oil (approximately)	⅔ cup olive oil (approximately)
½ onion, peeled and chopped	½ onion, peeled and chopped
7 tablespoons dry white wine	7 tablespoons dry white wine
salt and freshly ground black pepper	salt and freshly ground black pepper
4 slices bread	4 slices bread
parsley sprigs to garnish	parsley sprigs to garnish

Scrub the mussels under cold running water, then place in a large bowl. Cover with cold water and leave to stand for 30 minutes. Drain and discard any with open shells.

Heat 7 tablespoons oil in a large pan, add the onion and fry gently for 5 minutes, stirring constantly. Add the mussels and wine to the pan and season with salt and pepper to taste. Cover and cook for about 5 minutes until the shells open. Discard any that have not opened.

Meanwhile, fry the bread in the remaining oil until crisp and golden on both sides. Cut each slice into 4 pieces and arrange in individual soup plates. Spoon the mussels over the bread and pour over the cooking juices. Serve immediately, garnished with parsley.
SERVES 4

PESCE PERSICO ALLA COMASCA

Marinated Perch

Metric/Imperial	American
4 tablespoons olive oil	¼ cup olive oil
juice of 1 lemon	juice of 1 lemon
1 small onion, peeled and chopped	1 small onion, peeled and chopped
salt and freshly ground black pepper	salt and freshly ground black pepper
4 perch, skinned and filleted	4 perch, skinned and filleted
plain flour for coating	all-purpose flour for coating
2 eggs, beaten with a pinch of salt	2 eggs, beaten with a pinch of salt
dried breadcrumbs for coating	dried bread crumbs for coating
75 g/3 oz butter	⅓ cup butter

SARDE RIPIENE
Stuffed Sardines

Metric/Imperial
8 large fresh sardines
100 g/4 oz dried
   breadcrumbs
1 garlic clove, peeled and
   crushed
1 tablespoon chopped
   parsley
8 capers, mashed
6 tablespoons olive oil
50 g/2 oz Parmesan
   cheese★, grated
salt and freshly ground
   black pepper

American
8 large fresh sardines
1 cup dried bread crumbs
1 garlic clove, peeled and
   crushed
1 tablespoon chopped
   parsley
8 capers, mashed
6 tablespoons olive oil
$\frac{1}{2}$ cup grated Parmesan
   cheese★
salt and freshly ground
   black pepper

Slit the sardines open on one side and clean thoroughly, removing the backbones but leaving the heads and tails intact.

Put three quarters of the breadcrumbs in a bowl with the garlic, parsley, capers, oil, half the cheese and salt and pepper to taste. Mix well.

Place a little of the mixture inside each sardine and spread evenly. Fold the sardines, enclosing the filling.

Place in an oiled ovenproof dish and sprinkle with the remaining breadcrumbs and cheese. Bake in a preheated moderate oven (180°C/350°F/Gas Mark 4) for 20 minutes. Serve immediately.

SERVES 4

GRANSEOLE ALLA VENEZIANA
Dressed Crab Venetian Style

If you are able to obtain live crabs for this recipe, plunge them into a large pan of boiling salted water and cook for 20 minutes. Drain and cool, then prepare as described below.

Metric/Imperial
2 cooked crabs, each
   weighing about 1 kg/2 lb
3–4 tablespoons olive oil
juice of 1 lemon
salt and freshly ground
   black pepper

American
2 cooked crabs, each
   weighing about 2 lb
3–4 tablespoons olive oil
juice of 1 lemon
salt and freshly ground
   black pepper

Twist the large claws and legs off the crabs, crack open and extract all the meat. Remove any white meat and all the brown meat from the body shells, discarding the grey stomach sacs and the feathered gills. Trim and clean the shells and set aside.

Flake the crabmeat into a bowl and sprinkle with the oil, lemon juice and salt and pepper to taste. Pile the meat into the crab shells and serve cold.

SERVES 4

ABOVE: **Granseole alla veneziana; Sarde ripiene**
RIGHT: **Baccalà alla fiorentina**

BACCALÀ MANTECATO

Salt Cod Mantecato

Metric/Imperial	American
575 g/1¼ lb salt cod, soaked in cold water overnight	1¼ lb salt cod, soaked in cold water overnight
5 tablespoons olive oil	5 tablespoons olive oil
1 tablespoon chopped parsley	1 tablespoon chopped parsley
2 garlic cloves, peeled and crushed	2 garlic cloves, peeled and crushed
3 tablespoons cream	3 tablespoons cream
freshly ground black pepper	freshly ground black pepper

Drain the salt cod, rinse in fresh cold water and drain thoroughly. Place in a flameproof casserole and barely cover with cold water. Bring to the boil, lower the heat and simmer for 20 to 30 minutes until the fish is tender. Drain, remove the skin and bones, then flake the fish.

Transfer to a bowl standing over a pan of simmering water. Add the oil a few drops at a time, beating vigorously after each addition with an electric beater or wooden spoon.

Continue beating until smooth. Stir in the parsley, garlic, cream and pepper to taste. Serve warm or cold, with toasted or fried bread.

SERVES 4

ANGUILLE ALLA COMACCHIESE

Eels in Tomato Sauce

Metric/Imperial	American
4 tablespoons olive oil	¼ cup olive oil
1 onion, peeled and chopped	1 onion, peeled and chopped
1 tablespoon chopped parsley	1 tablespoon chopped parsley
3 tablespoons tomato purée	3 tablespoons tomato paste
150 ml/¼ pint warm water	⅔ cup warm water
salt and freshly ground black pepper	salt and freshly ground black pepper
2 small eels, each weighing about 750 g/1¾ lb, skinned, cleaned and cut into 5 cm/2 inch pieces	2 small eels, each weighing about 1¾ lb, skinned, cleaned and cut into 2 inch pieces
3–4 tablespoons vinegar	3–4 tablespoons vinegar
7 tablespoons fish stock	7 tablespoons fish stock

Heat the oil in a heavy pan, add the onion and parsley and fry gently for 5 minutes. Mix the tomato purée (paste) with the warm water and stir into the pan. Season liberally with salt and pepper and simmer for 10 minutes.

Pour half this sauce into the bottom of a flameproof casserole. Arrange the eel pieces in a single layer on top. Spoon over the remaining sauce and the vinegar. Simmer gently for 5 minutes. Add the stock, cover and cook for a further 20 minutes until the fish is tender. Serve hot with polenta (see page 87), if liked.

SERVES 6

BACCALÀ ALLA FIORENTINA

Salt Cod Florentine

Metric/Imperial	American
750 g/1¾ lb salt cod, soaked in cold water overnight and drained	1¾ lb salt cod, soaked in cold water overnight and drained
plain flour for coating	all-purpose flour for coating
5 tablespoons olive oil	5 tablespoons olive oil
½ onion, peeled and chopped	½ onion, peeled and chopped
1 garlic clove, peeled and crushed	1 garlic clove, peeled and crushed
pinch of dried thyme	pinch of dried thyme
1 dried bay leaf, crumbled	1 dried bay leaf, crumbled
450 g/1 lb tomatoes, skinned and mashed	2 cups skinned and mashed tomatoes
freshly ground black pepper	freshly ground black pepper
1 tablespoon chopped parsley	1 tablespoon chopped parsley

Remove the skin and bones from the fish, then cut into serving pieces and coat with flour. Heat 3 tablespoons of the oil in a large frying pan (skillet), add the fish and fry, turning, until golden brown on both sides. Remove from the pan and drain on absorbent kitchen paper.

Add the remaining oil to the pan, add the onion and garlic and fry gently for 5 minutes. Stir in the herbs, tomatoes and pepper to taste. Return the fish to the pan.

Bring to the boil, lower the heat and simmer for 15 minutes. Serve hot, sprinkled with the parsley.

SERVES 4

The Italians are great lovers of *baccalà*, white fish (usually cod) which has been salted and dried. It is particularly popular in Rome and Venice, and both cities have their own special ways of serving it. It is an Italian tradition to eat *baccalà* on Fridays (Good Friday in particular), and on Christmas Eve.

CIECHE ALLA PISANA

Eel au Gratin

Metric/Imperial	American
7 tablespoons olive oil	7 tablespoons olive oil
4 garlic cloves, peeled and crushed	4 garlic cloves, peeled and crushed
4 sage leaves, chopped	4 sage leaves, chopped
1 kg/2 lb eels, cleaned	2 lb eels, cleaned
200 ml/⅓ pint warm water	1 cup warm water
salt and freshly ground black pepper	salt and freshly ground black pepper
4 eggs	4 eggs
50 g/2 oz dried breadcrumbs	½ cup dried bread crumbs
75 g/3 oz Parmesan cheese★, grated	¾ cup grated Parmesan cheese★
juice of ½ lemon	juice of ½ lemon
sage leaves to garnish	sage leaves to garnish

Heat the oil in a flameproof casserole, add the garlic and sage and fry gently until browned. Add the eels, cover and cook for 5 minutes. Add the warm water and salt and pepper to taste. Cover and cook in a preheated moderate oven (180°C/350°F/Gas Mark 4) for 30 minutes or until the eels are tender.

Put the eggs in a bowl with the breadcrumbs, Parmesan, lemon juice and a pinch of salt and pepper. Stir well to mix. Spread this mixture over the eels, then grill (broil) under a preheated hot grill (broiler) until a crisp crust has formed. Serve immediately, garnished with sage.

SERVES 4

TRIGLIE ALLA LIVORNESE

Red Mullet Casserole

Metric/Imperial	American
olive oil for shallow-frying	olive oil for shallow-frying
2 garlic cloves, peeled and sliced	2 garlic cloves, peeled and sliced
1 small onion, peeled and chopped	1 small onion, peeled and chopped
450 g/1 lb tomatoes, skinned and chopped	2 cups skinned and chopped tomatoes
salt and freshly ground black pepper	salt and freshly ground black pepper
2 red mullet, each weighing about 450 g/1 lb, cleaned	2 red mullet, each weighing about 1 lb, cleaned
plain flour for coating	all-purpose flour for coating
1 tablespoon chopped parsley	1 tablespoon chopped parsley

Heat 3 tablespoons oil in a flameproof casserole, add the garlic and fry gently for 5 minutes. Discard the garlic, add the onion and fry gently for 5 minutes. Add the tomatoes and season liberally with salt and pepper. Cover and simmer for 15 minutes.

Meanwhile, heat 4 tablespoons oil in a frying pan (skillet). Coat the fish with flour and fry in the hot oil until golden brown on all sides. Remove and drain on absorbent kitchen paper, then sprinkle with salt and pepper.

Add the mullet to the casserole and simmer for 5 minutes. Sprinkle with parsley and serve immediately.

SERVES 4

Capitoni eels from
Grosseto in Tuscany are
the most highly prized of
all the eels, mainly
because their plump flesh
is so sweet and succulent.
They are exported all
over Italy, but
particularly to Rome,
where they are sold in the
fish markets on
Christmas Eve for the
traditional Christmas
Eve meal. The eels used
in the recipe for *Cieche
alla pisana* (opposite) are
a different kind from
capitoni. *Cieche* (the
blind) are blind elvers
which are caught at the
mouth of the river Arno,
near the town of Pisa.
They are peculiar to this
area and considered a
great delicacy, although
the recipe can equally
well be made with any
kind of eel.

TRIGLIE IN GRATICOLA

Marinated Mullet

Metric/Imperial	American
1 garlic clove, peeled and crushed	1 garlic clove, peeled and crushed
1 tablespoon chopped parsley	1 tablespoon chopped parsley
2 dried bay leaves, crumbled	2 dried bay leaves, crumbled
7 tablespoons olive oil	7 tablespoons olive oil
salt and freshly ground black pepper	salt and freshly ground black pepper
2 grey or red mullet, each weighing about 450 g/ 1 lb, cleaned with head and tail intact	2 grey or red mullet, each weighing about 1 lb, cleaned with head and tail intact
dried bay leaves to garnish	dried bay leaves to garnish

Mix the garlic, parsley, bay leaves and oil with a little
salt and pepper. Put the mullet in a shallow dish, pour
over the marinade and leave to marinate for 1 hour,
turning the fish over occasionally.

Score the fish, making a criss-cross pattern, and cook
under a preheated hot grill (broiler) for 10 minutes on
each side, brushing frequently with the marinade.
Serve immediately, garnished with bay leaves.
SERVES 4

BRODETTO ALL' ANCONETANA

Fish Stew Ancona Style

*For this chowder, choose a selection of fish and shellfish to
provide a variety of textures and flavours. Red or grey
mullet, bass, sole, halibut, shrimp, clams and mussels are
popular ingredients in Italy.*

Metric/Imperial	American
1.5 kg/3 lb mixed fish and shellfish, cleaned	3 lb mixed fish and shellfish, cleaned
3–5 tablespoons olive oil	3–5 tablespoons olive oil
plain flour for coating	all-purpose flour for coating
1 onion, peeled and chopped	1 onion, peeled and chopped
3 garlic cloves, peeled	3 garlic cloves, peeled
2 bay leaves	2 bay leaves
1 piece of canned pimento	1 piece of canned pimiento
450 g/1 lb tomatoes, skinned and chopped	2 cups skinned and chopped tomatoes
1 tablespoon chopped parsley	1 tablespoon chopped parsley
salt and freshly ground black pepper	salt and freshly ground black pepper
2 tablespoons wine vinegar	2 tablespoons wine vinegar
6 slices toasted bread	6 slices toasted bread

If the shellfish is raw, place in a pan with 2 tablespoons
of the oil and cook until the shells open. Remove the
shells and set the shellfish aside. Cut the other fish into
serving pieces and coat with flour.

Heat the remaining oil in a large flameproof
casserole, add the onion, garlic, bay leaves and pimento. Cook gently for 10 minutes, then discard the
garlic. Add the tomatoes, parsley and salt and pepper to
taste. Simmer for 20 minutes, stirring occasionally,
then strain.

Return the sauce to the casserole and add all the fish,
except the shellfish. Cover and simmer for 15 minutes
until the fish is tender. Add the shellfish and vinegar
and cook for a further 5 minutes.

Place a slice of toast in each individual soup bowl and
spoon over the fish stew. Serve immediately.
SERVES 6

ALICI A SCAPECE
Marinated Anchovies

Metric/Imperial	American
575 g/1¼ lb fresh anchovies	1¼ lb fresh anchovies
plain flour for coating	all-purpose flour for coating
vegetable oil for shallow-frying	vegetable oil for shallow-frying
salt and freshly ground black pepper	salt and freshly ground black pepper
150 ml/¼ pint water	⅔ cup water
4 tablespoons wine vinegar	4 tablespoons wine vinegar
1 small onion, peeled and finely chopped	1 small onion, peeled and finely chopped
2 garlic cloves, peeled and crushed	2 garlic cloves, peeled and crushed
3 bay leaves	3 bay leaves
pinch of dried marjoram	pinch of dried marjoram
few black peppercorns	few black peppercorns

Slit the anchovies along one side, open flat and clean thoroughly. Remove the heads, tails and backbones. Coat the anchovies with flour.

Heat the oil in a frying pan (skillet), add the anchovies and fry until golden brown on both sides. Drain on absorbent kitchen paper, sprinkle with salt and pepper to taste and place in a shallow dish.

Put the water, vinegar, onion, garlic, bay leaves, marjoram and peppercorns in a small pan.

Bring to the boil, lower the heat and simmer for 5 minutes.

Pour this marinade over the anchovies, cover and leave to stand for 24 hours. Serve cold.

SERVES 4

ACCIUGHE IN COTOLETTA
Deep-fried Anchovies

Metric/Imperial	American
575 g/1¼ lb fresh anchovies	1¼ lb fresh anchovies
2 eggs, beaten with a pinch of salt	2 eggs, beaten with a pinch of salt
200 g/7 oz dried breadcrumbs (approximately)	1¾ cups dried bread crumbs (approximately)
vegetable oil for deep-frying	vegetable oil for deep-frying
salt	salt
lemon slices to serve	lemon slices to serve

Slit the anchovies along one side, clean thoroughly and remove the heads and backbones. Press each anchovy flat, then combine them in pairs with their open sides face to face. Press firmly so that they adhere to each other.

Dip each pair of anchovies into the beaten eggs, then coat with breadcrumbs. Heat the oil in a deep-fryer and deep-fry the anchovies until golden brown. Drain on absorbent kitchen paper, then sprinkle with salt. Serve immediately, with lemon slices.

SERVES 4

The Italians are lucky to have plentiful supplies of fresh anchovies, but these are not so common outside Italy. Small fresh sardines can be used as a substitute, or even smelts or sprats when these are available.

'MPEPATA DI COZZE
Mussels with Lemon

Metric/Imperial	American
1.5 kg/3 lb mussels	3 lb mussels
1 garlic clove, peeled	1 garlic clove, peeled
3–4 tablespoons water	3–4 tablespoons water
1 lemon	1 lemon
1 tablespoon chopped parsley	1 tablespoon chopped parsley
freshly ground black pepper	freshly ground black pepper

SGOMBRI ALLA BARESE

Marinated Mackerel with Herbs

Metric/Imperial	American
4 mackerel, each weighing about 225 g/8 oz, cleaned	4 mackerel, each weighing about ½ lb, cleaned
250 ml/8 fl oz white wine vinegar	1 cup white wine vinegar
salt and freshly ground black pepper	salt and freshly ground black pepper
150 ml/¼ pint olive oil	⅔ cup olive oil
3 garlic cloves, peeled and chopped	3 garlic cloves, peeled and chopped
1 tablespoon chopped parsley	1 tablespoon chopped parsley
6 mint leaves, chopped	6 mint leaves, chopped
mint sprigs to garnish	mint sprigs to garnish

Lay the fish in a large frying pan (skillet) and pour over just enough water to cover. Bring slowly to the boil, cover and simmer gently for 10 minutes. Drain and leave to cool.

Divide each mackerel into four fillets, removing the skin. Place in a shallow dish, pour over the vinegar and sprinkle with a little salt and pepper. Leave to marinate for 30 minutes.

Mix the remaining ingredients with a pinch of salt. Drain the mackerel, then return to the dish and pour over the oil marinade. Leave to marinate again for 1 hour, then drain off the oil. Serve cold, garnished with mint.

SERVES 4

POLPI IN UMIDO

Octopus in Tomato Sauce

Metric/Imperial	American
4 tablespoons olive oil	¼ cup olive oil
750 g/1¾ lb octopus, cleaned and cut into 2.5 cm/1 inch pieces	1¾ lb octopus, cleaned and cut into 1 inch pieces
4 tablespoons dry white wine	¼ cup dry white wine
450 g/1 lb tomatoes, skinned and chopped	2 cups skinned and chopped tomatoes
salt and freshly ground black pepper	salt and freshly ground black pepper
1 garlic clove, peeled and chopped	1 garlic clove, peeled and chopped
1 tablespoon chopped parsley	1 tablespoon chopped parsley

Heat the oil in a flameproof casserole, add the octopus and fry, turning, over moderate heat for 10 minutes. Add the wine and simmer until it has evaporated, then add the tomatoes and salt and pepper to taste. Lower the heat, cover and cook gently for about 45 minutes until the octopus is tender.

Sprinkle the octopus with the garlic and parsley and serve hot.

SERVES 4

Scrub the mussels under cold running water, then place in a large bowl. Cover with cold water and leave to stand for 30 minutes. Drain and discard any with open shells.

Put the mussels in a large frying pan (skillet) with the garlic and water. Cover and cook for about 5 minutes until the shells open. Discard any that have not opened. Drain, reserving the cooking liquid.

Peel the lemon and divide into segments, discarding all pith and pips. Put the mussels and cooking liquor into a clean pan. Add the parsley and lemon segments and sprinkle liberally with pepper. Simmer for a further 5 minutes. Serve immediately.

SERVES 4

ABOVE: **Polpi in umido; 'Mpepata di cozze; Sgombri alla barese; Acciughe in cotoletta**

COZZE ALLA PUGLIESE

Mussels Apulian Style

Metric/Imperial	American
1 kg/3 lb mussels	3 lb mussels
4 tablespoons olive oil	4 tablespoons olive oil
2 garlic cloves, peeled and crushed	2 garlic cloves, peeled and crushed
7 tablespoons dry white wine	7 tablespoons dry white wine
2 tablespoons tomato purée	2 tablespoons tomato paste
4 tablespoons water	4 tablespoons water
salt and freshly ground black pepper	salt and freshly ground black pepper
25 g/1 oz butter	2 tablespoons butter
25 g/1 oz plain flour	¼ cup all-purpose flour
250 ml/8 fl oz milk	1 cup milk
2 tablespoons grated Parmesan cheese★	2 tablespoons grated Parmesan cheese★
3 tablespoons breadcrumbs	3 tablespoons bread crumbs

Scrub the mussels under cold running water, then soak in cold water for 30 minutes. Drain and discard any that are open.

Put the mussels in a pan with half the oil. Cook over high heat for 5 minutes or until the mussels open, discarding any that do not. Strain the cooking liquid and reserve. Remove the mussels from their shells.

Heat the remaining oil in a pan, add the garlic and fry gently until golden brown. Add the wine and cooking liquid. Simmer for 5 minutes, then add the tomato purée (paste) diluted with the water. Season with salt and pepper to taste and simmer for 5 minutes.

Meanwhile, melt the butter in a small pan, add the flour and cook, stirring, for 1 minute. Stir in the milk gradually and cook, stirring, over low heat until the sauce thickens.

Stir the mussels into the tomato mixture and spoon into a shallow ovenproof dish. Pour over the sauce and sprinkle with the cheese and breadcrumbs. Bake in a preheated moderately hot oven (190°C/375°F, Gas Mark 5) for 15 minutes. Serve hot.

SERVES 4

SARDE A BECCAFICO

Deep-Fried Sardines with Cheese Stuffing

Metric/Imperial	American
750 g/1¾ lb fresh sardines	1¾ lb fresh sardines
200 ml/⅓ pint white wine vinegar	1 cup white wine vinegar
75 g/3 oz pecorino cheese★, grated	¾ cup grated pecorino cheese★
3 garlic cloves, peeled and crushed	3 garlic cloves, peeled and crushed
1 tablespoon chopped parsley or basil	1 tablespoon chopped parsley or basil
salt and freshly ground black pepper	salt and freshly ground black pepper
2 eggs, beaten	2 eggs, beaten
dried breadcrumbs for coating	dried bread crumbs for coating
vegetable oil for shallow-frying	vegetable oil for shallow-frying
basil or parsley sprigs to garnish	basil or parsley sprigs to garnish

Slit the sardines open along one side and clean thoroughly, removing the backbones but leaving the heads and tails intact. Open the fish out and place in a shallow bowl. Pour over the vinegar and leave to marinate for 2 hours, turning occasionally.

Drain the sardines. Mix the pecorino, garlic and parsley with salt and pepper to taste. Spread this mixture over the insides of the sardines and fold to close. Dip the sardines in the eggs and coat with breadcrumbs.

Pour the oil into a frying pan (skillet) to a depth of 5 mm/¼ inch and place over moderate heat. Fry the sardines until brown on both sides. Drain on absorbent kitchen paper and serve immediately, garnished with basil or parsley sprigs.

SERVES 4 TO 6

The recipe Sarde a beccafico is named after the tiny Sicilian birds known as beccafichi or figpeckers. These are a great delicacy in Italy, as are other kinds of small birds, and are most often served grilled (broiled) on skewers. It is easy to see why this dish has this title – when the sardines are stuffed and deep-fried they do in fact bear a striking resemblance to small birds.

COTOLETTE DI TONNO

Grilled (Broiled) Tuna Fish Steaks

Metric/Imperial	American
4 tuna fish steaks, each weighing about 175 g/6 oz	4 tuna fish or bonito steaks, each weighing about 6 oz
2 garlic cloves, peeled and chopped	2 garlic cloves, peeled and chopped
1 sprig rosemary, chopped	1 sprig rosemary, chopped
salt and freshly ground black pepper	salt and freshly ground black pepper
200 ml/⅓ pint dry white wine	1 cup dry white wine
4 tablespoons olive oil	¼ cup olive oil
25 g/1 oz dried breadcrumbs	¼ cup dried bread crumbs
juice of 1 lemon	juice of 1 lemon

Sarde a beccafico;
Agghiotta di pesce spada

Put the fish in a deep dish and sprinkle with the garlic, rosemary and salt and pepper to taste. Pour the wine over the fish and leave to marinate for 1 hour, turning the fish from time to time.

Drain the fish, reserving the marinade, and brush with some of the oil. Grill (broil) under a preheated moderate grill (broiler) for 7 to 8 minutes on each side, basting with the marinade from time to time. Sprinkle with the breadcrumbs and grill (broil) for a further 5 minutes.

Blend the remaining oil with the lemon juice and salt and pepper to taste. Arrange the fish on a warmed serving platter and sprinkle over the dressing. Serve immediately.

SERVES 4

NOTE: Salmon steaks can be used instead of tuna, if preferred.

AGGHIOTTA DI PESCE SPADA

Swordfish or Salmon with Tomatoes and Olives

Metric/Imperial	American
4 swordfish or salmon steaks, each weighing about 175 g/6 oz	4 swordfish or salmon steaks, each weighing about 6 oz
plain flour for coating	all-purpose flour for coating
4 tablespoons olive oil	4 tablespoons olive oil
salt and freshly ground black pepper	salt and freshly ground black pepper
1 small onion, peeled and chopped	1 small onion, peeled and chopped
1 celery stick, chopped	1 celery stalk, chopped
2 garlic cloves, peeled and crushed	2 garlic cloves, peeled and crushed
450 g/1 lb tomatoes, skinned and mashed	2 cups skinned and mashed tomatoes
25 g/1 oz seedless raisins, soaked in lukewarm water for 15 minutes and drained	2 tablespoons seedless raisins, soaked in lukewarm water for 15 minutes and drained
25 g/1 oz pine kernels	¼ cup pine kernels
1 tablespoon capers	1 tablespoon capers
100 g/4 oz green olives, halved and stoned	¾ cup pitted green olives
2 bay leaves	2 bay leaves

Coat the fish with flour. Heat the oil in a flameproof casserole, add the fish and fry until golden brown on both sides. Remove and drain on absorbent kitchen paper, then sprinkle with salt and pepper.

Add the onion, celery and garlic to the casserole and fry gently for 5 minutes. Add the tomatoes, with salt and pepper to taste, and simmer for 15 minutes. Stir in the raisins, pine kernels, capers and olives and cook for a further 5 minutes.

Return the fish to the casserole, add the bay leaves and enough water to just cover the fish. Cover and cook in a preheated moderate oven (180°C/350°F/Gas Mark 4) for 15 to 20 minutes until the fish is tender. Remove the bay leaves and serve hot.

SERVES 4

ABOVE: **Naselli alla palermitana; Calamari ripieni al forno**
RIGHT: **Cassola**

PESCE ALLA MESSINESE

Fish Casseroled in Wine

Metric/Imperial	American
750 g/1¾ lb white fish (swordfish, bass, cod, etc)	1¾ lb white fish (swordfish, bass, cod, etc)
450 g/1 lb potatoes, peeled	1 lb potatoes, peeled
salt	salt
5 tablespoons olive oil	⅓ cup olive oil
1 onion, peeled and chopped	1 onion, peeled and chopped
1 garlic clove, peeled and chopped	1 garlic clove, peeled and chopped
150 ml/¼ pint dry white wine	⅔ cup dry white wine
575 g/1¼ lb tomatoes, skinned and chopped	2½ cups skinned and chopped tomatoes
freshly ground black pepper	freshly ground black pepper
225 g/8 oz black olives	1½ cups pitted ripe olives
25 g/1 oz capers	¼ cup capers

Remove the skin and bones from the fish, then cut into serving pieces. Parboil the potatoes in boiling salted water for 10 minutes. Drain and slice.

Heat the oil in a flameproof casserole, add the onion and garlic and fry gently for 5 minutes. Add the fish and fry, turning, for 2 to 3 minutes. Pour in the wine and simmer for a few minutes, then stir in the tomatoes and salt and pepper to taste.

Add the potatoes, olives and capers. Cover and bake in a preheated moderate oven (180°C/350°F/Gas Mark 4) for 20 minutes or until the fish and potatoes are tender. Serve hot.
SERVES 4

NASELLI ALLA PALERMITANA
Hake with Rosemary and Anchovies

Metric/Imperial	American
1 hake, weighing about 1 kg/2 lb, cleaned and filleted	1 hake, weighing about 2 lb, cleaned and fileted
salt and freshly ground black pepper	salt and freshly ground black pepper
10–12 sprigs rosemary	10–12 sprigs rosemary
3 tablespoons olive oil	3 tablespoons olive oil
6 canned anchovies, soaked in milk, drained and chopped	6 canned anchovies, soaked in milk, drained and chopped
50 g/2 oz dried breadcrumbs	½ cup dried bread crumbs
1 lemon twist to garnish	1 lemon twist to garnish

Sprinkle the fish with salt and pepper. Dip half the rosemary sprigs into the oil and place in a flameproof casserole. Lay the fish on top.

Heat the remaining oil in a small pan, add the anchovies and cook gently until dissolved, breaking them down with a fork. Pour over the fish, then sprinkle with the breadcrumbs. Bake in a preheated moderate oven (180°C/350°F/Gas Mark 4) for 30 minutes or until the fish is tender. Garnish with the remaining rosemary sprigs and a twist of lemon. Serve immediately.

SERVES 4

CALAMARI RIPIENI AL FORNO
Baked Stuffed Squid

Metric/Imperial	American
750 g/1¾ lb squid	1¾ lb squid
salt	salt
4 canned anchovies, mashed	4 canned anchovies, mashed
1 garlic clove, peeled and crushed	1 garlic clove, peeled and crushed
1 tablespoon dried breadcrumbs	1 tablespoon dried bread crumbs
1 tablespoon chopped parsley	1 tablespoon chopped parsley
1 egg, beaten	1 egg, beaten
freshly ground black pepper	freshly ground black pepper
3 tablespoons olive oil	3 tablespoons olive oil
fennel leaves to garnish	fennel leaves to garnish

Clean the squid, discarding the heads, inksacs and backbones. Cut off the tentacles and set aside the squid. Cook the tentacles in boiling salted water for 10 minutes. Drain, chop and place in a bowl. Add the remaining ingredients, except the oil, seasoning with salt and pepper to taste.

Stuff the squid with this mixture, and sew up the opening with thread. Place the squid in an ovenproof dish and sprinkle with the oil.

Bake in a preheated moderate oven (180°C/350°F/Gas Mark 4) for 1 hour or until tender. Serve immediately, garnished with fennel.

SERVES 4

CASSOLA
Seafood Casserole

Metric/Imperial	American
4 tablespoons olive oil	4 tablespoons olive oil
1 onion, peeled and chopped	1 onion, peeled and chopped
1 garlic clove, peeled and chopped	1 garlic clove, peeled and chopped
1 piece of canned pimento, chopped	1 piece of canned pimiento, chopped
450 g/1 lb tomatoes, skinned, seeded and chopped	2 cups skinned, seeded and chopped tomatoes
4 tablespoons white wine or water	¼ cup white wine or water
salt and freshly ground black pepper	salt and freshly ground black pepper
1.25 kg/2½ lb mixed fish (squid, sole, halibut, red mullet, eel, etc), cleaned, filleted and cut into pieces if large	2½ lb mixed fish (squid, sole, halibut, red mullet, eel, etc), cleaned, fileted and cut into pieces if large
6 slices hot toasted bread	6 slices hot toasted bread

Heat half the oil in a large flameproof casserole, add the onion, garlic and pimento and fry gently for 5 minutes. Add the tomatoes, wine or water, and salt and pepper to taste. Bring slowly to the boil.

Sauté the squid in the remaining oil for 4 to 5 minutes, then add to the tomato mixture. Cover and simmer for 30 minutes. Add the remaining fish, cover and simmer for 15 minutes or until all the fish are tender.

Place a slice of toast in each individual soup bowl and pour over the fish stew. Serve immediately.

SERVES 6

Sardinia's fishing industry is almost as important as her sheep farming. Everyone knows the sardine owes its name to the island, but there are many other kinds of fish in Sardinia which are equally prolific. Tuna and swordfish provide the island's fishermen with a thriving business, although the fishing industry here is still very much steeped in the past; to this very day local fishermen can be seen using wooden hooks and tridents.

Meat Dishes

In the past, meat was not considered to be one of the staple foodstuffs of Italy – fish, pasta, vegetables and cheese were more widely consumed. Today, however, the quantity of meat eaten, particularly veal and pork, is quite considerable.

Beef is eaten more in the north of the country than elsewhere, for the rich pasturelands and alpine slopes breed excellent cattle. By and large these cattle are bred more for their milk than their meat, but a certain amount of good quality beef does find its way to the table. Oxen are used as working animals in Italy, and some of the beef is therefore tougher than non-Italians are used to, but the flavoursome stews of the north, with their long slow cooking, are eminently suitable for this kind of beef. Italians prefer to eat good quality beef as steaks, either plain or charcoal grilled (broiled).

Veal is a very popular meat in Italy, and there are countless recipes using it. The different kinds of veal to choose from include *vitello da latte*; this is meat from calves slaughtered when only a few weeks old, which were therefore entirely milk-fed. This is the most expensive and highly prized veal, and it is particularly suitable for veal escalopes. Meat from older calves from six to nine months is known as *vitello*, and this is the most common type of veal on sale in Italy and other countries. *Vitellone* is neither veal nor beef, but what some butchers call 'baby beef' and it is not suitable for escalopes. Apart from the numerous ways in which they serve escalopes, Italians also like to serve other cuts of veal in casseroles, as in *Ossibuchi alla milanese* (see page 128), and in roasts, such as *Cima alla genovese* (see page 127) and *Arrosto di vitello al latte* (see page 128).

Lamb and kid are popular roasting meats, especially in the central regions around Rome and *abbacchio* (whole spit-roasted lamb) and *capretto* (whole spit-roasted kid) are common sights in these areas. Roast joints of young (spring) lamb are also popular, so too is the occasional casserole or stew.

Pork is very popular and the Italians are as fond of eating the fresh meat as they are of eating it cured, in the form of hams, bacon, sausages and salami. Spit-roasting whole young pigs, known as *porchetta* or *porceddu* is another, much-favoured, way of eating pork.

Offal (variety meats) are used a great deal. The Italians waste very little that is edible, so recipes for sausages, rissoles, meat loaves, stuffings and *ragù* often combine offal (variety meats) with minced (ground) veal, beef or pork.

PIEMONTE & VALLE D'AOSTA

BRASATO DI BUE AL BAROLO

Beef Casseroled in Barolo Wine

Metric/Imperial	American
1 kg/2 lb piece topside or top rump	2 lb piece beef top round or top rump
1 bottle Barolo or other red wine	1 bottle Barolo or other red wine
2 onions, peeled and chopped	2 onions, peeled and chopped
2 carrots, peeled and chopped	2 carrots, peeled and chopped
1 celery stick, chopped	1 celery stalk, chopped
1 garlic clove, peeled and thinly sliced	1 garlic clove, peeled and thinly sliced
1 bay leaf	1 bay leaf
1 rosemary sprig	1 rosemary sprig
pinch of dried thyme	pinch of dried thyme
1 cinnamon stick	1 cinnamon stick
2 whole cloves	2 whole cloves
4 tablespoons olive oil	$\frac{1}{4}$ cup olive oil
2 tablespoons tomato purée	2 tablespoons tomato paste
3–4 tablespoons beef stock	3–4 tablespoons beef stock
salt and freshly ground black pepper	salt and freshly ground black pepper
1 small glass brandy	1 small glass brandy

Put the meat in a large bowl with the wine, vegetables, herbs and spices. Leave to marinate in a cool place for 12 hours.

Drain the meat thoroughly, reserving the marinade. Heat the oil in a flameproof casserole and fry the meat over brisk heat, turning, until browned on all sides. Add the reserved marinade, vegetables, herbs and spices and cook over moderate heat for 10 minutes.

Mix the tomato purée (paste) with the stock, then add to the pan with salt and pepper to taste. Lower the heat, cover and simmer gently for 2 to $2\frac{1}{2}$ hours until the meat is tender.

Drain the meat and keep hot. Work the cooking liquid in an electric blender or through a sieve (strainer). Return to the casserole, add the brandy and heat through. Slice the meat and arrange on a warmed serving platter. Pour over the sauce and serve immediately.

SERVES 4

RIGHT: **Brasato di bue al barolo**

CARBONATA VALDOSTANA

Beef Casserole, Valle d'Aosta Style

Metric/Imperial	American
750 g/1¾ lb stewing beef, cut into large chunks	1¾ lb stewing beef, cut into large chunks
plain flour for coating	all-purpose flour for coating
40 g/1½ oz beef dripping or 3 tablespoons oil	3 tablespoons beef dripping or oil
1 onion, peeled and chopped	1 onion, peeled and chopped
300 ml/½ pint robust red wine	1¼ cups robust red wine
salt and freshly ground black pepper	salt and freshly ground black pepper

Coat the meat with flour. Heat the dripping or oil in a flameproof casserole, add the meat and fry over brisk heat until browned on all sides. Remove the meat with a slotted spoon and set aside.

Add the onion to the casserole and fry gently for 5 minutes. Return the meat to the casserole, then add the wine and salt and pepper to taste. Cover and simmer for 2 hours or until the meat is tender. Stir a little water into the casserole if it becomes dry during cooking. Serve hot, with polenta (see page 87).

SERVES 4

COSTATA DI MANZO ALLA VALTELLINESE

Braised Beef Valtellina Style

Metric/Imperial	American
4 large, thin slices beef topside	4 large, thin slices beef top round
salt and freshly ground black pepper	salt and freshly ground black pepper
350 g/12 oz mushrooms, thinly sliced	3 cups thinly sliced mushrooms
8 tomatoes, skinned and chopped	8 tomatoes, skinned and chopped
100 g/4 oz butter	½ cup butter
6-8 tablespoons beef stock	6-8 tablespoons beef stock
450 g/1 lb small pickling onions, peeled	1 lb baby onions, peeled

Sprinkle the meat slices with salt and pepper to taste. Divide the mushrooms and tomatoes equally between the beef slices, placing it in the centre. Roll up each slice, enclosing the filling, and tie securely with string.

Melt the butter in a flameproof casserole, add the beef rolls and spoon over the butter and stock. Cover and simmer gently for 1 hour, basting occasionally.

Meanwhile, boil the onions in salted water for 10 minutes. Drain and add to the casserole. Cook for a further 30 minutes or until the meat and onions are tender.

Remove the string from the meat and transfer the meat and onions to a serving dish. Pour over the cooking juices and serve immediately.

SERVES 4

Meat Dishes/119

ABOVE: **Mondeghili**

MONDEGHILI
Fried Meatballs

Metric/Imperial	American
50 g/2 oz fresh bread-crumbs, soaked in milk	1 cup fresh bread crumbs, soaked in milk
450 g/1 lb cooked minced beef	2 cups cooked ground beef
1 tablespoon chopped parsley	1 tablespoon chopped parsley
finely grated rind of $\frac{1}{2}$ lemon	finely grated rind of $\frac{1}{2}$ lemon
pinch of grated nutmeg	pinch of grated nutmeg
salt and freshly ground black pepper	salt and freshly ground black pepper
1 egg, beaten	1 egg, beaten
dried breadcrumbs for coating	dried bread crumbs for coating
vegetable oil for shallow-frying	vegetable oil for shallow-frying
rosemary sprigs to garnish	rosemary sprigs to garnish

Squeeze the breadcrumbs dry and place in a bowl with the meat, parsley, lemon rind, nutmeg and salt and pepper to taste. Stir well and mix in enough egg to bind.

Shape the mixture into small balls, then press into flat oval shapes and coat with dried breadcrumbs. Heat the oil in a frying pan (skillet) until very hot and fry the meatballs until golden brown. Drain on absorbent kitchen paper.

Garnish with rosemary and serve hot.

SERVES 4

NOTE: Leftover cooked beef is ideal for this dish.

INVOLTINI DI VERZA
Stuffed Cabbage Rolls

Metric/Imperial	American
8 large green cabbage leaves	8 large green cabbage leaves
100 g/4 oz cooked luganega sausage,★ chopped	½ cup cooked chopped luganega sausage★
350 g/12 oz cooked minced beef	1½ cups cooked ground beef
100 g/4 oz Parmesan cheese★, grated	1 cup grated Parmesan cheese★
100 g/4 oz stale bread-crumbs, soaked in milk and squeezed dry	2 cups stale bread crumbs, soaked in milk and squeezed dry
1 tablespoon chopped parsley	1 tablespoon chopped parsley
1 garlic clove, peeled and crushed	1 garlic clove, peeled and crushed
pinch of grated nutmeg	pinch of grated nutmeg
salt and freshly ground black pepper	salt and freshly ground black pepper
1 egg, beaten	1 egg, beaten
2 ripe tomatoes, peeled and chopped	2 ripe tomatoes, peeled and chopped
7 tablespoons hot beef stock	7 tablespoons hot beef stock

Parboil the cabbage leaves in boiling water for 30 seconds. Drain thoroughly, then spread flat on a work surface and leave to cool.

Put the sausage in a bowl with the beef, cheese, breadcrumbs, parsley, garlic, nutmeg and salt and pepper to taste. Stir well and mix in enough beaten egg to bind. Divide equally between the cabbage leaves. Roll the leaves around the filling and secure with string.

Arrange the cabbage rolls in a single layer in an oiled ovenproof dish. Cook in a preheated moderate oven (180°C/350°F/Gas Mark 4) for 10 minutes, then add the tomatoes, stock and a pinch of salt. Lower the heat to cool (140°C/275°F/Gas Mark 1) and bake for a further 30 minutes, basting the cabbage rolls with the cooking juices from time to time. Serve hot.

SERVES 4

COTECHINO IN GALERA
Stuffed Beef Roll

Metric/Imperial	American
1 cotechino★, weighing 675 g/1½ lb	1 cotechino★, weighing 1½ lb
450 g/1 lb slice beef topside, about 1 cm/½ inch thick	1 lb slice beef top round, about ½ inch thick
2 large slices cured or cooked ham	2 large slices cured or cooked ham
4 tablespoons olive oil	4 tablespoons olive oil
1 onion, peeled and chopped	1 onion, peeled and chopped
300 ml/½ pint red wine	1¼ cups red wine
300 ml/½ pint hot beef stock	1¼ cups hot beef stock
salt and freshly ground black pepper	salt and freshly ground black pepper

Puncture the sausage, wrap in a cloth and place in a large pan. Cover with water, bring to the boil, lower the heat and simmer for 1 hour. Drain, remove the cloth and skin from the sausage, then leave to cool.

Beat the slice of beef with a mallet to flatten. Place the ham on top and the sausage in the centre, then roll the beef around the ham and sausage. Tie securely with thread or string.

Heat the oil in a flameproof casserole, add the onion and fry gently for 5 minutes. Add the beef roll and fry, turning, until evenly browned. Pour in the wine and stock. Add salt and pepper to taste. Cover and simmer for 1 hour or until the meat is tender.

Remove the roll from the casserole, leave to cool for 1 to 2 minutes, then remove the thread. Slice neatly, arrange on a warmed serving platter, and pour over the cooking juices. Serve immediately.

SERVES 4

STUFATO AL LATTE ALLA RAVENNATE
Beef Casseroled in Rum and Milk

Metric/Imperial	American
50 g/2 oz lard	2 tablespoons lard
1 kg/2 lb stewing beef, cut into chunks	2 lb stewing beef, cut into chunks
7 tablespoons rum	7 tablespoons rum
300 ml/½ pint milk	1¼ cups milk
1 onion, peeled and chopped	1 onion, peeled and chopped
1 carrot, peeled and chopped	1 carrot, peeled and chopped
1 celery stick, chopped	1 celery stalk, chopped
2 basil leaves, finely chopped	2 basil leaves, finely chopped
2 tablespoons tomato purée	2 tablespoons tomato paste
salt and freshly ground black pepper	salt and freshly ground black pepper
50 g/2 oz butter	¼ cup butter
350 g/12 oz pickling onions, peeled	¾ lb baby onions, peeled

Heat the lard in a flameproof casserole, add the meat and brown evenly. Add the rum, milk, onion, carrot, celery, basil, tomato purée (paste) and salt and pepper to taste. Cover and simmer for 2 to 2½ hours until the meat is almost tender.

Melt the butter in another pan, add the onions and sauté until golden. Add the onions to the casserole and bring to the boil. Lower the heat, cover and simmer for a further 30 minutes until the meat and onions are tender. Serve hot.

SERVES 4 TO 6

One of Italy's most odd dishes is the Elephant Platter'. Believed to be Balkan in origin, the legend goes that in the sixteenth century an elephant came to the town of Bressanone, not far from Bolzano in Trentino-Alto Adige. He was on his way from Portugal to Austria, but because the mountains were impassable, he and his handlers spent the winter in the town. They lodged at the Elefante Hotel, where you can still order the 'Elephant Platter' - a concoction of meat, fish, cheese, eggs, fruit, vegetables and sweetmeats.

POLPETTE ALLA FIORENTINA
Beef Rissoles

Metric/Imperial	American
350 g/12 oz cooked minced beef	1½ cups ground cooked beef
2 garlic cloves, peeled and crushed	2 garlic cloves, peeled and crushed
2 potatoes, boiled and mashed	2 potatoes, boiled and mashed
1 tablespoon chopped parsley	1 tablespoon chopped parsley
75 g/3 oz Parmesan cheese★, grated	¾ cup grated Parmesan cheese★
1 stale bread roll, soaked in milk and squeezed dry	1 stale bread roll, soaked in milk and squeezed dry
salt and freshly ground black pepper	salt and freshly ground black pepper
1–2 eggs, beaten	1–2 eggs, beaten
dried breadcrumbs for coating	dried bread crumbs for coating
vegetable oil for shallow-frying	vegetable oil for shallow-frying
parsley sprigs to garnish	parsley sprigs to garnish

Put the beef in a bowl with the garlic, potato, parsley, Parmesan, bread and salt and pepper to taste. Add enough beaten egg to bind the mixture and stir until the ingredients are thoroughly combined. Shape the mixture into oval rissoles, then coat in breadcrumbs.

Heat the oil in a frying pan (skillet). Add the rissoles and fry over moderate heat until golden brown on all sides. Drain on absorbent kitchen paper. Serve hot, garnished with parsley.

SERVES 4

Tuscan beef ranks amongst the finest in the world, and *Bistecca alla fiorentina*, charcoal-grilled (broiled) steak, is one of the greatest of all Italian dishes. In Tuscany, only beef from the Chianina breed of cattle is used for this dish. It is a huge rib steak which is always served plain – any sauce or accompaniment would only detract from the superb flavour and tender texture of the meat. Chianina cattle are reputed to be the oldest breed of cattle in the world, and probably the tallest and heaviest. They are noted for their speedy growth – by the time other breeds of cattle could reach a comparable size to the Chianina, their meat would be tough and sinewy.

BELOW: Bistecchine alla napoletana; Polpette alla fiorentina; Stufato di manzo alla fiorentina

STUFATO DI MANZO ALLA FIORENTINA
Tuscan Beef Stew

Metric/Imperial	American
3–4 tablespoons olive oil	3–4 tablespoons olive oil
2 garlic cloves, peeled and crushed	2 garlic cloves, peeled and crushed
1 teaspoon chopped rosemary	1 teaspoon chopped rosemary
750 g/1¾ lb stewing beef, cut into cubes	1¾ lb stewing beef, cut into cubes
pinch of ground mixed spice	pinch of ground allspice
salt and freshly ground black pepper	pinch of ground cinnamon
7 tablespoons red wine	salt and freshly ground black pepper
5 tablespoons tomato purée	7 tablespoons red wine
rosemary sprigs to garnish	5 tablespoons tomato paste
	rosemary sprigs to garnish

Heat the oil in a flameproof casserole, add the garlic and rosemary and fry gently for 5 minutes until browned. Add the meat, spice(s) and salt and pepper to taste and fry until the meat is browned on all sides.

Add the wine and simmer until reduced slightly. Stir in the tomato purée (paste), dissolved in a little warm water. Simmer, stirring, for 3 minutes, then add enough water to cover the meat. Bring to the boil.

Cover the casserole, lower the heat and simmer for 2 hours or until the meat is tender, stirring occasionally and adding more water as necessary to cover the meat. Serve hot, garnished with rosemary.

SERVES 4

STUFATO DI MANZO
Beef Casseroled in White Wine

Metric/Imperial	American
25 g/1 oz lard	2 tablespoons lard
50 g/2 oz raw ham or bacon, chopped	¼ cup chopped raw ham or bacon
½ onion, peeled and chopped	½ onion, peeled and chopped
1 garlic clove, peeled and crushed	1 garlic clove, peeled and crushed
1 kg/2 lb stewing beef, sliced	2 lb stewing beef, sliced
pinch of dried marjoram	pinch of dried marjoram
salt and freshly ground black pepper	salt and freshly ground black pepper
7 tablespoons dry white wine	7 tablespoons dry white wine
2 tablespoons tomato purée	2 tablespoons tomato paste

Melt the lard in a flameproof casserole, add the ham or bacon, onion and garlic and fry gently until browned. Add the meat, marjoram and salt and pepper to taste and fry over moderate heat until the meat is browned on all sides.

Add the wine and simmer until reduced slightly. Stir in the tomato purée (paste), dissolved in a few tablespoons of water, and simmer for 3 minutes, stirring frequently. Pour in enough water to cover the meat and bring to the boil.

Cover the casserole, lower the heat and simmer for 2 hours or until the meat is tender, stirring occasionally and adding more water as necessary. Serve hot.

SERVES 4 TO 6

BISTECCHINE ALLA NAPOLETANA
Fillet Steak with Ham and Mushrooms

Metric/Imperial	American
3 tablespoons olive oil	3 tablespoons olive oil
100 g/4 oz prosciutto* or raw smoked ham, chopped	½ cup chopped prosciutto* or raw smoked ham
225 g/8 oz mushrooms, sliced	2½ cups sliced mushrooms
salt and freshly ground black pepper	salt and freshly ground black pepper
1 tablespoon chopped parsley	1 tablespoon chopped parsley
8 slices beef fillet, each weighing 50 g/2 oz	8 slices beef filet, each weighing 2 oz
juice of ½ lemon	juice of ½ lemon

Heat half the oil in a flameproof casserole, add the ham, mushrooms and salt and pepper to taste and sauté for 5 minutes. Sprinkle with the parsley.

Arrange the beef slices on top, without overlapping the slices. Sprinkle with a little salt, the lemon juice and the remaining oil. Cook in a preheated moderate oven (180°C/350°F/Gas Mark 4) for 20 minutes, turning the steaks and basting them with the cooking juices halfway through cooking. Serve immediately.

SERVES 4

There are few great meat dishes to come from Sicily, for the simple reason that the Sicilians are not the greatest of meat eaters. The rugged character of the island's landscape does not lend itself to vast tracts of grazing land – the most common animals are the sheep and goats that graze on the hillsides. The recipes for stuffed beef rolls on this page illustrate how easy it is to make a small amount of meat 'stretch' with the addition of other ingredients.

INVOLTINI ALLA BARESE

Stuffed Beef Olives

Metric/Imperial	American
2 garlic cloves, peeled and crushed	2 garlic cloves, peeled and crushed
2 teaspoons chopped parsley	2 teaspoons chopped parsley
2 teaspoons chopped basil	2 teaspoons chopped basil
50 g/2 oz pecorino cheese,★ grated	$\frac{1}{2}$ cup grated pecorino cheese★
4 slices beef top rump, each weighing about 100 g/4 oz	4 slices beef top round, each weighing about $\frac{1}{4}$ lb
4 thin slices cooked ham	4 thin slices cooked ham
salt and freshly ground black pepper	salt and freshly ground black pepper
3 tablespoons olive oil	3 tablespoons olive oil
$\frac{1}{2}$ onion, peeled and sliced	$\frac{1}{2}$ onion, peeled and sliced
6 tablespoons dry white wine	6 tablespoons dry white wine
6–8 tablespoons hot beef stock	6–8 tablespoons hot beef stock
400 g/14 oz tomatoes, skinned and chopped	$1\frac{3}{4}$ cups skinned and chopped tomatoes

Put the garlic, parsley, basil and pecorino in a bowl and stir well to mix. Beat the beef slices with a mallet to flatten. Place a slice of ham on each, then top with the cheese and herb mixture and sprinkle with salt and pepper to taste. Roll the meat around the stuffing, then tie securely with string.

Heat the oil in a flameproof casserole, add the onion and fry gently for 5 minutes. Add the meat rolls and fry until browned on all sides, then add the wine, stock, tomatoes and salt and pepper to taste.

Lower the heat, cover the casserole and cook gently for about 45 minutes or until the meat is tender. Turn the meat during cooking and add more stock to moisten if necessary.

Remove the meat from the casserole and untie the string. Arrange on a warmed serving plate and pour over the cooking juices. Serve immediately.
SERVES 4

FARSUMAGRU

Stuffed Beef or Veal Roll

Metric/Imperial	American
100 g/4 oz ham or bacon, minced	$\frac{1}{2}$ cup ground ham or bacon
175 g/6 oz salsiccia a metro★, finely chopped	6 oz salsiccia a metro★, finely chopped
100 g/4 oz gruyère cheese, cut into cubes	$\frac{1}{4}$ lb gruyère cheese, cut into cubes
2 garlic cloves, peeled and crushed	2 garlic cloves, peeled and chopped
1 tablespoon chopped parsley	1 tablespoon chopped parsley
1 egg, beaten	1 egg, beaten
salt and freshly ground black pepper	salt and freshly ground black pepper
1 large slice beef topside or leg of veal, weighing about 575 g/1$\frac{1}{4}$ lb	1 large slice beef top round or leg of veal, weighing about 1$\frac{1}{4}$ lb
2 hard-boiled eggs, sliced	2 hard-cooked eggs, sliced
4 tablespoons olive oil	$\frac{1}{4}$ cup olive oil
pinch of dried marjoram	pinch of dried marjoram
1 small onion, peeled and sliced	1 small onion, peeled and sliced
$\frac{1}{2}$ carrot, peeled and chopped	$\frac{1}{2}$ carrot, peeled and chopped
1 bay leaf	1 bay leaf
120 ml/4 fl oz beef stock	$\frac{1}{2}$ cup beef stock
3–4 tablespoons red wine	3–4 tablespoons red wine

Put the ham in a bowl with the sausage, cheese, half the garlic, the parsley, egg and salt and pepper to taste. Stir well to mix.

Beat the meat with a mallet to flatten. Spread with the stuffing and top with the sliced egg. Roll the meat up to enclose the stuffing, then tie securely with string.

Heat the oil in a flameproof casserole. Add the meat and sprinkle with the marjoram, then add the onion, carrot, bay leaf and remaining garlic. Fry, turning the meat until browned on all sides.

Add half the stock, cover the casserole and cook in a preheated moderate oven (180°C/350°F/Gas Mark 4) for 1 to 1$\frac{1}{2}$ hours until the meat is tender, basting frequently and adding a little stock as necessary to prevent the meat sticking.

Transfer the meat to a plate; keep hot. Place the casserole over moderate heat, add the wine and boil until reduced by half. Discard the bay leaf. Slice the meat and arrange on a warmed serving plate. Pour over the cooking juices and serve immediately.
SERVES 4 TO 6

INVOLTINI COI CARCIOFI

Beef Olives with Artichokes

Metric/Imperial	American
2 young globe artichokes	2 young globe artichokes
salt	salt
juice of 1 lemon	juice of 1 lemon
8 slices beef topside, each weighing 50 g/2 oz	8 slices beef top round, each weighing 2 oz
100 g/4 oz prosciutto★ or raw smoked ham, finely chopped	¼ lb prosciutto★ or raw smoked ham, finely chopped
50 g/2 oz butter	¼ cup butter
2 tablespoons olive oil	2 tablespoons olive oil
1 small onion, peeled and chopped	1 small onion, peeled and chopped
flour for coating	flour for coating
4–5 tablespoons dry white wine	4–5 tablespoons dry white wine
freshly ground black pepper	freshly ground black pepper
6–8 tablespoons hot beef stock	6–8 tablespoons hot beef stock

Discard the outer leaves, tips and chokes from the artichokes. Cook them in plenty of boiling salted water, with the lemon juice added, for 20 minutes. Drain and cut each one into 8 sections.

Beat the meat slices with a mallet to flatten. Mix the ham with a third of the butter and spread this mixture over the slices. Top each one with 2 artichoke sections, then roll the slices around the stuffing and tie securely with string.

Heat the remaining butter and the oil in a flame-proof casserole, add the onion and fry gently for 5 minutes. Coat the meat rolls with flour, add to the casserole and fry, turning, until browned on all sides.

Add the wine and salt and pepper to taste. Lower the heat, cover the casserole and cook gently for about 45 minutes or until the meat is tender. Turn the meat during cooking and add the stock as necessary to prevent the meat sticking.

Remove the meat from the casserole and untie the string. Arrange the meat on a warmed serving platter, then pour over the cooking juices. Serve immediately.
SERVES 4

ABOVE: **Farsumagru**;
LEFT: **Involtini coi carciofi**

The Italians have always been great veal eaters – one glance at a menu in an Italian restaurant will bear this out – and there are many splendid classic veal dishes to come out of Italy. The Italians insist on using only the youngest and very best quality veal, especially in any dish that calls for *scaloppine di vitello* or veal escalopes. Its texture is so fine that it will cook in minutes, and it should be almost white in colour.

SUBRICS
Veal and Apple Rissoles

Metric/Imperial	American
2 sharp eating apples, peeled, cored and finely chopped	2 sharp dessert apples, peeled, cored and finely chopped
450 g/1 lb minced veal	2 cups ground veal
1 egg, beaten	1 egg, beaten
1½ teaspoons sugar	1½ teaspoons sugar
salt and freshly ground black pepper	salt and freshly ground black pepper
50 g/2 oz plain flour	½ cup all-purpose flour
65 g/2½ oz butter	5 tablespoons butter
4 tablespoons red wine	¼ cup red wine

Put the apples in a bowl and add the meat, egg, sugar and salt and pepper to taste. Stir well to mix, adding a little of the flour to bind the mixture. Shape the mixture into rissoles and coat with flour.

Melt the butter in a large frying pan (skillet), add the rissoles and fry over moderate heat until browned on all sides. Add the wine, cover and cook gently for a further 15 minutes. Serve hot.

SERVES 4

COSTOLETTE ALLA VALDOSTANA
Veal Cutlets Valle d'Aosta Style

Metric/Imperial	American
4 veal cutlets	4 veal cutlets
4 slices fontina cheese★	4 slices fontina cheese★
salt and freshly ground black pepper	salt and freshly ground black pepper
plain flour for coating	all-purpose flour for coating
1–2 eggs, beaten	1–2 eggs, beaten
100 g/4 oz dried breadcrumbs	1 cup dried bread crumbs
75 g/3 oz butter	⅓ cup butter

Cut the cutlets horizontally through the centre towards the bone. Place a slice of cheese inside each 'pocket' and press well to flatten slightly. Sprinkle with salt and pepper on both sides, then coat with flour. Dip the cutlets in the beaten egg, then coat with breadcrumbs.

Melt the butter in a large frying pan (skillet), add the cutlets and fry gently for about 8 minutes on each side until the cutlets are golden and tender. Serve immediately.

SERVES 4

ABOVE: **Costolette alla valdostana; Vitello all'uccelletto; Subrics**

CIMA ALLA GENOVESE
Cold Stuffed Breast of Veal

Metric/Imperial	American
175 g/6 oz calf's sweetbreads, soaked in cold water for 15 minutes	6 oz veal sweetbreads, soaked in cold water for 15 minutes
350 g/12 oz pork loin, finely chopped	1½ cups finely chopped pork loin
100 g/4 oz streaky bacon, finely chopped	½ cup finely chopped fatty bacon
100 g/4 oz fresh breadcrumbs, soaked in milk and squeezed dry	2 cups fresh bread crumbs, soaked in milk and squeezed dry
225 g/8 oz cooked peas	2 cups cooked peas
50 g/2 oz Parmesan cheese★, grated	½ cup grated Parmesan cheese★
50 g/2 oz pistachio nuts, blanched	½ cup pistachio nuts, blanched
2 teaspoons chopped marjoram	2 teaspoons chopped marjoram
pinch of grated nutmeg	pinch of grated nutmeg
salt and freshly ground black pepper	salt and freshly ground black pepper
1 egg, beaten	1 egg, beaten
1.25 kg/2½ lb slice breast of veal	2½ lb slice breast of veal
3 hard-boiled eggs, sliced	3 hard-cooked eggs, sliced
1 onion, peeled and chopped	1 onion, peeled and chopped
1 carrot, peeled and chopped	1 carrot, peeled and chopped
½ bay leaf	½ bay leaf
few black peppercorns	few black peppercorns

Drain the sweetbreads and rinse thoroughly under cold running water. Parcook them in boiling salted water for 5 minutes, then skin and dice.

Put the sweetbreads in a bowl with the pork, bacon, breadcrumbs, peas, Parmesan, pistachio nuts, marjoram, nutmeg and salt and pepper to taste. Stir well to mix, then add enough beaten egg to bind the mixture.

Spread a quarter of the stuffing mixture over the meat, then arrange egg slices on top. Continue these layers until all the stuffing and eggs are used, finishing with a layer of stuffing. Roll the meat around the stuffing and tie securely with string.

Place the meat in a flameproof casserole and sprinkle with salt and pepper. Add cold salted water to cover the meat, then add the onion, carrot, bay leaf and peppercorns. Bring to the boil, lower the heat, cover and simmer for 1½ to 2 hours until the meat is tender.

Drain the meat and place in a dish into which it just fits. Cover with a plate, place a weight on top and leave to cool. Slice neatly before serving.

SERVES 6

VITELLO ALL'UCCELLETTO
Sautéed Veal in White Wine

Metric/Imperial	American
25 g/1 oz butter	2 tablespoons butter
2 tablespoons olive oil	2 tablespoons olive oil
2 bay leaves	2 bay leaves
575 g/1¼ lb veal escalope, cut into strips	1¼ lb veal scallopini, cut into strips
7 tablespoons dry white wine	7 tablespoons dry white wine
salt and freshly ground black pepper	salt and freshly ground black pepper

Melt the butter and oil in a flameproof casserole, add the bay leaves and fry gently for a few minutes. Increase the heat, add the meat and fry quickly until browned on all sides. Add the wine and salt and pepper to taste and boil until reduced. Remove the bay leaves and serve immediately.

SERVES 4

RIGHT: **Ossibuchi alla milanese served with Risotto alla milanese; Costolette alla milanese**

RUSTIN NEGAÀ
Veal Cutlets with Sage and Rosemary

Metric/Imperial	American
4 large veal cutlets	4 large veal cutlets
plain flour for coating	all-purpose flour for coating
50 g/2 oz butter	¼ cup butter
75 g/3 oz streaky bacon, diced	⅓ cup diced fatty bacon
salt and freshly ground black pepper	salt and freshly ground black pepper
4 sage leaves, chopped	4 sage leaves, chopped
1 teaspoon chopped rosemary	1 teaspoon chopped rosemary
300 ml/½ pint dry white wine	1¼ cups dry white wine
200 ml/⅓ pint beef stock	1 cup beef stock

Coat the veal with flour. Melt the butter in a frying pan (skillet). Add the bacon and fry gently for 5 minutes. Add the cutlets, sprinkle with salt and pepper and brown on both sides.

Add the sage, rosemary and wine and simmer until the wine has evaporated. Gradually stir in the stock, lower the heat and simmer for 30 minutes.

Transfer the cutlets to a warmed serving dish; keep hot. Boil the cooking juices until reduced and thickened, then pour over the meat. Serve hot with Risotto alla milanese (see page 88) or mashed potatoes.
SERVES 4

ARROSTO DI VITELLO AL LATTE
Veal Cooked in Milk

Metric/Imperial	American
750 g/1¾ lb boned and rolled loin of veal	1¾ lb boned and rolled veal loin
75 g/3 oz lean bacon, cut into strips	⅓ cup lean bacon strips
salt and freshly ground black pepper	salt and freshly ground black pepper
plain flour for coating	all-purpose flour for coating
75 g/3 oz butter	⅓ cup butter
1 litre/1¾ pints milk (approximately)	4¼ cups milk (approximately)

Make deep incisions over the surface of the meat and insert the strips of bacon. Sprinkle with salt and pepper to taste, then coat lightly with flour.

Melt the butter in a flameproof casserole, add the meat and fry, turning over moderate heat to brown on all sides. Bring the milk to the boil and pour over the meat. Lower the heat and simmer, uncovered, for 1½ hours or until the meat is tender, basting with the milk from time to time.

Lift out the meat, slice and arrange on a serving platter. Beat the milk remaining in the pan over low heat for a few minutes until creamy. Pour over the meat and serve immediately.
SERVES 4

OSSIBUCHI ALLA MILANESE
Braised Shin of Veal

Ossibuchi are veal slices, about 5 cm/2 inches thick, cut across the top of the leg. Each piece consists of a piece of bone with marrow in the centre, surrounded by meat. You may need to order ossibuchi in advance from your butcher.

Metric/Imperial	American
4 ossibuchi	4 ossibuchi
plain flour for coating	all-purpose flour for coating
65 g/2½ oz butter	5 tablespoons butter
½ onion, peeled and chopped	½ onion, peeled and chopped
120 ml/4 fl oz dry white wine	1 cup dry white wine
350 g/12 oz tomatoes, peeled and diced	¾ lb tomatoes, peeled and diced
7 tablespoons stock	7 tablespoons stock
salt and freshly ground black pepper	salt and freshly ground black pepper
1 garlic clove, peeled and chopped	1 garlic clove, peeled and chopped
1 small bunch parsley, chopped	1 small bunch parsley, chopped
finely grated rind of ½ lemon	finely grated rind of ½ lemon

Coat the veal lightly with flour. Melt the butter in a flameproof casserole, add the onion and fry gently for 5 minutes. Remove and set aside. Add the veal and fry quickly to brown on both sides. Replace the onion.

Add the wine, tomatoes, stock and seasoning to taste. Cover and simmer for 1¼ hours, basting occasionally.

Mix together the garlic, parsley and lemon rind and sprinkle over the meat. Cook for a further 10 minutes. Serve hot with Risotto alla milanese (see page 88).
SERVES 4

COSTOLETTE ALLA MILANESE
Milanese Veal Escalopes

Metric/Imperial	American
4 veal escalopes, each weighing 100 g/4 oz	4 veal scallopini, each weighing ¼ lb
1–2 eggs, beaten	1–2 eggs, beaten
dried breadcrumbs for coating	dried bread crumbs for coating
75 g/3 oz butter	⅓ cup butter
salt and freshly ground black pepper	salt and freshly ground black pepper
TO GARNISH:	TO GARNISH:
lemon twists	lemon twists
parsley sprigs	parsley sprigs

Beat the veal lightly with a mallet to flatten. Dip into the beaten egg and coat with breadcrumbs.

Melt the butter in a large frying pan (skillet), and fry the veal for 2 to 3 minutes on each side until tender and golden brown. Transfer to a warmed serving dish and sprinkle with salt and pepper to taste. Garnish with lemon and parsley and serve immediately.
SERVES 4

Ossibucchi alla milanese is one of the great classic Italian dishes. Strictly speaking, it should be made with the marrow bones of tender young veal – the marrow is 'dug' out of the centre of each bone with a special marrow spoon by the diner. It is considered to be a great delicacy by the Milanese who created this dish. The traditional garnish of garlic, parsley and grated lemon rind is known as *gremolata* in Milan, and no dish of *ossibucchi* is complete without it, nor its saffron-coloured rice accompaniment, *Risotto alla milanese*.

COTOLETTE ALLA BOLOGNESE

Veal Escalopes with Ham, Cheese and Tomatoes

Metric/Imperial	American
4 tablespoons olive oil	¼ cup olive oil
½ onion, peeled and chopped	½ onion, peeled and chopped
225 g/8 oz tomatoes, skinned and mashed	1 cup skinned and mashed tomatoes
salt and freshly ground black pepper	salt and freshly ground black pepper
4 veal escalopes, each weighing 100 g/4 oz	4 veal scallopini, each weighing ¼ lb
plain flour for coating	all-purpose flour for coating
2 eggs, beaten	2 eggs, beaten
dried breadcrumbs for coating	dried bread crumbs for coating
75 g/3 oz butter	⅓ cup butter
4 slices prosciutto★ or cooked ham	4 slices proscuitto★ or cooked ham
4 slices gruyère cheese	4 slices gruyère cheese

Heat the oil in a heavy pan, add the onion and fry gently for 5 minutes. Add the tomatoes and salt and pepper to taste, then cook gently for 20 minutes, stirring occasionally.

Meanwhile, beat the veal slices slightly, then coat lightly with flour. Dip into the beaten egg, then coat with breadcrumbs.

Melt two thirds of the butter in a large frying pan (skillet), add the veal and brown quickly on both sides. Transfer to a buttered ovenproof dish. Cover each piece of veal with a slice of ham and a slice of cheese. Sprinkle with a little salt and pepper.

Bake in a preheated moderately hot oven (190°C/375°F/Gas Mark 5) for 5 to 10 minutes or until the cheese has melted. Place the veal on a warmed serving platter, pour over the sauce and serve immediately.

SERVES 4

ARROSTO DI VITELLO RIPIENO

Veal Roll with Spinach

Metric/Imperial	American
2 eggs	2 eggs
75 g/3 oz Parmesan cheese★, grated	¾ cup grated Parmesan cheese★
salt and freshly ground black pepper	salt and freshly ground black pepper
100 g/4 oz butter	½ cup butter
450 g/1 lb cooked spinach, well drained and chopped	2 cups chopped cooked spinach, well drained
100 g/4 oz bacon rashers, derinded	6 bacon slices, derinded
750 g/1¾ lb slice leg of veal	1¾ lb slice leg of veal
3 tablespoons olive oil	3 tablespoons olive oil
120 ml/4 fl oz beef stock	½ cup beef stock
parsley sprigs to garnish	parsley sprigs to garnish

Put the eggs in a bowl with a third of the Parmesan and a pinch each of salt and pepper. Beat well to mix. Melt 1 tablespoon of the butter in a frying pan (skillet), add the egg mixture and fry on both sides to make an omelet. Remove from the pan and set aside.

Melt 1½ tablespoons butter in a heavy pan, add the remaining Parmesan and the spinach and cook, stirring, for a few minutes. Add salt and pepper to taste, remove from the heat and leave to cool.

Spread the bacon over the veal, cover with the omelet, then top with the spinach. Roll the veal around the stuffing, then sew or tie securely with thread or string.

Heat the oil and the remaining butter in a flame-proof casserole, add the veal roll and fry, turning until browned on all sides. Sprinkle with salt and pepper to taste and add the stock. Cover and simmer for 1½ hours or until the meat is tender, basting occasionally with the pan juices.

Remove the thread or string, then cut the veal into fairly thick slices. Serve hot, garnished with parsley.

SERVES 4

ABOVE: **Cotolette alla bolognese; Arrosto di vitello ripieno; Saltimbocca alla romana**

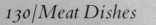

OSSIBUCHI ALLA REGGIANA

Roman Shin of Veal Casserole

Metric/Imperial	American
50 g/2 oz butter	1/4 cup butter
1 small onion, peeled and finely chopped	1 small onion, peeled and finely chopped
1 garlic clove, peeled and crushed	1 garlic clove, peeled and crushed
4 ossibuchi (see page 128)	4 ossibuchi (see page 128)
pinch of ground mixed spice	pinch each of ground allspice and cinnamon
salt and freshly ground black pepper	salt and freshly ground black pepper
7 tablespoons dry Marsala wine	7 tablespoons dry Marsala wine
450 g/1 lb tomatoes, skinned and mashed	2 cups skinned and mashed tomatoes
Risotto alla parmigiana (see page 91), to serve	Risotto alla parmigiana (see page 91), to serve

Melt the butter in a flameproof casserole, add the onion and garlic and fry gently for 5 minutes. Add the veal, spice(s) and salt and pepper to taste and fry until the veal is browned on all sides.

Add the Marsala and simmer until evaporated. Add the tomatoes and enough hot water to cover the veal. Cover and simmer for $1\frac{1}{2}$ hours until the veal is tender. Serve hot with the risotto.

SERVES 4

SALTIMBOCCA ALLA ROMANA

Veal and Ham Slices in Wine

Metric/Imperial	American
8 slices raw ham or bacon	8 slices raw ham or bacon
8 veal escalopes, each weighing 75 g/3 oz	8 veal scallopini, each weighing 3 oz
8–12 sage leaves	8–12 sage leaves
50 g/2 oz butter	1/4 cup butter
7 tablespoons dry white wine	7 tablespoons dry white wine
salt and freshly ground black pepper	salt and freshly ground black pepper
sage leaves to garnish	sage leaves to garnish

Place a slice of ham on each slice of veal, then top with the sage leaves. Secure with cocktail sticks (toothpicks).

Melt the butter in a large frying pan (skillet), add the veal and fry until browned on both sides. Add the wine and salt and pepper to taste. Simmer for about 6 to 8 minutes until the meat is tender.

Transfer the saltimbocca to a warmed serving platter, removing the cocktail sticks (toothpicks). Add 1 tablespoon water to the pan and simmer, stirring, for 1 minute, then pour the pan juices over the saltimbocca. Garnish with sage and serve immediately.

SERVES 4

Meat Dishes/131

ABOVE: **Agnello al forno;**
Involtini al sugo
RIGHT: **Agnello imbottito**

ABRUZZI & MOLISE

INVOLTINI AL SUGO
Stuffed Veal Rolls in Tomato Sauce

Metric/Imperial

4 tablespoons olive oil
225 g/8 oz mushrooms,
    chopped
1 garlic clove, peeled and
    crushed
1 tablespoon chopped
    parsley
4–6 tablespoons beef stock
salt and freshly ground
    black pepper
225 g/8 oz cooked pork,
    minced
75 g/3 oz Parmesan
    cheese★, grated
1 egg, beaten
1 piece canned red pimento,
    chopped
8 veal escalopes, each
    weighing 50 g/2 oz
350 g/12 oz tomatoes,
    skinned and mashed

American

$\frac{1}{4}$ cup olive oil
2$\frac{1}{2}$ cups chopped mushrooms
1 garlic clove, peeled and
    crushed
1 tablespoon chopped
    parsley
4–6 tablespoons beef stock
salt and freshly ground
    black pepper
1 cup ground cooked pork
$\frac{3}{4}$ cup grated Parmesan
    cheese★
1 egg, beaten
1 piece canned red pimiento,
    chopped
8 veal scallopini, each
    weighing 2 oz
1$\frac{1}{2}$ cups skinned and mashed
    tomatoes

Heat half the oil in a flameproof casserole, add the mushrooms, garlic and parsley and cook gently for 15 minutes, adding a little of the stock to moisten if necessary. Add salt and pepper to taste, then transfer to a bowl. Add the pork, Parmesan, egg, pimento and a pinch of salt; stir well to mix.

Beat the veal with a mallet to flatten, then sprinkle lightly with salt and pepper and spread with the stuffing. Roll the veal around the stuffing and tie securely with string.

Heat the remaining oil in the casserole, add the veal rolls and fry over moderate heat for 5 minutes until browned on all sides. Add the tomatoes with salt and pepper to taste, then cover and cook gently for about 45 minutes until the meat is tender. Turn the meat during cooking and add a few tablespoons of stock to moisten if necessary.

Remove the meat from the casserole and untie the string. Arrange in a warmed serving dish and pour over the cooking juices. Serve immediately.
SERVES 4

ABBACCHIO ALLA ROMANA

Leg of Lamb Roman Style

Metric/Imperial	American
7 tablespoons olive oil	7 tablespoons olive oil
2 garlic cloves, peeled	2 garlic cloves, peeled
1 kg/2 lb leg of lamb	2 lb leg of lamb
salt and freshly ground black pepper	salt and freshly ground black pepper
1 rosemary sprig, chopped	1 rosemary sprig, chopped
2 canned anchovies, soaked in milk and drained	2 canned anchovies, soaked in milk and drained
3–4 tablespoons wine vinegar	3–4 tablespoons wine vinegar

Heat half the oil in a flameproof casserole, add 1 garlic clove and fry until browned. Remove the garlic, then add the meat to the casserole. Fry the meat over moderate heat, turning until browned on all sides. Sprinkle with salt and pepper to taste. Cover and cook in a preheated moderately hot oven (190°C/375°F/Gas Mark 5) for 1½ hours or until tender, basting and turning frequently.

Pound the rosemary, remaining garlic and the anchovies together using a mortar and pestle, then stir in the remaining oil and the vinegar. Transfer the meat to a warmed serving dish. Add the rosemary mixture to the casserole and simmer until reduced. Pour the juices over the meat and serve immediately.

SERVES 4

AGNELLO IMBOTTITO

Stuffed Breast of Lamb

Metric/Imperial	American
100 g/4 oz salami★, diced	½ cup diced salami★
100 g/4 oz provolone cheese★, diced	1 cup diced provolone cheese★
25 g/1 oz Parmesan cheese★, grated	¼ cup grated Parmesan cheese★
25 g/1 oz fresh breadcrumbs	½ cup fresh bread crumbs
25 g/1 oz parsley, chopped	¾ cup chopped parsley
salt and freshly ground black pepper	salt and freshly ground black pepper
1–2 eggs, beaten	1–2 eggs, beaten
1 kg/2 lb piece boned breast or shoulder of lamb	2 lb piece boned breast or shoulder of lamb
3–4 tablespoons olive oil	3–4 tablespoons olive oil
1 onion, peeled and chopped	1 onion, peeled and chopped
1 carrot, peeled and chopped	1 carrot, peeled and chopped
1 celery stick, chopped	1 celery stalk, chopped
1 garlic clove, peeled and crushed	1 garlic clove, peeled and crushed
150 ml/¼ pint dry white wine	⅔ cup dry white wine

Put the salami in a bowl with the cheeses, breadcrumbs, parsley and salt and pepper to taste. Stir well and mix in enough beaten egg to bind the stuffing. Leave to stand for 20 minutes.

Spread the mixture over the lamb and roll the meat around the stuffing. Tie securely with string. Heat the oil in a flameproof casserole, add the onion, carrot, celery and garlic, then place the meat on top. Sprinkle with salt and pepper to taste, then fry over moderate heat, turning the meat until it is browned on all sides.

Add the wine and 2 tablespoons water, then cover and cook gently for 1½ hours until the meat is tender, adding a little more water to moisten as necessary.

Remove the meat from the casserole, untie and cut into neat slices. Arrange the slices on a warmed serving platter. Strain the cooking juices and pour over the meat. Serve immediately.

SERVES 4

AGNELLO AL FORNO

Roast Lamb

Metric/Imperial	American
1 kg/2 lb leg of lamb	2 lb leg of lamb
100 g/4 oz lean bacon, chopped	½ cup chopped lean bacon
3 garlic cloves, peeled and slivered	3 garlic cloves, peeled and slivered
2 rosemary sprigs	2 rosemary sprigs
4 tablespoons olive oil	4 tablespoons olive oil
salt and freshly ground black pepper	salt and freshly ground black pepper

Make deep incisions in the meat and insert the bacon, garlic and rosemary leaves. Use half of the oil to grease a roasting pan and put the lamb into the pan.

Sprinkle with salt and pepper and the remaining oil. Roast in a preheated moderately hot oven (190°C/375°F/Gas Mark 5) for 1½ hours or until the meat is tender, basting occasionally. Transfer to a warmed serving dish and serve immediately.

SERVES 4

Agnello is the Italian word for lamb; *abbacchio* is a very special kind of lamb which is most often found in the region of Lazio. It is highly prized by the Romans, especially around Eastertime when whole baby lambs can be seen roasting on spits in the open air. *Abbacchio* is an unweaned lamb that has never eaten grass (like *vitello da latte*); it is therefore very tender with a sweet flavour. The Romans like to enhance this natural flavour by cooking it with fresh rosemary.

AGNELLO CASCE E OVA

Lamb in Egg and Cheese Sauce

Metric/Imperial	American
5 tablespoons olive oil	5 tablespoons olive oil
1 kg/2 lb boned leg or shoulder of lamb, cut into cubes	2 lb boned leg or shoulder of lamb, cut into cubes
1 rosemary sprig, chopped	1 rosemary sprig, chopped
2 garlic cloves, peeled and sliced	2 garlic cloves, peeled and sliced
1 piece of canned pimento, chopped	1 piece of canned pimiento, chopped
300 ml/½ pint chicken stock	1¼ cups chicken stock
salt and freshly ground black pepper	salt and freshly ground black pepper
3 eggs, beaten	3 eggs, beaten
50 g/2 oz pecorino cheese★, grated	½ cup grated pecorino cheese★
50 g/2 oz Parmesan cheese,★ grated	½ cup grated Parmesan cheese★

Heat the oil in a flameproof casserole, then add the meat, rosemary, garlic and pimento. Fry over moderate heat, turning the meat until evenly browned. Add the stock and salt and pepper to taste.

Cover and cook in a preheated moderate oven (180°C/350°F/Gas Mark 4) for 1 hour or until the meat is tender, stirring occasionally.

Mix the eggs with the cheeses and pour over the meat. Stir well, then cook on top of the stove, over low heat, stirring constantly, until the sauce has thickened; do not boil. Serve immediately.

SERVES 4 TO 6

ABBACCHIO BRODETTATO

Lamb in Egg and Lemon Sauce

Metric/Imperial	American
50 g/2 oz lard	¼ cup lard
½ onion, peeled and finely chopped	½ onion, peeled and finely chopped
50 g/2 oz raw ham or bacon, finely chopped	¼ cup finely chopped raw ham or bacon
1 kg/2 lb boned shoulder of lamb, cut into cubes	2 lb boned shoulder of lamb, cut into cubes
pinch of grated nutmeg	pinch of grated nutmeg
salt and freshly ground black pepper	salt and freshly ground black pepper
4 tablespoons dry white wine	¼ cup dry white wine
450 ml/¾ pint chicken stock	2 cups chicken stock
2 egg yolks	2 egg yolks
juice of ½ lemon	juice of ½ lemon
25 g/1 oz Parmesan cheese★, grated	¼ cup grated Parmesan cheese★
1 garlic clove, peeled and crushed	1 garlic clove, peeled and crushed
1 tablespoon chopped parsley	1 tablespoon chopped parsley

Melt the lard in a flameproof casserole, add the onion and ham and fry gently for 5 minutes. Add the lamb, nutmeg and salt and pepper to taste. Fry over moderate heat, turning the meat until it is browned on all sides. Add the wine and simmer until almost completely evaporated. Stir in the stock, cover and simmer for 1 hour or until the meat is tender.

Put the egg yolks in a bowl with the lemon juice and Parmesan cheese. Beat well to mix, then stir in a little of the hot cooking liquid. Add the garlic and parsley to the casserole, then gradually stir in the egg yolk mixture. Cook very gently, stirring constantly, until the sauce thickens; do not allow to boil or the sauce will curdle. Serve immediately.

SERVES 4 TO 6

ABOVE: Abbacchio brodettato; Agnello coi funghi; Cutturiddi

Sheep-rearing is as important to the peasant farmers of Abruzzi & Molise today as it was hundreds of years ago, and old-fashioned methods of farming still survive. Shepherds can be seen tending small flocks of sheep on the beautiful herb-ridden pastures; it is a region which has remained relatively untouched by modern technology.

AGNELLO COI FUNGHI

Lamb and Mushrooms Casseroled in Wine

Metric/Imperial	American
3 tablespoons olive oil	3 tablespoons olive oil
1 kg/2 lb boned shoulder or leg of lamb, cut into serving pieces	2 lb boned shoulder or leg of lamb, cut into serving pieces
450 g/1 lb mushrooms	1 lb mushrooms
4 fl oz/120 ml dry white wine	1 cup dry white wine
salt and freshly ground black pepper	salt and freshly ground black pepper
chopped parsley to garnish	chopped parsley to garnish

Heat the oil in a flameproof casserole, add the meat and fry over moderate heat until browned on all sides. Add the mushrooms, wine and enough water to just cover the meat. Season with salt and pepper to taste.

Cover and cook in a preheated moderately hot oven (190°C/375°F/Gas Mark 5) for 1 hour or until the meat is tender, stirring occasionally. Serve hot, garnished with parsley.

SERVES 4

CUTTURIDDI

Lamb with Celery and Onions

Metric/Imperial	American
3 tablespoons olive oil	3 tablespoons olive oil
2 celery sticks, chopped	2 celery stalks, chopped
350 g/12 oz pickling onions, peeled	¾ lb baby onions, peeled
1 kg/2 lb boned leg or shoulder of lamb, cut into serving pieces	2 lb boned leg or shoulder of lamb, cut into serving pieces
2–3 rosemary sprigs, cut into pieces	2–3 rosemary sprigs, cut into pieces
2 bay leaves	2 bay leaves
salt and freshly ground black pepper	salt and freshly ground black pepper
450 ml/¾ pint chicken stock	2 cups chicken stock

Heat the oil in a flameproof casserole, add the celery and onions and fry gently for 5 minutes. Add the meat, half the rosemary, the bay leaves and salt and pepper to taste. Fry over moderate heat until the meat is browned on all sides. Stir in the stock and enough water to just cover the meat. Cover and simmer for 1 hour or until the meat is tender. Discard the herbs.

Serve hot, garnished with the remaining rosemary.

SERVES 4

AGNELLO ALLA LUCANA

Leg of Lamb with Tomatoes

Metric/Imperial	American
50 g/2 oz lard	¼ cup lard
1 kg/2 lb boned leg of lamb, cut into serving pieces	2 lb boned leg of lamb, cut into serving pieces
pinch of dried marjoram	pinch of dried marjoram
400 g/14 oz potatoes, peeled and diced	14 oz potatoes, peeled and diced
225 g/8 oz pickling onions, peeled	½ lb baby onions, peeled
225 g/8 oz tomatoes, skinned and chopped	1 cup skinned and chopped tomatoes
50 g/2 oz pecorino cheese★, grated	½ cup grated pecorino cheese★
750 ml/1¼ pints chicken stock	3 cups chicken stock
salt and freshly ground black pepper	salt and freshly ground black pepper

Heat the lard in a flameproof casserole. Add the meat and fry, turning, until evenly browned. Add the remaining ingredients, with salt and pepper to taste. Cover and cook in a preheated moderately hot oven (190°C/375°F/Gas Mark 5) for 1 hour or until the meat is tender, stirring occasionally during cooking. Serve hot.

SERVES 4

AGNELLO COI FINOCCHIETTI

Lamb with Fennel and Tomatoes

Metric/Imperial	American
5 tablespoons olive oil	5 tablespoons olive oil
1kg/2 lb boned leg of lamb, cut into serving pieces	2 lb boned leg of lamb, cut into serving pieces
1 onion, peeled and chopped	1 onion, peeled and chopped
400 g/14 oz tomatoes, skinned and mashed	1¾ cups skinned and mashed tomatoes
salt and freshly ground black pepper	salt and freshly ground black pepper
675 g/1½ lb fennel, quartered	1½ lb fennel, quartered

Heat the oil in a flameproof casserole, add the meat and fry over moderate heat until lightly browned on all sides. Stir in the onion and fry for a further 5 minutes, then add the tomatoes and salt and pepper to taste. Lower the heat, cover and simmer for 40 minutes, adding a little water if the casserole becomes too dry during cooking.

Cook the fennel in boiling salted water for 20 minutes. Drain and reserve 200 ml/⅓ pint/1 cup of the cooking liquid.

Add the fennel and the reserved cooking liquid to the casserole and continue cooking for about 20 minutes until the meat is tender; the casserole should be fairly dry. Serve hot.

SERVES 4

Spit-roasting whole baby lambs over charcoal is a fairly common cooking method throughout central and southern Italy. The Sardinians have a most unusual way of cooking lambs.

The whole ungutted animal is placed in a leaf-lined hole in the ground, which is packed with glowing embers. It is covered with soil, a fire is lit on top and the meat cooks slowly for several hours. The idea was developed long ago by sheep thieves as a means of cooking lambs without being seen. These days this method is reserved for feast days.

ABOVE: **Agnello coi finocchietti; Impanadas; Agnello alla lucana**

AGNELLO AL VERDETTO

Lamb Casserole with Peas

Metric/Imperial	American
4 tablespoons olive oil	$\frac{1}{4}$ cup olive oil
1 onion, peeled and sliced	1 onion, peeled and sliced
1 kg/2 lb boned shoulder of lamb, cut into serving pieces	2 lb boned shoulder of lamb, cut into serving pieces
200 ml/8 fl oz dry white wine	1 cup dry white wine
salt and freshly ground black pepper	salt and freshly ground black pepper
300 g/11 oz fresh or frozen peas	2$\frac{3}{4}$ cups fresh or frozen peas
3 eggs, beaten	3 eggs, beaten
50 g/2 oz pecorino cheese★, grated	$\frac{1}{2}$ cup grated pecorino cheese★
50 g/2 oz Parmesan cheese★, grated	$\frac{1}{2}$ cup grated Parmesan cheese★
1 tablespoon chopped parsley	1 tablespoon chopped parsley

Heat the oil in a flameproof casserole, add the onion and fry gently for 5 minutes. Add the meat and fry until browned on all sides, then add the wine, an equal quantity of water and salt and pepper to taste.

Cover and cook in a preheated moderate oven (180°C/350°F/Gas Mark 4) for 1 hour. Add the peas and continue cooking for a further 30 minutes or until the meat is tender.

Mix the eggs with the cheeses and parsley. Pour this mixture over the lamb and cook for 5 minutes over a low heat on top of the stove, without stirring. Serve immediately.

SERVES 4

IMPANADAS

Meat Pasties

Metric/Imperial	American
7 tablespoons olive oil	7 tablespoons olive oil
1 garlic clove, peeled and chopped	1 garlic clove, peeled and chopped
675 g/1$\frac{1}{2}$ lb minced lamb or pork	3 cups ground lamb or pork
2 tomatoes, skinned and chopped	2 tomatoes, skinned and chopped
1 tablespoon chopped parsley	1 tablespoon chopped parsley
pinch of saffron powder	pinch of saffron powder
salt and freshly ground black pepper	salt and freshly ground black pepper
275 g/10 oz wholewheat flour	2$\frac{1}{2}$ cups wholewheat flour
6 tablespoons water (approximately)	6 tablespoons water (approximately)

Heat 2 tablespoons of the oil in a heavy pan, add the garlic and fry gently until browned. Add the meat and tomatoes and cook, stirring, over low heat for 15 minutes.

Transfer the mixture to a bowl, then add the parsley, saffron and salt and pepper to taste. Mix well, then set aside to cool.

Mix the flour with the remaining oil and a pinch of salt then mix in enough water to form a smooth dough. Knead well, then roll out to a thin sheet. Cut the dough into 8 circles, making 4 of them 2.5 cm/1 inch larger than the other four.

Place the 4 larger circles on a greased baking tray (cookie sheet). Divide the meat mixture between them, then brush the edges of the dough with a little water. Cover with the smaller circles of dough, press the edges together firmly to seal, then flute.

Bake in a preheated moderate oven (180°C/350°F/Gas Mark 4) for 30 minutes until well risen and golden brown. Serve hot or cold.

SERVES 4

ARROSTO DI MAIALE AL LATTE

Pork Cooked in Milk

Metric/Imperial	American
1 kg/2 lb leg of pork	2 lb leg of pork
450 ml/¾ pint dry white wine	2 cups dry white wine
1 garlic clove, peeled and sliced	1 garlic clove, peeled and sliced
plain flour for coating	all-purpose flour for coating
50 g/2 oz butter	¼ cup butter
1 rosemary sprig, chopped	1 rosemary sprig, chopped
750 ml/1¼ pints milk	3 cups milk
salt and freshly ground black pepper	salt and freshly ground black pepper

Put the meat in a dish. Add the wine and garlic, then leave to marinate in the refrigerator for 2 days.

Drain the meat, dry thoroughly, then sprinkle lightly with flour. Melt the butter in a flameproof casserole, add the meat and rosemary and fry over moderate heat until browned on all sides. Add the milk and salt and pepper to taste, lower the heat, cover and simmer for 2 hours or until the meat is tender.

Transfer the meat to a warmed serving platter; keep hot. Boil the cooking liquor until reduced to a creamy consistency. Slice the meat and serve hot, with the sauce.

SERVES 4

POLENTA CON OSELETI SCAMPAI

Meat Kebabs with Polenta

Metric/Imperial	American
1.5 litres/2½ pints water	6¼ cups water
salt	salt
400 g/14 oz maize flour	3½ cups maize flour
225 g/8 oz lean veal, cut into 2 cm/¾ inch cubes	½ lb lean veal, cut into ¾ inch cubes
225 g/8 oz lean pork, cut into 2 cm/¾ inch cubes	½ lb lean pork, cut into ¾ inch cubes
100 g/4 oz calf's liver, cut into 2 cm/¾ inch cubes	¼ lb veal liver, cut into ¾ inch cubes
100 g/4 oz pig's liver, cut into 2 cm/¾ inch cubes	¼ lb pork liver, cut into ¾ inch cubes
100 g/4 oz streaky bacon or belly pork, cut into 2 cm/¾ inch cubes	¼ lb fatty bacon or pork belly, cut into ¾ inch cubes
12–16 sage leaves	12–16 sage leaves
4 tablespoons olive oil	¼ cup olive oil
freshly ground black pepper	freshly ground black pepper
7 tablespoons dry white wine	7 tablespoons dry white wine
3–4 tablespoons beef stock	3–4 tablespoons beef stock

Bring a large pan of salted water to the boil. Stir in the maize flour and cook, stirring frequently over low heat for about 40 minutes, until the polenta is smooth and thickened.

Meanwhile thread the meat onto skewers, alternating the different kinds and interspersing them with sage leaves. Place the skewers in a single layer in the grill (broiler) pan. Sprinkle with the oil and salt and pepper to taste.

Grill (broil) the meat under a preheated hot grill (broiler) for about 20 minutes, turning the skewers over from time to time.

Transfer the kebab skewers to a deep roasting tin (pan) into which they fit snugly. Add the wine and stock and roast in a preheated hot oven (220°C/425°F/Gas Mark 7) for 20 minutes.

Spread the polenta in a warmed serving dish, then top with the skewers of meat. Sprinkle with the meat juices and serve immediately.

SERVES 4

BELOW: **Polenta con oseleti scampai; Braciole di maiale alla romagnola**

BRACIOLE DI MAIALE ALLA ROMAGNOLA

Pork Chops with Sage and Rosemary

Metric/Imperial	American
4 pork chops, trimmed	4 pork chops, trimmed
salt and freshly ground black pepper	salt and freshly ground black pepper
1 garlic clove, peeled and chopped	1 garlic clove, peeled and chopped
1 rosemary sprig, chopped	1 rosemary sprig, chopped
few sage leaves, chopped	few sage leaves, chopped
7 tablespoons dry white wine	7 tablespoons dry white wine

Sprinkle the chops with salt and pepper and place in an oiled baking tin (pan). Sprinkle with the garlic, rosemary and sage, then add the wine and enough water to just cover the chops.

Bake in a preheated moderately hot oven (200°C/400°F/Gas Mark 6) for about 30 minutes until tender. Transfer the chops to a warmed serving dish, pour over the cooking juices and serve immediately.
SERVES 4

BRACIOLE DI MAIALE UBRIACHE

Pork Chops with Fennel Seeds

Metric/Imperial	American
4 pork chops, trimmed	4 pork chops, trimmed
salt and freshly ground black pepper	salt and freshly ground black pepper
2 tablespoons olive oil	2 tablespoons olive oil
1 garlic clove, peeled and chopped	1 garlic clove, peeled and chopped
1 tablespoon chopped parsley	1 tablespoon chopped parsley
pinch of fennel seeds	pinch of fennel seeds
7 tablespoons dry red wine	7 tablespoons dry red wine

Sprinkle the chops with salt and pepper. Heat the oil in a flameproof casserole, add the chops, garlic, parsley and fennel seeds and fry over brisk heat until the chops are browned on both sides. Pour in the wine. Lower the heat, cover and cook gently for about 30 minutes or until the meat is tender and the wine is reduced completely. Serve immediately.
SERVES 4

ARISTA DI MAIALE ALLA FIORENTINA

Loin of Pork with Rosemary

Metric/Imperial	American
1.5 kg/3 lb boned and rolled pork loin	3 lb boneless pork top loin roast
1 garlic clove, peeled and finely chopped	1 garlic clove, peeled and finely chopped
1 rosemary sprig, finely chopped	1 rosemary sprig, finely chopped
salt and freshly ground black pepper	salt and freshly ground black pepper
2 tablespoons dripping	2 tablespoons drippings

Make deep incisions in the meat with a sharp knife. Mix the garlic with the rosemary, adding salt and pepper to taste. Insert this mixture into the incisions in the meat.

Place the dripping(s) and meat in a baking tin (pan) and bake in a preheated moderately hot oven (200°C/400°F/Gas Mark 6) for 30 minutes. Lower the heat to moderate (180°C/350°F/Gas Mark 4) and cook for a further 1½ hours, turning the meat and basting with the cooking juices occasionally.

Serve the meat sliced, hot or cold, with the cooking juices poured over.
SERVES 6

SALSICCE CON BROCCOLETTI

Sausages with Broccoli

Metric/Imperial	American
25 g/1 oz dripping or lard	2 tablespoons drippings or lard
2 garlic cloves, peeled and chopped	2 garlic cloves, peeled and chopped
1 piece of canned pimento	1 piece of canned pimiento
450 g/1 lb salamelle★	1 lb salamelle★
salt and freshly ground black pepper	salt and freshly ground black pepper
675 g/1½ lb broccoli	1½ lb broccoli

Melt the dripping or lard in a flameproof casserole, add the garlic and fry gently until browned. Stir in the pimento, sausages and salt and pepper to taste. Cover the casserole and bake in a preheated moderately hot oven (190°C/375°F/Gas Mark 5) for about 45 minutes until the sausages are cooked.

Meanwhile, cook the broccoli in boiling salted water for 15 minutes until tender. Drain and place in a warmed serving dish. Add the sausages, toss well and serve immediately.
SERVES 4

MUSET E BROVADE

Pork Sausage with Turnips

Metric/Imperial	American
575 g/1¼ lb new turnips, peeled and sliced	1¼ lb new turnips, peeled and sliced
2 garlic cloves, peeled and thinly sliced	2 garlic cloves, peeled and thinly sliced
300 ml/½ pint beef stock	1¼ cups beef stock
salt and freshly ground black pepper	salt and freshly ground black pepper
350 g/12 oz cotechino★	¾ lb cotechino★
parsley sprigs to garnish	parsley sprigs to garnish

Put the turnips in a pan with the garlic and stock. Sprinkle with salt and pepper to taste, then cover and simmer very gently for 20 minutes or until tender.

Cook the sausage in boiling water for 1 hour. Drain, slice and arrange on a warmed serving plate with the turnips. Serve hot, garnished with parsley sprigs.
SERVES 4

SALSICCE IN UMIDO

Pork Sausages in Herb Sauce

Metric/Imperial	American
450 g/1 lb salamelle★	1 lb salamelle★
1 tablespoon olive oil	1 tablespoon olive oil
25 g/1 oz butter	2 tablespoons butter
2 tablespoons plain flour	2 tablespoons all-purpose flour
3–4 tablespoons dry white wine	3–4 tablespoons dry white wine
4 tablespoons vinegar	¼ cup vinegar
7 tablespoons beef stock	7 tablespoons beef stock
salt and freshly ground black pepper	salt and freshly ground black pepper
3–4 bay leaves	3–4 bay leaves
2 sage leaves	2 sage leaves

Parboil the sausages in boiling water for 10 minutes, leave to cool in the water, then drain. Leave to dry for 10 minutes, then cut into serving pieces.

Heat the oil and butter in a flameproof casserole, add the pieces of sausage and fry over moderate heat for 2 minutes. Stir in the flour, then add the wine, vinegar, stock and salt and pepper to taste.

Stir over moderate heat until the sauce thickens, then add the herbs and cook for a further 6 to 8 minutes, stirring frequently. Remove the herbs and serve hot, with polenta (see page 87).
SERVES 4

FRIZON ALLA MODENESE

Sausage Casserole

Metric/Imperial	American
3 tablespoons olive oil	3 tablespoons olive oil
450 g/1 lb onions, peeled and sliced	1 lb onions, peeled and sliced
2 green peppers, cored, seeded and sliced	2 green peppers, cored, seeded and sliced
225 g/8 oz tomatoes, skinned and mashed	1 cup skinned and mashed tomatoes
450 g/1 lb salamelle★	1 lb salamelle★
salt and freshly ground black pepper	salt and freshly ground black pepper
chopped parsley to garnish	chopped parsley to garnish

Heat the oil in a flameproof casserole, add all the ingredients and stir well. Cover and cook gently, stirring frequently, for 1 hour or until the sausages are tender. Serve hot, garnished with parsley.
SERVES 4

ABOVE: **Muset e brovade;
Frizon alla modenese;
Braciole di maiale in salsa**
LEFT: **Salsicce con
broccoletti**

BRACIOLE DI MAIALE IN SALSA

Pork Chops with Artichoke and Tomato Sauce

Metric/Imperial	American
5 tablespoons olive oil	5 tablespoons olive oil
175 g/6 oz tomatoes, skinned and chopped	¾ cup skinned and chopped tomatoes
4 pickled artichokes, sliced	4 pickled artichokes, sliced
4 pickled mushrooms, sliced	4 pickled mushrooms, sliced
6 basil leaves, chopped	6 basil leaves, chopped
salt and freshly ground black pepper	salt and freshly ground black pepper
4 pork chops, trimmed	4 pork chops, trimmed

Heat half the oil in pan and add the tomatoes, artichokes, mushrooms, basil and salt and pepper to taste. Fry, stirring, for a few minutes, then cover and cook gently for about 10 minutes.

Meanwhile, brush the chops with the remaining oil. Cook under a preheated hot grill (broiler) for 8 to 10 minutes on each side. Transfer to a warmed serving plate and pour over the sauce. Serve immediately.

SERVES 4

FAVATA

Bean and Sausage Stew

Metric/Imperial	American
300 g/11 oz dried cannellini or haricot beans	1½ cups dried cannellini or navy beans
350 g/12 oz belly pork, diced	1½ cups diced belly pork
350 g/12 oz salsiccia a metro★, diced	1½ cups diced salsiccia a metro★
100 g/4 oz bacon, diced	⅓ cup diced bacon
100 g/4 oz finocchiona★ (optional)	¼ lb finocchiona★ (optional)
1 whole canned pimento	1 whole canned pimiento
2 garlic cloves, peeled	2 garlic cloves, peeled
salt	salt
8 slices stale bread	8 slices stale bread

Soak the beans in lukewarm water overnight. Drain, then place in a flameproof casserole and cover with cold water. Bring to the boil, then lower the heat and cook gently for 40 minutes.

Add the remaining ingredients, except the bread. Cover and cook gently for 2 hours, stirring frequently.

Place 2 slices of bread in each individual soup bowl. Discard the garlic and pimento and spoon the stew over the bread. Serve immediately.

SERVES 4 TO 6

Pigs have been common livestock in Italy for centuries; Pope Clement VIII had to issue a special edict to liberate the city of Rome from their unsavoury presence at the turn of the sixteenth century. He authorized anyone coming across a pig in the streets of Rome to take it home and eat it immediately!

The regions of Umbria and Emilia-Romagna produce most of the pork in Italy, but large quantities of this are used to make sausages and salami-type products – the pigs are bred to an incredibly large size expressly for this purpose – and for bacon and hams. For this reason, the Italians tend to eat rather less fresh pork than they might, although pork chops cooked with herbs or in a sauce are popular.

FRITTO MISTO
Mixed Fried Meats and Vegetables

Metric/Imperial	American
600 ml/1 pint milk	2½ cups milk
finely grated rind of 1 lemon	finely grated rind of 1 lemon
75 g/3 oz sugar	⅓ cup sugar
few drops of vanilla essence	few drops of vanilla extract
100 g/4 oz semolina	⅔ cup semolina
8 macaroons	8 macaroons
4 eggs	4 eggs
salt and freshly ground black pepper	salt and freshly ground black pepper
100 g/4 oz calf's brains, cleaned and cut into serving pieces	¼ lb veal brains, cleaned and cut into serving pieces
100 g/4 oz calf's sweetbreads, cleaned and cut into serving pieces	¼ lb veal sweetbreads, cleaned and cut into serving pieces
100 g/4 oz pig's liver, sliced	¼ lb pork liver, sliced
4 small lamb cutlets, boned and well beaten	4 small lamb cutlets, boned and well beaten
4 veal escalopes, well beaten	4 veal scallopini, well beaten
100 g/4 oz button mushrooms	1¼ cups button mushrooms
1 courgette, sliced lengthways	1 zucchini, sliced lengthways
1 aubergine, sliced, salted and drained	1 eggplant, sliced, salted and drained
1 apple, peeled, cored and cut into rings	1 apple, peeled, cored and cut into rings
plain flour for coating	all-purpose flour for coating
dried breadcrumbs for coating	dried bread crumbs for coating
vegetable oil for deep-frying	vegetable oil for deep-frying
lemon wedges to garnish	lemon wedges to garnish

There are numerous versions of *fritto misto* or 'mixed fry' to give it its English name, and these can vary from being mostly pieces of offal (variety meats), as in the recipe on page 146, to the much grander and more complicated version on this page. Most versions have offal (variety meats) as their main ingredient, but veal escalopes, small lamb or pork cutlets, and even chicken breasts are often included. Young, tender vegetables are a must in a good *fritto misto*. Two unusual ingredients are a sort of sweet custard made from semolina, and macaroons; these are not absolutely vital and can easily be omitted if preferred – they are peculiar to the *fritto misto* from Piemonte.

Pour 500 ml/18 fl oz/2¼ cups milk into a heavy pan, add the lemon rind, sugar and vanilla essence (extract), then add the semolina. Cook gently for 5 minutes, stirring constantly. Turn the mixture onto a cold work surface, then flatten with the hands.

Leave to cool, then roll into balls, about the size of walnuts. Soak the macaroons in the remaining milk, then squeeze dry and roll into similar-sized balls.

Beat the eggs with salt and pepper to taste. Coat the meat, vegetables, apple, semolina and macaroon balls with flour. Dip in the beaten eggs and coat with breadcrumbs.

Heat the oil in a deep-fat fryer until very hot, then deep-fry the coated ingredients separately until golden brown and cooked through. Drain on absorbent kitchen paper and keep hot while cooking the remaining ingredients. Serve immediately, garnished with lemon wedges.
SERVES 4

RUSTIDA
Braised Mixed Meats

Metric/Imperial	American
50 g/2 oz butter	¼ cup butter
1 large onion, peeled and sliced	1 large onion, peeled and sliced
225 g/8 oz pork loin, thinly sliced	½ lb pork loin, thinly sliced
100 g/4 oz salsiccia a metro★, thinly sliced	¼ lb salsiccia a metro★, thinly sliced
100 g/4 oz calf's sweetbreads, cleaned and thinly sliced	¼ lb veal sweetbreads, cleaned and thinly sliced
450 g/1 lb tomatoes, skinned and chopped	1 lb tomatoes, skinned and chopped
200 ml/8 fl oz beef stock	1 cup beef stock
salt and freshly ground black pepper	salt and freshly ground black pepper

Melt the butter in a flameproof casserole, add the onion and fry gently for 5 minutes. Add the pork, sausage and sweetbreads. Cook, stirring, over high heat for 5 minutes.

Add the tomatoes, stock and salt and pepper to taste. Cover and cook gently for 20 minutes until the meat is tender and the sauce is thick. Serve hot with polenta (see page 87) or mashed potatoes.
SERVES 4

FEGATO DI VITELLO ALLA PAESANA
Veal Liver, Peasant Style

Metric/Imperial	American
50 g/2 oz butter	¼ cup butter
50 g/2 oz streaky bacon, chopped	¼ cup chopped fatty bacon
2 garlic cloves, peeled and chopped	2 garlic cloves, peeled and chopped
1 tablespoon chopped parsley	1 tablespoon chopped parsley
2 onions, peeled and sliced	2 onions, peeled and sliced
450 g/1 lb calf's liver, cut into serving pieces	1 lb veal liver, cut into serving pieces
25 g/1 oz plain flour	¼ cup all-purpose flour
7 tablespoons red wine	7 tablespoons red wine
freshly ground black pepper	freshly ground black pepper
salt	salt

Melt the butter in a frying pan (skillet), add the bacon, garlic and half the parsley. Fry gently for 5 minutes. Add the onions and cook gently for 5 minutes, stirring frequently.

Coat the liver with the flour, add to the pan and brown lightly on both sides. Add the wine and a pinch of pepper. Cook for 5 to 6 minutes, stirring occasionally.

Add salt to taste and serve immediately, garnished with the remaining parsley.
SERVES 4

ANIMELLA DI VITELLO IN AGRODOLCE

Sweet and Sour Veal Sweetbreads

Metric/Imperial	American
25 g/1 oz butter	2 tablespoons butter
1 onion, peeled and chopped	1 onion, peeled and chopped
½ carrot, peeled and chopped	½ carrot, peeled and chopped
1 small celery stick, chopped	1 small celery stalk, chopped
25 g/1 oz streaky bacon, chopped	2 fatty bacon slices, chopped
pinch of dried thyme	pinch of dried thyme
½ bay leaf, crumbled	½ bay leaf, crumbled
450 g/1 lb calf's sweetbreads, cleaned and sliced	1 lb veal sweetbreads, cleaned and sliced
salt and freshly ground black pepper	salt and freshly ground black pepper
3–4 tablespoons vinegar	3–4 tablespoons vinegar
25 g/1 oz sugar	2 tablespoons sugar
3–4 tablespoons olive oil	3–4 tablespoons olive oil
25 g/1 oz capers	¼ cup capers

Melt the butter in a flameproof casserole, add the onion, carrot, celery, bacon, thyme and bay leaf and cook gently for 10 minutes. Add the sweetbreads and salt and pepper to taste. Cook gently for 15 to 20 minutes.

Meanwhile, heat the remaining ingredients in a small pan and cook gently, without boiling, for 5 minutes, stirring frequently with a wooden spoon. Put the sweetbread mixture in a warmed serving dish, pour over the sauce and serve immediately.

SERVES 4

TRIPPA ALLA GENOVESE

Tripe Genoa–Style

Metric/Imperial	American
1 kg/2 lb dressed tripe, cut into strips	2 lb dressed tripe, cut into strips
4 tablespoons olive oil	¼ cup olive oil
25 g/1 oz butter	2 tablespoons butter
1 onion, peeled and chopped	1 onion, peeled and chopped
1 celery stick, chopped	1 celery stalk, chopped
1 carrot, peeled and chopped	1 carrot, peeled and chopped
75 g/3 oz mushrooms, chopped	1 cup chopped mushrooms
salt and freshly ground black pepper	salt and freshly ground black pepper
450 g/1 lb tomatoes, skinned and mashed	2 cups skinned and mashed tomatoes
450 g/1 lb potatoes, peeled and cut into pieces	1 lb potatoes, peeled and cut into pieces

Blanch the tripe in boiling water for 5 minutes, drain, then plunge into cold water.

Heat the oil and butter in a flameproof casserole, add the chopped vegetables and fry gently for 5 minutes. Drain the tripe and add to the casserole with salt and pepper to taste. Cook for 15 minutes, stirring frequently.

Add the tomatoes and 7 tablespoons warm water. Cover and simmer for 30 minutes. Add the potatoes and cook for a further 30 minutes, stirring occasionally. Serve hot.

SERVES 6

Animella di vitello in agrodolce; Fegato di vitello alla milanese; Fegato alla tirolese

FEGATO DI VITELLO ALLA MILANESE

Milanese Fried Veal Liver

Metric/Imperial	American
450 g/1 lb calf's liver, sliced	1 lb veal liver, sliced
1 tablespoon chopped parsley	1 tablespoon chopped parsley
salt and freshly ground black pepper	salt and freshly ground black pepper
4 tablespoons olive oil	$\frac{1}{4}$ cup olive oil
plain flour for coating	all-purpose flour for coating
2 eggs, beaten with a pinch of salt	2 eggs, beaten with a pinch of salt
dried breadcrumbs for coating	dried bread crumbs for coating
75 g/3 oz butter	$\frac{1}{3}$ cup butter
TO GARNISH:	TO GARNISH
lemon slices	lemon slices
parsley sprigs	parsley sprigs

Place the liver in a shallow dish and sprinkle with the parsley, salt and pepper to taste and 2 tablespoons oil. Leave to marinate for 2 hours, turning occasionally.

Drain the liver, then coat lightly with flour. Dip in the beaten eggs, then coat with breadcrumbs.

Heat the remaining oil and the butter in a frying pan (skillet). Add the liver and fry over high heat for 4 to 5 minutes on each side until tender. Drain and serve immediately, garnished with lemon slices and parsley.
SERVES 4

FEGATO ALLA TIROLESE

Liver Tyrolese-Style

Metric/Imperial	American
450 g/1 lb calf's liver, thinly sliced	1 lb veal liver, thinly sliced
250 ml/8 fl oz milk	1 cup milk
50 g/2 oz butter	$\frac{1}{4}$ cup butter
$\frac{1}{2}$ onion, peeled and chopped	$\frac{1}{2}$ onion, peeled and chopped
50 g/2 oz streaky bacon, diced	$\frac{1}{4}$ cup diced fatty bacon
25 g/1 oz plain flour	$\frac{1}{4}$ cup all-purpose flour
3 tablespoons stock	3 tablespoons stock
200 ml/$\frac{1}{3}$ pint double cream	1 cup heavy cream
1 tablespoon chopped capers	1 tablespoon chopped capers
salt and freshly ground black pepper	salt and freshly ground black pepper
sage leaves to garnish	sage leaves to garnish

Put the liver and milk in a dish and leave for 1 hour.

Melt the butter in a frying pan (skillet), add the onion and bacon and fry gently for 5 minutes. Drain the liver, then add to the pan and fry for 7 to 8 minutes.

Transfer the liver to a serving plate; keep hot. Mix the flour and stock to a smooth paste, then stir into the pan juices with the cream. Simmer for 10 minutes, stirring frequently. Add the capers and salt and pepper to taste. Pour over the liver and serve immediately, garnished with sage.
SERVES 4

The Italians invariably use calf's (veal) tripe because it is more delicate in flavour and less coarse in texture than other tripe. This is also true of calf's (veal) liver, which is considered very much a delicacy in Italy. The tripe and liver from other animals may be substituted in Italian recipes calling for calf's (veal), but more care must be taken in the cooking if it is to be as good. Soaking in milk before cooking often helps tenderize offal (variety meats), especially liver.

FEGATO DI VITELLO ALLA VENEZIANA

Veal Liver Venetian Style

Metric/Imperial	American
3–4 tablespoons olive oil	3–4 tablespoons olive oil
25 g/1 oz butter	2 tablespoons butter
450 g/1 lb onions, peeled and sliced	1 lb onions, peeled and sliced
1 tablespoon chopped parsley	1 tablespoon chopped parsley
450 g/1 lb calf's liver, sliced	1 lb veal liver, sliced
4 tablespoons beef stock	¼ cup beef stock
salt and freshly ground black pepper	salt and freshly ground black pepper

Heat the oil and butter in a frying pan (skillet), add the onions and parsley, cover and cook gently for 20 to 30 minutes until softened.

Add the liver, increase the heat and stir in the stock. Cook for 5 minutes, then remove from the heat and add salt and pepper to taste. Serve immediately with grilled (broiled) slices of polenta (see page 87), or fried bread.

SERVES 4

ROGNONE ALLA BOLOGNESE

Kidneys Braised with Onion

Metric/Imperial	American
4 tablespoons olive oil	¼ cup olive oil
2 calf's kidneys, thinly sliced	2 veal kidneys, thinly sliced
3–4 tablespoons vinegar	3–4 tablespoons vinegar
50 g/2 oz butter	¼ cup butter
1 onion, peeled and finely chopped	1 onion, peeled and finely chopped
1 garlic clove, peeled	1 garlic clove, peeled
1 tablespoon chopped parsley	1 tablespoon chopped parsley
3–4 tablespoons beef stock	3–4 tablespoons beef stock
salt and freshly ground black pepper	salt and freshly ground black pepper

Heat the oil in a heavy pan, add the kidneys and fry gently for 4 to 5 minutes. Add half the vinegar and cook for a further 2 minutes, then drain the kidneys and keep hot.

Meanwhile, melt the butter in another pan. Add the onion, garlic and parsley and fry gently until browned. Discard the garlic and add the kidneys.

Increase the heat and cook, stirring, for a few minutes until the mixture is dry. Add the remaining vinegar and the stock and simmer for 5 minutes. Sprinkle with salt and pepper to taste and serve immediately.

SERVES 4

FRITTO MISTO ALLA ROMANA

Fried Kidneys and Sweetbreads, Roman-Style

Metric/Imperial	American
4 globe artichokes	4 globe artichokes
575 g/1¼ lb mixed lamb's offal (brains, kidneys, sweetbreads), cleaned and cut into serving pieces	1¼ lb mixed lamb's variety meats (brains, kidneys, sweetbreads), cleaned and cut into serving pieces
plain flour for coating	all-purpose flour for coating
2 eggs, beaten with a pinch of salt	2 eggs, beaten with a pinch of salt
vegetable oil for deep-frying	vegetable oil for deep-frying
salt and freshly ground black pepper	salt and freshly ground black pepper
2 lemons, quartered, to serve	2 lemons, quartered, to serve

Discard the hard outer leaves of the artichokes and the choke. Cut the hearts into sections. Coat the artichokes and meat with flour, then dip in the beaten eggs.

Heat the oil in a deep-fat fryer and deep-fry the different meats and artichokes separately until golden brown and cooked through. Drain on absorbent kitchen paper. Sprinkle with salt and pepper to taste and keep hot while cooking the remaining ingredients. Serve hot, with lemon quarters.

SERVES 4

TRIPPA ALLA BOLOGNESE

Tripe with Eggs and Parmesan

Metric/Imperial	American
1 kg/2 lb tripe, dressed and chopped	2 lb tripe, dressed and chopped
5 tablespoons olive oil	⅓ cup olive oil
100 g/4 oz bacon, chopped	½ cup chopped bacon
1 small onion, peeled and chopped	1 small onion, peeled and chopped
1 garlic clove, peeled and crushed	1 garlic clove, peeled and crushed
1 tablespoon chopped parsley	1 tablespoon chopped parsley
salt and freshly ground black pepper	salt and freshly ground black pepper
1 beef stock cube	1 beef bouillon cube
2 eggs, beaten	2 eggs, beaten
75 g/3 oz Parmesan cheese*, grated	¾ cup grated Parmesan cheese*

Blanch the tripe in boiling water for 5 minutes, drain, then plunge into cold water.

Heat the oil in a heavy pan, add the bacon, onion, garlic and parsley and fry gently for 5 minutes. Add the tripe and salt and pepper to taste, then add the stock (bouillon) cube dissolved in a little warm water. Cook gently for 1 hour, stirring frequently.

Mix the eggs with half the Parmesan, stir into the tripe mixture and cook for a further 5 minutes. Transfer to a warmed serving dish. sprinkle with the remaining Parmesan and serve immediately.

SERVES 4

CODA ALLA VACCINARA

Oxtail Stew

Metric/Imperial	American
2 kg/4½ lb oxtail, cut into pieces	4½ lb oxtail, cut into pieces
2 onions, peeled	2 onions, peeled
2 carrots, peeled	2 carrots, peeled
575 g/1¼ lb celery	1¼ lb celery
2 bay leaves	2 bay leaves
salt	salt
1 tablespoon olive oil	1 tablespoon olive oil
225 g/8 oz lean bacon, chopped	1 cup chopped lean bacon
50 g/2 oz raw ham, chopped	¼ cup chopped raw ham
7 tablespoons dry white wine	7 tablespoons dry white wine
450 g/1 lb tomatoes, skinned and mashed	2 cups skinned and mashed tomatoes
pinch of ground cinnamon	pinch of ground cinnamon
freshly ground black pepper	freshly ground black pepper

Soak the oxtail in cold water for 2 hours. Put 1 onion, 1 carrot, 1 celery stick and the bay leaves in a large pan of salted water and bring to the boil. Add the oxtail pieces and bring to the boil. Boil for 1 hour, skimming frequently. Drain the oxtail, reserving the cooking liquid.

Chop the remaining onion and carrot. Heat the oil in a large clean pan, and add the onion, carrot, bacon, ham and oxtail. Fry, stirring, over moderate heat for 10 minutes, then add the wine and simmer until it has evaporated. Add the tomatoes, cover and simmer for 2½ hours, adding a little of the reserved cooking liquid from time to time as necessary.

Chop the remaining celery into 2 cm/¾ inch long pieces. Cook in boiling salted water for 10 minutes, then drain and add to the oxtail. Cook for a further 30 minutes, then add the cinnamon and a little pepper. Serve hot.

SERVES 8

ABOVE: **Coda alla vaccinara; Rognone alla bolognese**
LEFT: **Fegato di vitello alla veneziana**

Poultry & Game

Poultry, in the form of capon, chicken, duck, goose and turkey, is popular throughout Italy, and is generally of good quality.

There are many different chicken specialities throughout the country, both using whole birds and chicken portions. Chicken breasts are cooked with ham, cheese or wine, or in a tomato sauce or devilled dressing(*alla diavola*). Whole chickens are often served roasted and stuffed, with the chicken livers and giblets included in homemade stuffings. Older birds or boiling fowl are usually simmered with herbs and seasonings, or made into soup or stock.

Turkey is popular in Italy, and is available throughout the year, both as whole birds and as thick turkey steaks or portions, which Italian housewives slice or cut up and use like veal, for escalope dishes or in stews. Turkeys are bred to huge sizes specifically for selling in portions in this way. Capon was always the traditional bird for Christmas, but nowadays turkey seems to be taking its place. The stuffing for either bird is likely to be made with breadcrumbs, sausage-meat, livers from the bird, herbs and seasonings, as in the recipe *Cappone farcito al forno* (see page 39), which can equally well be made with turkey. Another delicious recipe for roast turkey is *Tacchinetta al melograno* (see page 151); it is served with a sauce of pomegranate juice.

There is a wide choice of game – both small birds and large game. The Italians do not impose rigid hunting and shooting restrictions so game is available most of the year. The Sardinians like to stuff large game with smaller game for celebration feasts and special occasions, then roast the animals and birds together over embers covered with myrtle leaves. In other regions of Italy game is cooked in a more conventional way – but very often in a sweet-sour (*agrodolce*) sauce, or marinated in wine and herbs. Rabbit is probably the most common game found in Italy, with hare another favourite, and both of these are often served with a sweet-sour sauce and slices of *polenta*.

TUSCANY

POLLO ALLO SPIEDO

Spit-Roasted Chicken

Metric/Imperial
1 × 1.5 kg/3 lb oven-ready chicken
7 tablespoons olive oil
few sage leaves, chopped
1 rosemary sprig, chopped
225 g/8 oz raw ham or bacon slices
2 garlic cloves, peeled and chopped
salt and freshly ground black pepper

American
1 × 3 lb oven-ready chicken
7 tablespoons olive oil
few sage leaves, chopped
1 rosemary sprig, chopped
½ lb raw ham or bacon slices
2 garlic cloves, peeled and chopped
salt and freshly ground black pepper

Brush the chicken with the oil, then sprinkle with half the sage and rosemary. Leave to stand for 2 to 3 hours.

Chop half the ham or bacon and mix with the garlic, remaining sage and rosemary, and salt and pepper to taste, then put inside the chicken. Sew the opening securely with trussing thread or string.

Wrap the chicken in the remaining slices of ham, then tie them on with more thread or string. Thread the chicken on the spit and spit roast for 1¼ hours until the skin is crunchy and the meat is tender. Alternatively, cook in a preheated moderately hot oven (200°C/400°F/Gas Mark 6) for 1¼ hours or until tender. Serve immediately.

SERVES 4

TUSCANY

POLLO ALLA DIAVOLA

Charcoal Grilled (Broiled) Chicken

Metric/Imperial
1 × 1.25 kg/2½ lb oven-ready chicken, halved
7 tablespoons olive oil
salt and freshly ground black pepper
1 lemon, sliced, to serve

American
1 × 2½ lb oven-ready chicken, halved
7 tablespoons olive oil
salt and freshly ground black pepper
1 lemon, sliced, to serve

Pound the 2 halves of chicken lightly with a mallet, taking care not to break the bones.

Rub the chicken halves with the oil and sprinkle with salt and pepper. Cook for about 40 minutes over a charcoal grill (broiler) until the skin is crisp and crunchy and the meat is tender.

Serve immediately, with lemon slices.

SERVES 4

POLLO IN POTACCHIO

Chicken Braised with Onion and Pimento

Metric/Imperial	American
3–4 tablespoons olive oil	3–4 tablespoons olive oil
1 small onion, peeled and sliced	1 small onion, peeled and sliced
2 garlic cloves, peeled and crushed	2 garlic cloves, peeled and crushed
1 × 1.25 kg/2½ lb oven-ready chicken, cut into serving pieces	1 × 2½ lb oven-ready chicken, cut into serving pieces
1 small piece canned pimento, chopped	1 small piece canned pimiento, chopped
salt and freshly ground black pepper	salt and freshly ground black pepper
1 tablespoon tomato purée	1 tablespoon tomato paste
3–4 tablespoons dry white wine	3–4 tablespoons dry white wine
few rosemary sprigs	few rosemary sprigs
6–8 tablespoons chicken stock	6–8 tablespoons chicken stock

Heat the oil in a flameproof casserole, add the onion and garlic and fry gently for 15 minutes. Add the chicken pieces with the pimento and salt and pepper to taste and fry, turning, over moderate heat until browned on all sides.

Mix the tomato purée (paste) with a little lukewarm water, then stir into the casserole with the wine. Lower the heat, cover and cook gently for 30 minutes. Chop one of the rosemary sprigs and sprinkle over the chicken. Cook for a further 20 minutes or until the chicken is tender, adding a little of the stock occasionally to moisten.

Serve hot, garnished with the remaining rosemary.
SERVES 4

ABOVE: **Pollo in potacchio**

The best chickens are said to come from Tuscany, specifically from the valley of the river Arno. They are noted for their plump tender flesh, which has an indescribably good flavour. The Tuscans rarely cook their chickens in elaborate sauces, for the simple reason that the birds are so good that this would only mar their flavour. Simple spit-roasting over a wood fire or charcoal grill (broiler) is the most favoured cooking method.

ABOVE: **Anatra farcita alla novarese; Gallina alla vernaccia**

POLLO RIPIENO AL FORNO

Roast Stuffed Chicken

Metric/Imperial	American
25 g/1 oz butter	2 tablespoons butter
1 × 1.5 kg/3 lb oven-ready chicken, with giblets	1 × 3 lb oven-ready chicken, with giblets
150 g/5 oz dried breadcrumbs	1¼ cups dried bread crumbs
3 tomatoes, skinned and chopped	3 tomatoes, skinned and chopped
1 egg, beaten	1 egg, beaten
100 g/4 oz pecorino cheese★, grated	1 cup grated pecorino cheese★
7 tablespoons milk	7 tablespoons milk
4 tablespoons cream	¼ cup cream
salt and freshly ground black pepper	salt and freshly ground black pepper
1 hard-boiled egg	1 hard-cooked egg
4 tablespoons olive oil	¼ cup olive oil

Melt the butter in a heavy pan, chop the chicken giblets and add to the pan. Fry gently for 10 minutes. Add the breadcrumbs and fry until browned, then add the tomatoes and simmer for 10 minutes. Remove from the heat and leave to cool.

Add the egg to the mixture with the cheese, milk, cream and salt and pepper to taste. Mix thoroughly. Stuff the chicken with this mixture, putting the hard-boiled (cooked) egg in the centre. Sew the opening securely with trussing thread or string.

Place the chicken in an oiled roasting tin (pan) and sprinkle with salt and pepper to taste and the oil. Roast in a preheated moderately hot oven (200°C/400°F/Gas Mark 6) for 1½ hours or until the chicken is tender. Serve immediately.

SERVES 6

GALLINA ALLA VERNACCIA

Chicken Casseroled with Garlic and White Wine

Metric/Imperial	American
4 tablespoons olive oil	$\frac{1}{4}$ cup olive oil
3 garlic cloves, peeled	3 garlic cloves, peeled
1 × 1.5 kg/3 lb oven-ready chicken, cut into serving pieces	1 × 3 lb oven-ready chicken, cut into serving pieces
salt and freshly ground black pepper	salt and freshly ground black pepper
500 ml/18 fl oz Vernaccia or other dry white wine	$2\frac{1}{4}$ cups Vernaccia or other dry white wine
chopped parsley to garnish	chopped parsley to garnish

Heat the oil in a flameproof casserole, add the garlic and fry gently until browned. Discard the garlic and add the chicken pieces to the casserole. Fry over high heat until browned on all sides, turning frequently. Add salt and pepper to taste, then add the wine.

Lower the heat, cover and cook gently for 1 hour or until the chicken is tender, stirring occasionally. Serve hot, garnished with parsley.
SERVES 6

TACCHINETTA AL MELOGRANO

Turkey with Pomegranates

Metric/Imperial	American
1 × 2 kg/4½ lb oven-ready turkey, with giblets	1 × 4½ lb oven-ready turkey, with giblets
salt	salt
50 g/2 oz butter, diced	$\frac{1}{4}$ cup butter, diced
150 ml/¼ pint olive oil	$\frac{2}{3}$ cup olive oil
4 juniper berries	4 juniper berries
1 rosemary sprig	1 rosemary sprig
200 ml/⅓ pint dry white wine	1 cup dry white wine
3 pomegranates	3 pomegranates
freshly ground black pepper	freshly ground black pepper
juice of ½ lemon	juice of ½ lemon
4 tablespoons chicken stock	¼ cup chicken stock

Sprinkle the turkey inside and out with salt, then place a third of the butter in the cavity. Sew the opening with trussing thread or string.

Place the turkey in an oiled roasting tin (pan). Top with the remaining butter, 7 tablespoons oil, the juniper berries and rosemary, then pour in the wine. Roast in a preheated moderate oven (180°C/350°F/Gas Mark 4) for 1½ hours, basting the turkey with the wine and cooking juices occasionally. Add the juice of 1 pomegranate and cook for a further 1 hour or until the turkey is almost tender.

Meanwhile, chop the turkey liver and gizzard finely. Heat the remaining oil in a heavy pan, add the liver and gizzard and fry until browned. Remove from the heat and set aside.

Add the juice of another pomegranate and salt and pepper to taste to the turkey. Roast for a further 10 minutes, then lift out the turkey and cut into serving pieces. Arrange in an ovenproof serving dish.

Skim the fat off the cooking juices and place the pan over moderate heat. Add the lemon juice and stock and boil until reduced by about half. Strain and stir into the giblet mixture. Pour this sauce over the turkey pieces, sprinkle with the grains of the remaining pomegranate and return to the oven for a further 7 to 8 minutes. Serve immediately.
SERVES 8

ANATRA FARCITA ALLA NOVARESE

Stuffed Duck Novara Style

Metric/Imperial	American
50 g/2 oz dripping	$\frac{1}{4}$ cup drippings
50 g/2 oz bacon, chopped	$\frac{1}{4}$ cup chopped bacon
1 onion, peeled and chopped	1 onion, peeled and chopped
225 g/8 oz minced beef	1 cup ground beef
225 g/8 oz minced pork	1 cup ground pork
100 g/4 oz salsiccia a metro★, skinned and diced	$\frac{1}{2}$ cup skinned and diced salsiccia a metro★
100 g/4 oz rice	scant $\frac{1}{2}$ cup rice
salt	salt
3 eggs, beaten	3 eggs, beaten
1 garlic clove, peeled and crushed	1 garlic clove, peeled and crushed
1 tablespoon chopped parsley	1 tablespoon chopped parsley
pinch of grated nutmeg	pinch of grated nutmeg
freshly ground black pepper	freshly ground black pepper
1 × 1.5 kg/3½ lb oven-ready duckling, boned	1 × 3½ lb oven-ready duckling, boned
1–2 tablespoons olive oil	1–2 tablespoons olive oil
1 rosemary sprig	1 rosemary sprig
6–8 tablespoons chicken stock	6–8 tablespoons chicken stock

Melt the dripping(s) in a heavy pan, add the bacon and onion and fry gently for 5 minutes. Add the beef, pork and sausage and fry for 10 minutes, stirring frequently. Remove from the heat.

Cook the rice in boiling salted water for 10 minutes, then drain thoroughly and add to the meat mixture. Add the eggs, garlic, parsley, nutmeg and salt and pepper to taste and mix thoroughly.

Stuff the duckling with this mixture, then sew up with trussing thread or string. Heat the oil with the rosemary in a roasting tin (pan). Add the duck and brown on all sides, then roast in a preheated moderate oven (180°C/350°F/Gas Mark 4) for 1½ to 2 hours until the duck is tender, basting occasionally with a little stock. Slice the duck and serve hot, with the cooking juices poured over, or serve cold with salad.
SERVES 6

The centre of the turkey producing industry is in the town of Vicenza, just north-east of Verona in the region of Veneto. Pomegranates are often served with turkey in this area, as they are in the recipe for *Tacchinetta al melograno*. Another local custom involving turkeys has died out now; it used to take place at the annual fair in Vicenza. Men were blindfolded and armed with long sticks which they used for bashing in the heads of turkeys. Thankfully, this cruel sport no longer takes place.

RIGHT: **Lepre in salsa peverada**; **Anatra con tagliatelle**; **Oca conservata**

ANATRA CON TAGLIATELLE

Duck Casserole with Tagliatelle

Metric/Imperial	American
75 g/3 oz butter	1/3 cup butter
1/2 onion, peeled and chopped	1/2 onion, peeled and chopped
1/2 carrot, peeled and chopped	1/2 carrot, peeled and chopped
1 celery stick, chopped	1 celery stalk, chopped
1 bay leaf	1 bay leaf
1 × 1.5 kg/3½ lb oven-ready duckling	1 × 3½ lb oven-ready duckling
50 g/2 oz mushrooms, sliced	¾ cup sliced mushrooms
450 g/1 lb tomatoes, skinned and mashed	2 cups skinned and mashed tomatoes
300 ml/½ pint chicken stock	1¼ cups chicken stock
salt and freshly ground black pepper	salt and freshly ground black pepper
300 g/11 oz tagliatelle	11 oz tagliatelle
TO SERVE:	TO SERVE:
25 g/1 oz butter, melted	2 tablespoons butter, melted
65 g/2½ oz Parmesan cheese★, grated	⅔ cup grated Parmesan cheese★

Melt the butter in a flameproof casserole, add the onion, carrot, celery and bay leaf and fry gently for 5 minutes. Add the duckling and fry, turning until browned on all sides, then add the mushrooms, tomatoes, stock and salt and pepper to taste. Bring to the boil, lower the heat, cover and simmer for 1½ hours or until the duckling is tender.

Meanwhile, cook the tagliatelle in boiling salted water until *al dente*. Drain thoroughly and pile into a warmed serving dish. Sprinkle with a little of the cooking juice from the duckling, then mix in the melted butter and Parmesan. Cut the duck into serving pieces and arrange on top of the tagliatelle. Keep hot.

Strain the cooking juices and boil until reduced by about half. Pour over the duck and serve immediately.

SERVES 6

OCA CONSERVATA

Conserve of Goose

Goose will keep for several months in the refrigerator if preserved in this way – as long as it remains covered with fat and oil.

Metric/Imperial	American
1 × 2 kg/4½ lb goose, cleaned	1 × 4½ lb goose, cleaned
150 ml/¼ pint olive oil	⅔ cup olive oil
2 garlic cloves, peeled and crushed	2 garlic cloves, peeled and crushed
1 rosemary sprig	1 rosemary sprig
salt and freshly ground black pepper	salt and freshly ground black pepper
few bay leaves	few bay leaves

Put the goose in a flameproof casserole and sprinkle with 3 tablespoons oil, the garlic, rosemary and salt and pepper to taste. Cover and cook very gently for 2 hours or until the goose is tender. Drain the goose, reserving

the fat, then cut into serving pieces, removing all skin and bones.

Cover the bottom of an earthenware or glass dish with a layer of goose fat and arrange a layer of goose meat over the fat. Top with a few bay leaves and another layer of goose fat. Continue layering the fat, goose and bay leaves in this way until all the ingredients are used; the goose should be completely covered in fat. Decorate the top with bay leaves, then pour over the remaining oil..

Cover with foil and secure with string. Store in the refrigerator until required. To serve, turn out and cut into slices.

SERVES 8

LEPRE IN SALSA PEVERADA

Hare with Sausages

Metric/Imperial	American
50 g/2 oz butter	¼ cup butter
100 g/4 oz streaky bacon, chopped	½ cup chopped fatty bacon
1 small onion, peeled and chopped	1 small onion, peeled and chopped
1 × 1.5 kg/3 lb hare, cleaned and cut into serving pieces	1 × 3 lb hare, cleaned and cut into serving pieces
300 ml/½ pint chicken stock	1¼ cups chicken stock
salt and freshly ground black pepper	salt and freshly ground black pepper
SAUCE:	SAUCE:
5 tablespoons olive oil	5 tablespoons olive oil
175 g/6 oz sopressata★, chopped	¾ cup chopped sopressata★
1 hare or chicken liver, chopped	1 hare or chicken liver, chopped
300 ml/½ pint chicken stock	1¼ cups chicken stock
25 g/1 oz parsley, chopped	¾ cup chopped parsley
juice of ½ lemon	juice of ½ lemon

Heat the butter in a flameproof casserole, add the bacon and onion and fry gently for 5 minutes. Add the hare, stock and salt and pepper to taste. Bring to the boil, lower the heat, cover and simmer gently for 2 hours.

Meanwhile, prepare the sauce: heat the oil in a heavy pan, add the sausage and liver and fry gently for 5 minutes. Add the stock, parsley and salt and pepper to taste. Simmer for 30 minutes until the sauce thickens. Stir in the lemon juice and add to the hare 10 minutes before the end of the cooking time. Serve hot with polenta (see page 87).

SERVES 4

Rabbit and hare are the most popular small game, but in the mountain areas of northern Italy the hunters kill rarer species for the table. The white hare, wild goat, chamois and wild boar are found in Valle d'Aosta. Wild goat is rather strong in flavour and something of an acquired taste; chamois on the other hand is more delicate, and quite delicious when braised in one of the local red wines.

CONIGLIO CON LE OLIVE

Rabbit with Olives

Metric/Imperial	American
7 tablespoons olive oil	7 tablespoons olive oil
1 × 1.25 kg/2½ lb rabbit, cleaned and cut into serving pieces	1 × 2½ lb rabbit, cleaned and cut into serving pieces
2 garlic cloves, peeled and chopped	2 garlic cloves, peeled and chopped
1 rosemary sprig, chopped	1 rosemary sprig, chopped
200 ml/⅓ pint red wine	1 cup red wine
salt and freshly ground black pepper	salt and freshly ground black pepper
6–8 tablespoons chicken stock	6–8 tablespoons chicken stock
2 tomatoes, skinned and mashed	2 tomatoes, skinned and mashed
225 g/8 oz black olives, halved and stoned	1 cup pitted ripe olives

Heat the oil in a flameproof casserole, add the rabbit and sprinkle with the garlic and rosemary. Fry gently until the rabbit is browned on all sides, turning frequently.

Add the wine and salt and pepper to taste. Cover and simmer for 30 minutes, adding a little stock to moisten as necessary.

Add the tomatoes and olives and cook for a further 40 minutes until the rabbit is tender. Serve hot.

SERVES 4

CONIGLIO ALLA REGGIANA

Rabbit with Herbs

Metric/Imperial	American
1 × 1.25 kg/2½ lb rabbit, cleaned and cut into serving pieces	1 × 2½ lb rabbit, cleaned and cut into serving pieces
1 garlic clove, peeled and crushed	1 garlic clove, peeled and crushed
1 rosemary sprig, chopped	1 rosemary sprig, chopped
4 sage leaves, chopped	4 sage leaves, chopped
8 juniper berries	8 juniper berries
salt and freshly ground black pepper	salt and freshly ground black pepper
3–4 tablespoons vinegar	3–4 tablespoons vinegar
7 tablespoons olive oil	7 tablespoons olive oil
6–8 tablespoons chicken stock	6–8 tablespoons chicken stock

Put the rabbit in a flameproof casserole, sprinkle with the garlic, herbs, juniper, salt and pepper to taste, vinegar and two thirds of the oil. Leave to marinate for 3 to 4 hours, turning the rabbit pieces occasionally.

Add the remaining oil, then place the casserole on top of the stove. Cover and cook gently for 40 minutes, basting occasionally with the stock. Remove the lid, increase the heat to moderate and cook for a further 30 minutes until the rabbit is tender. Serve hot.

SERVES 4

CONIGLIO IN PORCHETTA

Rabbit and Fennel Casserole

Metric/Imperial	American
225 g/8 oz fennel (green part only), quartered	½ lb fennel (green part only), quartered
salt	salt
3 garlic cloves, peeled	3 garlic cloves, peeled
1 × 1.25 kg/2½ lb rabbit, cleaned, with liver	1 × 2½ lb rabbit, cleaned, with liver
100 g/4 oz bacon or raw ham	¼ lb bacon or raw ham
7 tablespoons olive oil	7 tablespoons olive oil
100 g/4 oz fresh breadcrumbs, soaked in a little milk and squeezed dry	2 cups fresh bread crumbs, soaked in a little milk and squeezed dry
freshly ground black pepper	freshly ground black pepper
fennel slices to garnish	fennel slices to garnish

Coniglio in porchetta;
Coniglio coi peperoni;
Coniglio con le olive

Cook the fennel in boiling salted water to cover, with 2 cloves garlic, for 15 minutes. Drain thoroughly, reserving the cooking liquid, but discarding the garlic. Chop the fennel finely.

Mince (grind) the liver together with the bacon and the remaining garlic. Heat 2 tablespoons oil in a flameproof casserole, add the fennel and liver mixture. Cook gently for 10 minutes, then mix with the breadcrumbs and salt and pepper to taste. Stuff the rabbit with this mixture, then sew up the opening with trussing thread or string.

Place the rabbit in a roasting tin (pan) and sprinkle with the remaining oil, and salt and pepper to taste. Cover with foil and roast in a preheated moderate oven (180°C/350°F/Gas Mark 4) for 1½ hours or until the rabbit is tender, basting occasionally with the fennel cooking liquid.

Transfer the rabbit to a serving platter and garnish with fennel. Serve hot.
SERVES 4

CONIGLIO COI PEPERONI

Rabbit with Peppers

Metric/Imperial	American
50 g/2 oz butter	¼ cup butter
50 g/2 oz ham fat or streaky bacon, chopped	¼ cup chopped ham fat or fatty bacon
1 rosemary sprig, chopped	1 rosemary sprig, chopped
1 × 1.25 kg/2½ lb rabbit, cleaned and cut into serving pieces	1 × 2½ lb rabbit, cleaned and cut into serving pieces
1 bay leaf	1 bay leaf
salt and freshly ground black pepper	salt and freshly ground black pepper
7 tablespoons chicken stock	7 tablespoons chicken stock
2 tablespoons olive oil	2 tablespoons olive oil
4 green peppers, cored, seeded and sliced	4 green peppers, cored, seeded and sliced
4 canned anchovies, soaked in milk, drained and mashed	4 canned anchovies, soaked in milk, drained and mashed
2 garlic cloves, peeled and sliced	2 garlic cloves, peeled and sliced
4 tablespoons white wine vinegar	¼ cup white wine vinegar

Melt half the butter in a flameproof casserole, add the ham fat or bacon and rosemary and fry gently for 5 minutes. Add the rabbit, bay leaf and salt and pepper to taste. Fry, turning over high heat until evenly browned, then cover and cook gently for 20 minutes, turning frequently and basting with the stock.

Meanwhile, heat the remaining butter and the oil in a separate pan. Add the peppers, anchovies, garlic and salt and pepper to taste. Cook gently for 20 minutes, adding the vinegar a little at a time during cooking.

Add the pepper mixture to the rabbit and cook gently for a further 30 minutes or until the rabbit is tender. Discard the bay leaf. Serve hot.
SERVES 4

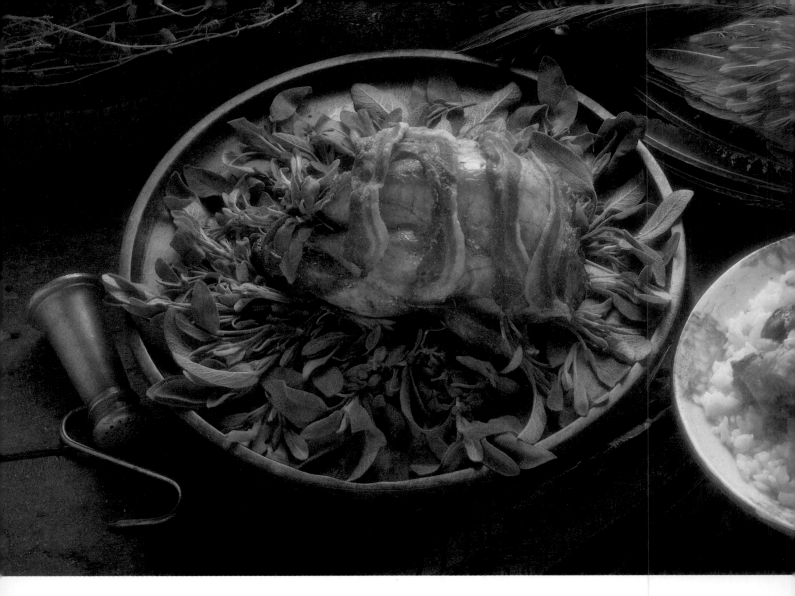

FAGIANO COL RISOTTO

Pheasant with Risotto

Metric/Imperial

1 × 1.25 kg/2½ lb pheasant, cleaned
salt
4 streaky bacon rashers, derinded
4 tablespoons olive oil
1 onion, peeled and chopped
1 carrot, peeled and chopped
1 celery stick, chopped
1 bay leaf
chicken stock (see method)
RISOTTO:
50 g/2 oz butter
1 small onion, peeled and chopped
300 g/11 oz rice
3–4 tablespoons dry white wine
1 litre/1¾ pints hot chicken stock
50 g/2 oz Parmesan cheese★, grated
freshly ground black pepper

American

1 × 2½ lb pheasant, cleaned
salt
4 fatty bacon slices
¼ cup olive oil
1 onion, peeled and chopped
1 carrot, peeled and chopped
1 celery stalk, chopped
1 bay leaf
chicken stock (see method)
RISOTTO:
¼ cup butter
1 small onion, peeled and chopped
1½ cups rice
3–4 tablespoons dry white wine
4¼ cups hot chicken stock
½ cup grated Parmesan cheese★
freshly ground black pepper

Sprinkle the pheasant inside and out with salt, then wrap the bacon around the outside and secure with string.

Heat the oil in a flameproof casserole, add the chopped vegetables and the bay leaf and fry gently until lightly coloured. Add the pheasant and fry until browned on all sides, then lower the heat, cover and cook gently for 40 minutes until the pheasant is tender, adding a little stock from time to time to prevent sticking.

Meanwhile, make the risotto. Melt the butter in a heavy pan, add the onion and cook gently for 5 minutes. Add the rice and stir for 2 to 3 minutes over moderate heat, then add the wine and boil until reduced, stirring constantly. Continue cooking for 20 minutes, adding the stock a cupful at a time, as the liquid is absorbed.

Remove from the heat, stir in the Parmesan and salt and pepper to taste, then turn into a warmed serving dish. Remove the pheasant from the casserole and cut into serving pieces. Place on top of the risotto and spoon over the vegetables and cooking liquid. Serve immediately.

SERVES 4 TO 6

Without the gaming restrictions common to other European countries, the Italians are at liberty to shoot almost anything that flies whenever they want. Shooting is therefore a popular sport, and the smaller and rarer the bird, the greater delicacy it is. Among the birds that are shot for the tables are thrushes, larks, figpeckers, swallows, woodcock, snipe and blackbirds. The most popular cooking method for such birds is spit-roasting on skewers.

TORRESANI IN TECIA

Casseroled Pigeon with Peas

Metric/Imperial	American
4 tablespoons olive oil	4 tablespoons olive oil
100 g/4 oz lean bacon, diced	½ cup diced lean bacn
1 onion, peeled and chopped	1 onion, peeled and chopped
1 carrot, peeled and chopped	1 carrot, peeled and chopped
1 celery stick, chopped	1 celery stalk, chopped
1 garlic clove, peeled and chopped	1 garlic clove, peeled and chopped
4 young pigeons, cleaned and halved	4 young pigeons, cleaned and halved
7 tablespoons dry white wine	7 tablespoons dry white wine
350 g/12 oz shelled fresh peas	3 cups shelled fresh peas
pinch of ground cinnamon	pinch of ground cinnamon
salt and freshly ground black pepper	salt and freshly ground black pepper
450 ml/¾ pint chicken stock	2 cups chicken stock

Heat the oil in a flameproof casserole, add the bacon, vegetables and garlic, and fry gently for 10 minutes. Add the pigeons and fry until browned on all sides, turning frequently. Add the wine and cook until it has evaporated.

Add the peas, cinnamon, salt and pepper to taste, and the stock. Cover and simmer for 30 minutes or until the pigeons are tender, basting the pigeons with the cooking liquor occasionally. Serve hot.

SERVES 4

LEFT: **Fagiano arrosto; Fagiano col risotto**
BELOW: **Torresani in tecia**

FAGIANO ARROSTO

Roast Pheasant with Sage

Metric/Imperial	American
100 g/4 oz raw ham, chopped	½ cup chopped raw ham
50 g/2 oz bacon, chopped	¼ cup chopped bacon
few sage leaves, chopped	few sage leaves, chopped
salt and freshly ground black pepper	salt and freshly ground black pepper
1 × 1.5 kg/3 lb pheasant, cleaned	1 × 3 lb pheasant, cleaned
4 bacon rashers	4 bacon slices
sage leaves to garnish	sage leaves to garnish

Mix the ham, bacon and sage together. Sprinkle the inside of the pheasant with salt and pepper, then fill with the ham mixture. Sew up the opening with trussing thread or string, then place the bacon on top and tie with string.

Place the pheasant in an oiled roasting tin (pan) and roast in a preheated moderately hot oven (190°C/375°F/Gas Mark 5) for 40 minutes until tender, basting occasionally with the pan juices.

Remove the thread or string from the pheasant and place on a warmed serving platter. Sprinkle with the cooking juices and garnish with sage leaves. Serve immediately.

SERVES 4

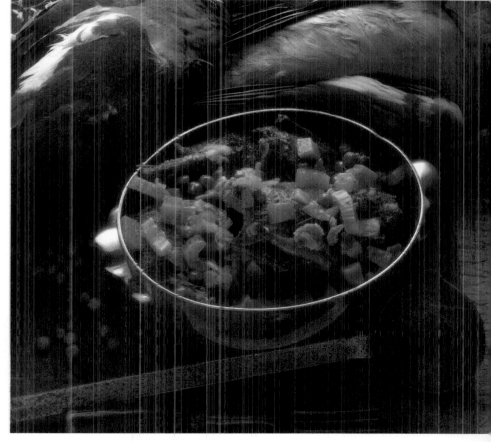

Vegetables

The Italians are blessed with an enormous variety of excellent vegetables, so it is hardly surprising to find that vegetables feature strongly in Italian cuisine. They may be included in soups or *antipasti*, or served as an accompaniment to a main course dish. Certain vegetables are often served as main courses in themselves.

Satisfying meals are made by stuffing artichokes, aubergines (eggplant), cabbage, peppers, onions, mushrooms or tomatoes, for example, with various mixtures of meat, cheese, rice, breadcrumbs, herbs and seasoning. Vegetables are also often served deep-fried, as *bignè* (fritters), or baked with cheese and other seasonings or sauces.

A popular, but unusual vegetable is the cardoon or *cardo*, an edible white thistle that is always served with *Bagna caôda* (see page 46). In their economical fashion, Italians cook the green leaves of beet and chard (turnip tops) in the same way as they cook spinach. One of the prettiest of Italian vegetables is *radicchio*, a type of lettuce eaten as a salad vegetable, which varies in colour from bright red to pale pink, with fine white veins. Some varieties can be rather bitter-tasting, but they make a welcome alternative to lettuce in salads, and are well worth seeking out at Italian shops in the winter months.

Another highly prized vegetable (if *funghi* can be categorized as such) is the white truffle (*tartufo*). Italians are fortunate to be able to grow a large number of truffles, both black and white, but it is the latter of which they are particularly proud. Both kinds of truffle are used in cooking, especially as a garnish for dishes with veal escalopes, chicken and turkey breasts, and for risotto and pasta, in which case they are usually sliced raw onto the dish at the point of serving.

Italians eat an immense variety of mushrooms, or *funghi* as they should correctly be called. These are not the cultivated mushrooms so common in Great Britain and the United States, but wild mushrooms. The most popular mushroom in Italy is the *porcino*, a very tasty variety that makes cultivated mushrooms seem completely flavourless in comparison. (See Mushrooms, Dried – page 27.)

Tomatoes, peppers, courgettes (zucchini) and aubergines (eggplant) feature extensively in the cuisine of southern Italy. Italian tomatoes are always full of flavour whether they are the large deep-red ones, the oddly shaped green and yellow ones used raw in salads and *antipasto*, or the plum-shaped ones used for sauces, purées and general cooking purposes. In the summer months fresh tomatoes are used in practically everything. In winter Italians use canned ones, tomato sauce and purée (paste).

Pulses are frequently served as a vegetable accompaniment to meat in Italy rather than eaten as a separate dish. They are also used a great deal in soups (see Pulses – page 26).

ABOVE: **Cipolle farcite; Cuori di carciofi con spinaci**

CUORI DI CARCIOFI CON SPINACI

Artichoke Hearts with Spinach

Metric/Imperial	American
6 tablespoons olive oil	6 tablespoons olive oil
1 small onion, peeled and finely chopped	1 small onion, peeled and finely chopped
1 garlic clove, peeled and crushed	1 garlic clove, peeled and crushed
4 canned anchovies, drained and crushed	4 canned anchovies, drained and crushed
1 kg/2 lb spinach, washed, drained and finely chopped	2 lb spinach, washed, drained and finely chopped
25 g/1 oz plain flour	¼ cup all-purpose flour
salt and freshly ground black pepper	salt and freshly ground black pepper
8 young globe artichokes	8 young globe artichokes
50 g/2 oz dried breadcrumbs	½ cup dried bread crumbs
50 g/2 oz Parmesan cheese★, grated	½ cup grated Parmesan cheese★

Heat half the oil in a large heavy pan. Add the onion, garlic and anchovies, and fry gently for 5 minutes. Add the spinach and cook for 2 minutes. Stir in the flour and salt and pepper to taste. Cover and cook gently for 5 minutes.

Clean the artichokes, discarding the hard outer leaves, spikes and chokes. Stand them close together in an oiled ovenproof dish, then cover with the spinach. Sprinkle with the remaining oil, breadcrumbs, cheese and pepper to taste. Bake in a preheated moderately hot oven (200°C/400°F/Gas Mark 6) for 20 minutes. Serve immediately.

SERVES 4 OR 8

Because the Italians serve vegetables more as complete dishes in their own right, than as mere accompaniments to meat, poultry or fish, vegetable recipes tend to be fairly involved. Stuffing vegetables is a very popular way of turning them into a substantial dish. Stuffed vegetables such as the ones on these pages are most likely to appear as first course dishes before the main course.

CIPOLLE FARCITE

Baked Stuffed Onions

Metric/Imperial	American
6 medium onions, peeled	6 medium onions, peeled
100 g/4 oz Parmesan cheese★, grated	1 cup grated Parmesan cheese★
75 g/3 oz butter	⅓ cup butter
3 eggs	3 eggs
salt and freshly ground black pepper	salt and freshly ground black pepper
3–4 tablespoons brandy	3–4 tablespoons brandy

Cook the onions in boiling water for 15 minutes. Drain, cut in half horizontally, then scoop out two thirds of the cores with a spoon. Chop the cores and place in a bowl with the cheese, one third of the butter, the eggs and salt and pepper to taste. Mix thoroughly, then spoon into the onion shells.

Melt the remaining butter in a flameproof casserole, put the onions in the dish and sprinkle with the brandy. Bake in a preheated moderately hot oven (200°C/400°F/Gas Mark 6) for 30 to 40 minutes. Serve immediately.

SERVES 6

PEPERONI RIPIENI DI RISO

Stuffed Peppers

Metric/Imperial	American
3 large green peppers	3 large green peppers
salt	salt
200 g/7 oz rice	1 cup rice
1 tablespoon chopped parsley	1 tablespoon chopped parsley
3 tablespoons olive oil	3 tablespoons olive oil
freshly ground black pepper	freshly ground black pepper
1 medium onion, peeled and sliced	1 medium onion, peeled and sliced
7 tablespoons dry white wine	7 tablespoons dry white wine

Halve the peppers lengthwise and remove the cores and seeds. Parboil the peppers in boiling salted water for 2 to 3 minutes, then drain and dry thoroughly. Cook the rice in boiling salted water for 10 minutes, then drain and mix with the parsley, 1 tablespoon oil and salt and pepper to taste.

Arrange the onion in an ovenproof dish. Fill the pepper halves with the rice mixture, then stand them upright on top of the onion. Sprinkle with the wine and the remaining oil, then cover and bake in a preheated moderately hot oven (200°C/400°F/Gas Mark 6) for 30 to 40 minutes. Serve hot or cold.

SERVES 6

FUNGHI AL FUNGHETTO

Mushrooms in Marjoram Sauce

Metric/Imperial	American
3 garlic cloves, peeled	3 garlic cloves, peeled
3–4 tablespoons olive oil	3–4 tablespoons olive oil
2 teaspoons chopped marjoram	2 teaspoons chopped marjoram
1 tablespoon tomato purée	1 tablespoon tomato paste
575 g/1½ lb mushrooms, sliced	1½ lb mushrooms, sliced
salt and freshly ground black pepper	salt and freshly ground black pepper

Chop 1 garlic clove. Heat the oil in a heavy pan, add the whole garlic cloves, chopped garlic, marjoram and tomato purée (paste) and fry gently for 5 minutes. Stir in the mushrooms and salt and pepper to taste. Simmer gently, stirring occasionally, for 15 minutes until just tender. Discard the whole garlic cloves and serve immediately.

SERVES 4 TO 6

FAGIOLI CON LE COTENNE

Bean, Bacon and Tomato Casserole

Metric/Imperial	American
200 g/7oz dried cannellini or haricot beans, soaked in lukewarm water overnight	1 cup dried cannellini or navy beans, soaked in lukewarm water overnight
1 rosemary sprig	1 rosemary sprig
3 garlic cloves, peeled	3 garlic cloves, peeled
½ lb streaky bacon, diced	½ lb fatty bacon, diced
½ onion, peeled and chopped	½ onion, peeled and chopped
1 small bunch parsley, chopped	1 small bunch parsley, chopped
4 basil leaves, chopped	4 basil leaves, chopped
2 tablespoons olive oil	2 tablespoons olive oil
450 g/1 lb tomatoes, skinned and chopped	2 cups skinned and chopped tomatoes
salt and freshly ground black pepper	salt and freshly ground black pepper

Drain the beans and place in a large pan with the rosemary and 2 whole garlic cloves. Cover with cold water and bring to the boil. Lower the heat, cover and simmer for 45 minutes to 1 hour until the beans are almost tender.

Meanwhile, chop the remaining garlic clove and mix with the bacon, onion, parsley and basil. Heat the oil in a flameproof casserole, add the mixture and fry gently until browned. Add the tomatoes and salt and pepper to taste. Cover and simmer gently for 30 minutes.

Drain the beans, discarding the garlic cloves and rosemary. Add the beans to the casserole and stir well. Cover and cook gently for a further 30 minutes. Adjust the seasoning and serve hot.

SERVES 4

CAVOLO ROSSO ALLA BOLZANESE

Red Cabbage Bolzano-Style

Metric/Imperial	American
75 g/3 oz smoked ham, diced	⅓ cup diced smoked ham
50 g/2 oz butter	¼ cup butter
3 tablespoons olive oil	3 tablespoons olive oil
½ onion, peeled and chopped	½ onion, peeled and chopped
7 tablespoons dry white wine	7 tablespoons dry white wine
1 large red cabbage, shredded	1 large red cabbage, shredded
salt and freshly ground black pepper	salt and freshly ground black pepper

Parboil the smoked ham in boiling water for 2 to 3 minutes, then drain and leave to cool.

Heat the butter and oil in a heavy pan, add the onion and ham and fry gently for 5 minutes. Add the wine and cabbage. Cover and simmer for 40 minutes, stirring occasionally. Add salt and pepper to taste before serving. Serve hot, with roast pork.

SERVES 4 TO 6

Liguria is renowned for its abundance of funghi. The Italians use every kind of edible funghi they can find, from the much coveted *funghi porcini*, to the somewhat strange-looking red, yellow and green varieties that are so common in the vegetable markets all over the country. *Funghi porcini* are often dried for winter use, so fond are the Italians of this variety.

The term *funghetti* can apply to any vegetable that has been cut into small pieces and fried with its skin on. It does not necessarily have to be mushrooms.

ASPARAGI ALLA MILANESE

Asparagus Milanese-Style

Metric/Imperial	American
1 kg/2 lb asparagus	2 lb asparagus
salt	salt
50 g/2 oz butter	¼ cup butter
4 eggs	4 eggs
freshly ground black pepper	freshly ground black pepper
50 g/2 oz Parmesan cheese★, grated	½ cup grated Parmesan cheese★

Scrape the lower part of the asparagus stems with a sharp knife, wash, then tie tightly together in small bundles. Stand the asparagus upright in a pan of boiling salted water so that the tips emerge just above water level. Cook for about 20 minutes or until the tips are soft to the touch, then drain, untie and place in individual warmed serving dishes: keep hot.

Heat half the butter in a large frying pan (skillet) until it turns brown. Break the eggs into the pan and sprinkle with salt and pepper to taste. Cook until the egg whites set slightly.

Using a spatula, remove the eggs and place them on top of the asparagus. Melt the remaining butter in the pan and sprinkle over the asparagus. Top with the Parmesan. Serve immediately.
SERVES 4

TORTA DI PATATE

Potato Cake

Metric/Imperial	American
575 g/1¼ lb potatoes, peeled	1¼ lb potatoes, peeled
125 g/4½ oz plain flour	1 cup plus 2 tablespoons all-purpose flour
salt and freshly ground black pepper	salt and freshly ground black pepper
3 eggs beaten	3 eggs, beaten
4 tablespoons olive oil	¼ cup olive oil

Grate the potato into a bowl. Sift in the flour, with ¼ teaspoon salt and a pinch of pepper. Stir well, then mix in the eggs to form a soft, pliable dough.

Heat the oil in a frying pan (skillet), add the mixture and level it. Fry for about 7 minutes on each side until golden brown. Turn onto a warmed serving dish and serve immediately.
SERVES 6

ABOVE: **Funghi al funghetto; Asparagi alla milanese; Cavolo rosso alla bolzanese**

ABOVE: **Asparagi in salsa;**
Radicchio alla trevisana
RIGHT: **Fave stufate**

ASPARAGI IN SALSA
Asparagus with Egg Sauce

Metric/Imperial	American
1 kg/2 lb asparagus	2 lb asparagus
salt	salt
4 hard-boiled eggs, finely chopped	4 hard-cooked eggs, finely chopped
7 tablespoons olive oil	7 tablespoons olive oil
2 tablespoons wine vinegar	2 tablespoons wine vinegar
freshly ground black pepper	freshly ground black pepper

Scrape the lower part of the asparagus stems with a sharp knife, wash, then tie tightly together in small bundles. Stand the asparagus upright in a pan of boiling salted water so that the tips emerge just above water level. Cook for about 20 minutes or until the tips are soft to the touch, then drain, untie and leave to cool.

Put the eggs in a bowl, then gradually blend in the oil, vinegar and salt and pepper to taste. Arrange the asparagus on a serving platter, pour over the sauce and serve cold.

SERVES 4 TO 6

VERZA AFFOGATA
Cabbage with Bacon

Metric/Imperial	American
100 g/4 oz streaky bacon, diced	½ cup diced fatty bacon
1 garlic clove, peeled and chopped	1 garlic clove, peeled and chopped
1 rosemary sprig	1 rosemary sprig
1 medium savoy cabbage, shredded	1 medium savoy cabbage, shredded
150 ml/¼ pint chicken stock	⅔ cup chicken stock
salt and freshly ground black pepper	salt and freshly ground black pepper

Put the bacon in a large heavy pan with the garlic and the rosemary leaves. Fry briskly for 5 minutes until browned.

Lower the heat and add the shredded cabbage, stock and salt and pepper to taste. Cover and cook gently for 40 minutes, stirring frequently. Serve immediately.

SERVES 4 TO 6

RADICCHIO ALLA TREVISANA

Grilled (Broiled) Radicchio

Metric/Imperial	American
1 kg/2 lb radicchio, halved	2 lb radicchio, halved
7 tablespoons olive oil	7 tablespoons olive oil
salt and freshly ground black pepper	salt and freshly ground black pepper

Sprinkle the radicchio with the oil and salt and pepper to taste. Cook under a preheated hot grill (broiler) for 10 minutes, turning frequently. Transfer to a warmed serving dish and serve immediately.
SERVES 4 TO 6

ASPARAGI ALLA PARMIGIANA

Asparagus Baked with Parmesan

Metric/Imperial	American
1 kg/2 lb asparagus	2 lb asparagus
salt	salt
100 g/4 oz butter, melted	½ cup butter, melted
75 g/3 oz Parmesan cheese*, grated	¾ cup grated Parmesan cheese*
freshly ground black pepper	freshly ground black pepper

Scrape the lower part of the asparagus stems with a sharp knife, wash, then tie tightly together in small bundles. Stand the asparagus upright in a pan of boiling salted water so that the tips just emerge above water level. Cook for 15 to 20 minutes until almost tender, then drain and untie them.

Arrange the asparagus in layers in an ovenproof dish, sprinkling each layer with the melted butter, Parmesan and pepper to taste. Bake in a preheated moderately hot oven (200°C/400°F/Gas Mark 6) for 15 to 20 minutes. Serve immediately.
SERVES 4

MELANZANE ALLA PARMIGIANA

Aubergines (Eggplants) with Tomatoes and Ham

Metric/Imperial	American
4 aubergines	4 eggplants
salt	salt
25 g/1 oz butter	2 tablespoons butter
2 tablespoons olive oil	2 tablespoons olive oil
1 onion, peeled and sliced	1 onion, peeled and sliced
100 g/4 oz prosciutto* or other raw cured ham, diced	½ cup diced prosciutto* or other raw cured ham
3 ripe tomatoes, skinned and chopped	3 ripe tomatoes, skinned and chopped
freshly ground black pepper	freshly ground black pepper

Cook the aubergines (eggplants) in plenty of boiling salted water for 10 minutes. Drain, then dry thoroughly and slice lengthways.

Heat the butter and oil in a flameproof casserole, add the onion and fry gently for 5 minutes. Add the ham and tomatoes and fry for a further 5 minutes. Add the aubergines (eggplants) and salt and pepper to taste, then cover and simmer for 20 to 30 minutes. Serve hot.
SERVES 4

FAVE STUFATE

Broad (Lima) beans with Mortadella

Metric/Imperial	American
25 g/1 oz chopped ham fat or lard	2 tablespoons chopped ham fat or lard
2 onions, peeled and sliced	2 onions, peeled and sliced
1 kg/2 lb fresh broad beans, shelled	2 lb fresh lima beans, shelled
salt and freshly ground black pepper	salt and freshly ground black pepper
50 g/2 oz mortadella*, chopped	¼ cup chopped mortadella*
200 ml/8 fl oz chicken stock	1 cup chicken stock
100 g/4 oz butter	½ cup butter
4–6 slices stale bread	4–6 slices stale bread

Heat the ham fat or lard in a flameproof casserole. Add the onions and cook for 5 minutes. Add the beans and salt and pepper to taste, then stir in the mortadella and stock. Cover and cook gently for 20 minutes or until tender.

Melt the butter in a large frying pan (skillet) and fry the bread slices until golden on both sides. Drain thoroughly and arrange on a warmed serving platter. Spoon over the beans and serve immediately
SERVES 4

Early in the morning, the gondolas in Venice can be seen laden with colourful fruit and vegetables, delivering to the shops and restaurants along the canal side. The Venetians are very proud of the high quality of their vegetables, particularly their young tender asparagus and early spring peas. Perhaps the most unusual vegetable to come from this region is *radicchio*, a bitter-tasting crisp vegetable which is mostly eaten raw in salads like lettuce. Its bright red colour makes an attractive addition to any salad bowl, especially in the winter months. It can also be grilled (broiled), or stuffed and baked like cabbage.

CAVOLFIORE FRITTO

Cauliflower Fritters

Metric/Imperial	American
100 g/4 oz plain flour	1 cup all-purpose flour
salt and freshly ground black pepper	salt and freshly ground black pepper
1 egg, beaten	1 egg, beaten
150 ml/¼ pint dry white wine (approximately)	⅔ cup dry white wine (approximately)
1 tablespoon aniseed liqueur (optional)	1 tablespoon aniseed liqueur (optional)
1 kg/2 lb cauliflower, divided into florets	2 lb cauliflower, divided into florets
vegetable oil for deep-frying	vegetable oil for deep-frying

Sift the flour with ¼ teaspoon salt and a pinch of pepper into a bowl, make a well in the centre, then add the egg and half the wine. Mix thoroughly, then stir in the aniseed liqueur, if using, and enough of the remaining wine to make a thick batter. Beat thoroughly, then cover and leave to stand for 1 hour.

Meanwhile, blanch the cauliflower in boiling salted water for 1 to 2 minutes. Drain and leave to cool.

Heat the oil in a deep-fat fryer. Dip the florets one at a time into the batter, then deep-fry a few at a time in the hot oil until golden brown. Drain on absorbent kitchen paper. Arrange on a warmed serving dish and sprinkle with salt. Serve immediately.

SERVES 4 TO 6

FAGIOLI ALL'UCCELLETTO

Broad (Lima) Beans in Tomato Sauce

Metric/Imperial	American
6 tablespoons olive oil	6 tablespoons olive oil
2 garlic cloves, peeled and chopped	2 garlic cloves, peeled and chopped
2 sage sprigs	2 sage sprigs
freshly ground black pepper	freshly ground black pepper
1 kg/2 lb fresh broad beans, shelled	2 lb fresh lima beans, shelled
salt	salt
350 g/12 oz tomatoes, skinned and chopped	1½ cups skinned and chopped tomatoes

Heat the oil in a flameproof casserole, add the garlic, sage and pepper to taste and fry gently for 5 minutes. Remove from the heat, add the beans and a pinch of salt and leave to stand for 3 to 4 minutes.

Add the tomatoes, cover and cook for 20 minutes or until the beans are tender, stirring occasionally. Remove the sage sprigs and serve immediately.

SERVES 4 TO 6

FAGIOLINI DI SANT'ANNA

French (Green) Beans in Garlic Sauce

Metric/Imperial	American
3 tablespoons olive oil	3 tablespoons olive oil
2 garlic cloves, peeled and crushed	2 garlic cloves, peeled and crushed
1 large ripe tomato, skinned and chopped	1 large ripe tomato, skinned and chopped
575 g/1¼ lb French beans, halved	1¼ lb green beans, halved
salt and freshly ground black pepper	salt and freshly ground black pepper

Heat the oil in a flameproof casserole, add the garlic and fry gently until browned. Stir in the tomato, then add the beans. Add enough water to barely cover the beans, then add salt and pepper to taste and bring to the boil. Lower the heat, cover and simmer for 20 to 25 minutes until the beans are tender. Remove the lid and increase the heat towards the end of the cooking time to reduce and thicken the liquor. Serve hot or cold.

SERVES 4

Carciofi alla guidea; Spinaci alla romana; Fagiolini di Sant'Anna

The Romans have the Jewish community in the city to thank for the pretty dish *Carciofi alla giudea*. In the Jewish quarter of Rome, this dish of deep-fried artichokes which look like roses is a speciality in many of the restaurants.

CARCIOFI ALLA GIUDEA

Fried Artichokes

Metric/Imperial	American
4 young globe artichokes	4 young globe artichokes
salt and freshly ground black pepper	salt and freshly ground black pepper
vegetable oil for shallow-frying	vegetable oil for shallow-frying

Remove the hard outer leaves, chokes and tips from the artichokes. Flatten the artichokes slightly by holding them upside down by their stems and pressing them against a work surface. Sprinkle the insides with salt and pepper.

Heat enough oil in a large frying pan (skillet) to cover the base of the pan, then place half the artichokes in the oil, stems downwards. Fry over moderate heat for 10 minutes, then turn over, increase the heat and fry for a further 10 minutes, turning frequently until golden brown and crunchy on all sides.

Drain the artichokes thoroughly on absorbent kitchen paper and keep hot while cooking the remainder. Serve immediately.

SERVES 4

SPINACI ALLA ROMANA

Spinach with Raisins and Pine Kernels

Metric/Imperial	American
1 kg/2 lb spinach	2 lb spinach
2 tablespoons olive oil	2 tablespoons olive oil
25 g/1 oz butter	2 tablespoons butter
1 garlic clove, peeled and sliced	1 garlic clove, peeled and sliced
25 g/1 oz pine kernels	$\frac{1}{4}$ cup pine kernels
25 g/1 oz seedless raisins, soaked in lukewarm water for 15 minutes and drained	$\frac{1}{3}$ cup seedless raisins, soaked in lukewarm water for 15 minutes and drained
salt and freshly ground black pepper	salt and freshly ground black pepper

Wash the spinach, then cook in a large pan, with only the water clinging to the leaves, until just tender. Drain well and squeeze out any excess water.

Heat the oil and butter in a heavy pan, add the garlic, fry gently until browned, then discard. Add the spinach to the pan with the pine kernels and raisins. Cook for 10 minutes, stirring frequently, then add salt and pepper to taste. Serve hot.

SERVES 4

Globe artichokes are one of the most popular vegetables in Italy, and they are readily available in most regions, although they are perhaps best liked in Lazio. Italian artichokes are usually very small and tender; some varieties are chokeless, so the whole artichoke can be eaten.

Many foods which we associate with France in fact originated in Italy. Petits pois, for instance, were brought to the court of Louis XIV from Genoa in the seventeenth century. They caused an immediate sensation and were considered a great luxury.

BROCCOLO STRASCINATO

Broccoli with Garlic

Metric/Imperial	American
1 kg/2 lb broccoli	2 lb broccoli
salt	salt
4 tablespoons olive oil	¼ cup olive oil
2 garlic cloves, peeled and sliced	2 garlic cloves, peeled and sliced
freshly ground black pepper	freshly ground black pepper

Cook the broccoli in boiling salted water for 15 minutes until almost tender. Drain and divide into florets.

Heat the oil in a heavy pan, add the garlic and fry gently until browned, then discard. Add the broccoli to the pan with salt and pepper to taste. Cook gently for 10 minutes, shaking the pan. Serve immediately.

SERVES 4 TO 6

FUNGHI ARROSTO ALLA ROMANA

Baked Mushrooms

Metric/Imperial	American
350 g/12 oz mushrooms, sliced	3 cups sliced mushrooms
salt and freshly ground black pepper	salt and freshly ground black pepper
1 tablespoon chopped parsley	1 tablespoon chopped parsley
1 garlic clove, peeled and crushed	1 garlic clove, peeled and crushed
2 tablespoons olive oil	2 tablespoons olive oil

Arrange the mushrooms in a single layer in an oiled ovenproof dish. Sprinkle with salt and pepper to taste, the parsley, garlic and oil. Bake in a preheated moderate oven (180°C/350°F/Gas Mark 4) for 20 minutes. Serve immediately.

SERVES 4

CARCIOFI COI PISELLI

Artichokes with Peas

Metric/Imperial	American
4 young globe artichokes	4 young globe artichokes
4 tablespoons olive oil	4 tablespoons olive oil
1 onion, peeled and finely chopped	1 onion, peeled and finely chopped
350 g/12 oz fresh shelled peas	¾ lb fresh shelled peas
75 g/3 oz raw ham or bacon, chopped	⅓ cup chopped raw ham or bacon
salt and freshly ground black pepper	salt and freshly ground black pepper
6–8 tablespoons chicken stock	6–8 tablespoons chicken stock

Remove the hard outer leaves and the chokes from the artichokes, then slice the artichokes lengthways.

Heat the oil in a large heavy pan, add the onion and fry gently for 5 minutes. Add the artichokes, cook for 15 minutes, then add the peas, ham and salt and pepper to taste. Stir in the stock and cook gently for 15 to 20 minutes, stirring occasionally, until the artichokes and peas are tender. Serve immediately.

SERVES 4

ABOVE: **Peperonata;**
Carciofi coi piselli
LEFT: **Funghi arrosto alla**
romana

PISELLI ALLA ROMANA COL PROSCIUTTO

Peas and Ham Roman-Style

Metric/Imperial	American
65 g/2½ oz butter	5 tablespoons butter
150 g/5 oz raw ham or bacon, with fat and lean chopped separately	5 oz raw ham or bacon, with fat and lean chopped separately
1 onion, peeled and sliced	1 onion, peeled and sliced
450 g/1 lb fresh shelled peas	1 lb fresh shelled peas
7 tablespoons chicken stock	7 tablespoons chicken stock
salt and freshly ground black pepper	salt and freshly ground black pepper

Melt half the butter in a heavy pan, add the ham or bacon fat and the onion and fry gently for 5 minutes. Add the peas, 2 tablespoons of the stock and a pinch each of salt and pepper. Cover and simmer for 10 minutes, stirring in the remaining stock a little at a time.

Stir in the remaining butter and the lean ham or bacon. Cook for a further 5 to 10 minutes until the peas are tender. Serve immediately.

SERVES 4

PEPERONATA

Peppers with Tomatoes and Onion

Metric/Imperial	American
6 tablespoons olive oil	6 tablespoons olive oil
1 onion, peeled and sliced	1 onion, peeled and sliced
1 garlic clove, peeled and sliced	1 garlic clove, peeled and sliced
4 large fleshy green or red peppers, cored, seeded and sliced	4 large fleshy green or red peppers, cored, seeded and sliced
salt and freshly ground black pepper	salt and freshly ground black pepper
350 g/12 oz tomatoes, skinned and chopped	1½ cups skinned and chopped tomatoes
1 tablespoon chopped parsley	1 tablespoon chopped parsley

Heat the oil in a heavy pan, add the onion and garlic and cook gently for 5 minutes. Add the peppers and salt and pepper to taste. Cook for a further 5 minutes, stirring occasionally.

Add the tomatoes and parsley. Adjust the seasoning, cover and simmer for 20 to 30 minutes, stirring frequently, until thickened. Serve hot or cold.

SERVES 4

Vegetables/167

MELANZANE RIPIENE
Stuffed Aubergines (Eggplants)

Metric/Imperial	American
4 small aubergines, cut in half lengthways	4 small eggplants, cut in half lengthways
2 tablespoons olive oil	2 tablespoons olive oil
1 onion, peeled and chopped	1 onion, peeled and chopped
225 g/8 oz tomatoes, skinned and chopped	1 cup skinned and chopped tomatoes
1 tablespoon chopped parsley	1 tablespoon chopped parsley
salt and freshly ground black pepper	salt and freshly ground black pepper
225 g/8 oz scamorza or mozzarella cheese★, sliced	½ lb scamorza or mozzarella cheese★, sliced
4 hard-boiled eggs, sliced	4 hard-cooked eggs, sliced
parsley sprigs to garnish	parsley sprigs to garnish

Scoop out the flesh of the aubergines (eggplants) with a spoon, leaving 1 cm/½ inch shells. Finely chop the flesh.

Heat the oil in a heavy pan, add the onion and fry gently for 5 minutes. Add the aubergine (eggplant) flesh, tomatoes, parsley and salt and pepper to taste. Stir well, then cook gently for 15 minutes.

Arrange the aubergine (eggplant) shells in an oiled shallow ovenproof dish and bake in a preheated moderate oven (180°C/350°F/Gas Mark 4) for 10 minutes. Spoon half the tomato mixture into the aubergine (eggplant) shells. Cover with alternate layers of cheese and egg slices. Spoon the remaining tomato mixture over the top, then return to the oven for a further 10 minutes. Serve hot or cold, garnished with parsley sprigs.

SERVES 4

MELANZANE A FUNGHETTI

Aubergines (Eggplants) with Tomato and Garlic Sauce

Metric/Imperial	American
2 large aubergines, cut into 2.5 cm/1 inch cubes	2 large eggplants, cut into 1 inch cubes
salt	salt
150 ml/$\frac{1}{4}$ pint olive oil	$\frac{2}{3}$ cup olive oil
2 garlic cloves, peeled and crushed	2 garlic cloves, peeled and crushed
350 g/12 oz tomatoes, skinned and chopped	1$\frac{1}{2}$ cups skinned and chopped tomatoes
1 tablespoon capers	1 tablespoon capers
freshly ground black pepper	freshly ground black pepper

Put the aubergines (eggplants) in a colander, sprinkle lightly with salt and leave to stand for 1 hour.

Rinse the aubergines (eggplants) under cold running water, then drain and dry thoroughly. Heat the oil in a heavy pan, add the garlic and fry gently until browned. Add the aubergines (eggplants) and fry for 10 minutes, then add the tomatoes, capers and salt and pepper to taste. Cover and simmer for 30 to 40 minutes, stirring occasionally. Serve hot or cold.
SERVES 4

CARCIOFI RIPIENI

Stuffed Artichokes

Metric/Imperial	American
4 young globe artichokes	4 young globe artichokes
125 g/4$\frac{1}{2}$ oz canned tuna fish in oil, drained and mashed	4$\frac{1}{2}$ oz canned tuna fish in oil, drained and mashed
4 canned anchovies, drained and mashed	4 canned anchovies, drained and mashed
1 garlic clove, peeled and crushed	1 garlic clove, peeled and crushed
50 g/2 oz capers, mashed	$\frac{1}{4}$ cup capers, mashed
1 tablespoon chopped parsley	1 tablespoon chopped parsley
salt and freshly ground black pepper	salt and freshly ground black pepper
6 tablespoons olive oil	6 tablespoons olive oil

Remove the hard outer leaves and chokes from the artichokes.

Mix the tuna with the anchovies, garlic, capers, parsley and salt and pepper to taste. Fill the centres of the artichokes with this mixture.

Place the artichokes very close together in a heavy pan and sprinkle with the oil. Add enough water to come halfway up the artichokes. Cover and cook for 30 minutes or until tender. Serve immediately.
SERVES 4

Carciofi ripiene; Insalata di rinforzo; Melanzane ripiene

INSALATA DI RINFORZO

Cauliflower Salad

This is a Christmas salad which Italian housewives often add to (or 'reinforce') with new ingredients each day.

Metric/Imperial	American
1 cauliflower, divided into florets	1 cauliflower, divided into florets
salt	salt
50 g/2 oz green olives, halved and stoned	$\frac{1}{3}$ cup pitted green olives
50 g/2 oz black olives, halved and stoned	$\frac{1}{3}$ cup pitted ripe olives
50 g/2 oz pickled gherkins, sliced	$\frac{1}{3}$ cup sliced sweet dill pickles
50 g/2 oz pickled peppers, chopped	$\frac{1}{3}$ cup chopped pickled peppers
1 tablespoon capers	1 tablespoon capers
6 canned anchovies, drained	6 canned anchovies, drained
6 tablespoons olive oil	6 tablespoons olive oil
1 tablespoon vinegar	1 tablespoon vinegar
freshly ground black pepper	freshly ground black pepper

Cook the cauliflower in boiling salted water for 5 minutes; it should still be quite crisp. Drain and leave to cool.

Put the cauliflower in a bowl with the olives, gherkins (dill pickles), peppers, capers and anchovies. Add the oil, vinegar and salt and pepper to taste and fold gently to mix. Chill for at least 30 minutes before serving, to allow the flavours to mingle. Serve cold.
SERVES 4 TO 5

ABOVE: **Funghi porcini al forno; Pomodori con pasta**
RIGHT: **Melanzane alla palermitana**

The region of Campania has extremely fertile soil, due to the volcanic action of Mt Vesuvius just behind the city of Naples. Fruit and vegetables grow in profusion, and sometimes as many as three crops can be harvested in one year from the same piece of land.

PARMIGIANA DI MELANZANE

Aubergine (Eggplant), Cheese and Tomato Bake

Metric/Imperial

4 large aubergines, sliced
   lengthways
salt
olive oil for shallow-frying
450 g/1 lb tomatoes,
   skinned, chopped and
   seeded
1 small onion, peeled and
   chopped
1 tablespoon chopped basil
freshly ground black pepper
plain flour for coating
175 g/6 oz mozzarella
   cheese★, sliced
2 hard-boiled eggs, sliced
100 g/4 oz Parmesan
   cheese★, grated

American

4 large eggplants, sliced
   lengthways
salt
olive oil for shallow-frying
2 cups skinned, chopped and
   seeded tomatoes
1 small onion, peeled and
   chopped
1 tablespoon chopped basil
freshly ground black pepper
all-purpose flour for coating
6 oz mozzarella cheese★,
   sliced
2 hard-cooked eggs, sliced
1 cup grated Parmesan
   cheese★

Put the aubergines (eggplants) in a colander, sprinkle lightly with salt, then leave to stand for 1 hour.

Heat 3 tablespoons oil in a heavy pan, add the tomatoes, onion, half the basil and salt and pepper to taste. Simmer for 30 minutes.

Meanwhile, rinse the aubergines (eggplants) under cold running water, then drain, dry thoroughly and coat with flour. Cover the base of a large frying pan (skillet) with a thin layer of oil. Place over moderate heat and fry the aubergine (eggplant) slices in batches until golden brown on both sides. Drain on absorbent kitchen paper.

Work the sauce through a sieve (strainer). Spread a thin layer over the bottom of an oiled ovenproof dish. Cover with a layer of aubergines (eggplants), then a layer of cheese and egg slices. Sprinkle with Parmesan and a little of the remaining basil.

Continue these layers until all the ingredients are used, finishing with a layer of sauce. Bake in a preheated moderate oven (180°C/350°F/Gas Mark 4) for 25 to 30 minutes. Serve hot or cold.
SERVES 4 TO 6

POMODORI CON PASTA

Tomatoes Stuffed with Pasta

*Any small pasta can be used for this recipe;
e.g. annellini, farfallette.*

Metric/Imperial	American
6 large firm tomatoes	6 large firm tomatoes
100 g/4 oz small pasta	¼ lb small pasta
salt	salt
2 teaspoons chopped parsley	2 teaspoons chopped parsley
1 teaspoon chopped mint	1 teaspoon chopped mint
3 tablespoons olive oil	3 tablespoons olive oil
freshly ground black pepper	freshly ground black pepper
parsley sprigs to garnish	parsley sprigs to garnish

Cut the tops off the tomatoes and reserve. Scoop out
the flesh from the tomatoes, discard the seeds and set
aside the flesh. Stand the tomatoes upside down on a
plate and leave to drain.

Meanwhile, cook the pasta in boiling salted water
until *al dente*; drain thoroughly. Put the pasta in a bowl,
add the tomato flesh, parsley, mint and half the oil and
mix well.

Sprinkle the insides of the tomatoes with salt and
pepper, then fill with the pasta. Cover each tomato
with its 'lid'. Stand upright in an oiled ovenproof dish
and sprinkle with the remaining oil. Bake in a
preheated moderate oven (180°C/350°F/Gas Mark 4)
for 20 minutes or until the tomatoes are tender. Serve
hot or cold, garnished with parsley.

SERVES 6

FUNGHI PORCINI AL FORNO

Baked Stuffed Mushrooms

Metric/Imperial	American
2 garlic cloves, peeled and crushed	2 garlic cloves, peeled and crushed
1 tablespoon chopped parsley	1 tablespoon chopped parsley
50 g/2 oz dried breadcrumbs	½ cup dried bread crumbs
4 tablespoons olive oil	¼ cup olive oil
salt and freshly ground black pepper	salt and freshly ground black pepper
12 large field mushrooms, peeled	12 large field mushrooms, peeled
1 tablespoon chopped marjoram	1 tablespoon chopped marjoram

Put the garlic in a bowl with the parsley, breadcrumbs,
3 tablespoons oil and salt and pepper to taste. Mix well.

Arrange the mushrooms in a single layer in an oiled
ovenproof dish, cup side uppermost. Fill with the
breadcrumb mixture and sprinkle with the remaining
oil and the marjoram. Bake in a preheated moderately
hot oven (190°C/375°F/Gas Mark 5) for 15 to 20
minutes. Serve immediately.

SERVES 4

MELANZANE ALLA PALERMITANA

Aubergines (Eggplants) Palermo-Style

Metric/Imperial	American
4 large aubergines	4 large eggplants
salt	salt
vegetable oil for deep-frying	vegetable oil for deep-frying
freshly ground black pepper	freshly ground black pepper

Slice the aubergines (eggplants) lengthways, keeping
them attached at the base. Cut each slice into thin strips.
Put them in a colander, sprinkle lightly with salt and
leave to stand for 1 hour.

Rinse the aubergines (eggplants) under cold running
water, then drain and dry thoroughly. Heat the oil in a
deep-fryer until very hot, then deep-fry each aubergine (eggplant) separately until golden brown. Drain
on absorbent kitchen paper and keep hot while frying
the remainder. Sprinkle with salt and pepper and serve
immediately.

SERVES 4

Moving south, sun-kissed
vegetables grow in
abundance. Peppers,
aubergines (eggplants),
tomatoes and courgettes
(zucchini) are common,
and the number of
recipes using these
vegetables seems to be
endless. The region of
Apulia is said to be the
best for growing
vegetables in Italy, and
vegetable connoisseurs
even rate highly the dried
vegetables from this area.
These are dried in the hot
summer sun for use later
on in the winter, and this
is said to be the reason for
their being so good.

ZUCCA ALL'AGRODOLCE

Sweet and Sour Pumpkin

Metric/Imperial	American
vegetable oil for shallow-frying	vegetable oil for shallow-frying
575 g/1¼ lb yellow pumpkin, skinned, seeded and thinly sliced	1¼ lb yellow pumpkin, skinned, seeded and thinly sliced
3–4 tablespoons wine vinegar	3–4 tablespoons wine vinegar
25 g/1 oz sugar	2 tablespoons sugar
1 tablespoon chopped mint	1 tablespoon chopped mint
2 garlic cloves, peeled and crushed	2 garlic cloves, peeled and crushed
salt and freshly ground black pepper	salt and freshly ground black pepper

Heat the oil to a depth of 5 mm/¼ inch in a large frying pan (skillet). Add the pumpkin slices and fry until golden brown on both sides. Drain off most of the oil from the pan, then add the vinegar, sugar, mint, garlic and salt and pepper to taste. Cook for a further 10 minutes, turning the pumpkin slices over halfway through cooking. Serve immediately.

SERVES 4

FUNGHI ALLA TRAPANESE

Mushrooms in Tomato and Wine Sauce

Metric/Imperial	American
450 g/1 lb mushrooms, sliced	5 cups sliced mushrooms
juice of 1 lemon	juice of 1 lemon
4 tablespoons olive oil	¼ cup olive oil
1 onion, peeled and chopped	1 onion, peeled and chopped
2 garlic cloves, peeled and crushed	2 garlic cloves, peeled and crushed
450 g/1 lb tomatoes, skinned, chopped and seeded	2 cups skinned, chopped and seeded tomatoes
salt and freshly ground black pepper	salt and freshly ground black pepper
7 tablespoons dry white wine	7 tablespoons dry white wine
chopped parsley to garnish	chopped parsley to garnish

Put the mushrooms in a bowl, sprinkle with the lemon juice and leave to stand.

Meanwhile, heat the oil in a heavy pan, add the onion and garlic and fry gently for 5 minutes. Add the tomatoes and simmer for 15 minutes, then add the mushrooms and salt and pepper to taste and simmer for a further 5 minutes.

Add the wine, increase the heat and boil until the wine has evaporated. Lower the heat and cook gently for about 10 minutes. Transfer to a warmed serving dish, sprinkle with parsley and serve immediately.

SERVES 4

ABOVE: **Carote in insalata; Caponata**

CAPONATA

Aubergines (Eggplants) with Tomatoes and Olives

Metric/Imperial	American
450 g/1 lb aubergines, diced	1 lb eggplants, diced
salt	salt
4 tablespoons vegetable oil	4 tablespoons vegetable oil
6 tablespoons olive oil	6 tablespoons olive oil
450 g/1 lb onions, peeled and finely chopped	1 lb onions, peeled and finely chopped
100 g/4 oz celery, parboiled and chopped	¼ lb celery, parboiled and chopped
150 g/5 oz green olives, halved and stoned	1 cup pitted green olives
450 g/1 lb tomatoes, skinned and mashed	2 cups skinned and mashed tomatoes
freshly ground black pepper	freshly ground black pepper
25 g/1 oz sugar	2 tablespoons sugar
7 tablespoons wine vinegar	7 tablespoons wine vinegar
2 tablespoons capers	2 tablespoons capers

CAROTE IN INSALATA

Carrot and Celery Salad

Metric/Imperial	American
1 head of celery, sliced	1 head of celery, sliced
450 g/1 lb young carrots, scrubbed and sliced diagonally	1 lb young carrots, scrubbed and sliced diagonally
3–4 tablespoons olive oil	3–4 tablespoons olive oil
juice of 1 lemon	juice of 1 lemon
1 tablespoon sugar	1 tablespoon sugar
salt and freshly ground black pepper	salt and freshly ground black pepper

Put the celery and carrots in a serving dish. Put the oil, lemon juice, sugar and a pinch each of salt and pepper in a screw-top jar and shake until thoroughly blended. Pour over the vegetables and toss well. Leave in a cool place for 1 hour before serving.
SERVES 6

FAGIOLI CON LE VERZE

Haricot (Navy) Beans and Cabbage

Metric/Imperial	American
350 g/12 oz dried haricot beans	1½ cups dried navy beans
2 pieces fennel, chopped	2 pieces fennel, chopped
1 onion, peeled and chopped	1 onion, peeled and chopped
1 green cabbage, shredded	1 green cabbage, shredded
4 tablespoons tomato purée	¼ cup tomato paste
salt and freshly ground black pepper	salt and freshly ground black pepper
2 tablespoons olive oil	2 tablespoons olive oil
100 g/4 oz streaky bacon, derinded and chopped	½ cup chopped fatty bacon
2 garlic cloves, peeled and crushed	2 garlic cloves, peeled and crushed

Soak the beans in lukewarm water overnight.

Drain the beans and place in a flameproof casserole. Cover with cold water and bring to the boil. Lower the heat, cover and simmer for 45 minutes, stirring occasionally.

Stir in the fennel, onion, cabbage, tomato purée (paste) and salt and pepper to taste and cook for a further 45 minutes or until the beans are tender.

Meanwhile, heat the oil in a small pan, add the bacon and garlic and fry until golden. Add to the casserole and cook for a further 5 minutes. Serve hot.
SERVES 6

Put the aubergines (eggplants) in a colander, sprinkle lightly with salt, then leave to stand for 1 hour.

Rinse the aubergines (eggplants) under cold running water, then drain and dry thoroughly. Heat the vegetable oil in a frying pan (skillet) and fry the aubergines (eggplants) until golden brown on all sides. Drain on absorbent kitchen paper.

Heat the olive oil in a heavy pan, add the onions and fry gently for 15 minutes. Add the celery, olives, tomatoes and a pinch each of salt and pepper. Cook for 5 minutes, then add the sugar, vinegar, capers and aubergines (eggplants). Cook for 10 minutes until the vinegar has evaporated.

Remove from the heat, adjust the seasoning and leave to cool. Serve cold.
SERVES 4

Vegetables in Italy are very often served as an *antipasto*, in which case they are usually either raw or only very lightly cooked and cooled. They are frequently tossed in a dressing of olive oil, lemon juice, herbs and seasonings. Globe artichokes, French (green) and broad (lima) beans, courgettes (zucchini), mushrooms, asparagus, fennel and carrots are among those served this way. Only freshly picked seasonal vegetables are used, when they are at the height of perfection. Italians rarely let any vegetable grow past its prime.

Desserts & Pâtisserie

Italians rarely finish a meal with a dessert; cheese and fresh fruit are normally served instead. They prefer to eat sweets, cakes and pastries at other times during the day. Possibly the only exceptions to this are *gelati* – ice creams, water ices and *granite* for which Italy is renowned. Many people say the Sicilians make the best ices, simply using fresh fruit purée and sugar for water ices, with eggs and cream added for ice cream.

Another area in which the Italians excel themselves is pastry-making. Italian pastry is rich but light, a combination that is difficult to achieve without some measure of skill and practice. For this reason, apart from on such special occasions as feast days, weddings and christenings, the Italian housewife buys most of her pastries from her local pâtisserie. Italian pastries contain delicious fillings;

fresh and candied fruit, preserves, nuts, honey and *ricotta* cheese are popular. *Cassata Siciliana* (see page 37), the famous dessert cake, has layers of *ricotta* frozen with sponge, and there are even ices made from *ricotta* mixed with fruit and sugar.

Throughout Italy, special yeast cakes are eaten on festive days, including the famous *panettone* at Christmas and *colomba* at Easter. Biscuits (cookies) are popular too, particularly the almond macaroons from Turin, called *amaretti* (see page 176). There are many different kinds of *amaretti*, from the tiny button-shaped ones to *pinoccate* which are made with pine nuts.

Frittelle (sweet fritters – see page 179), *bignè* (fritters) and *bomboloni* (doughnuts – see page 180) are sold on street corners, especially on festival and carnival days.

PIEMONTE & VALLE D'AOSTA

CIAMBELLINE VALDOSTANE

Ring-shaped Biscuits (Cookies)

Metric/Imperial	American
450 g/1 lb fine maize flour	4 cups fine maize flour
50 g/2 oz plain flour	½ cup all-purpose flour
250 g/9 oz butter, cut into small pieces	1 cup plus 2 tablespoons butter, cut into small pieces
225 g/8 oz sugar	1¼ cups sugar
3 eggs, beaten	3 eggs, beaten
finely grated rind of ½ lemon	finely grated rind of ½ lemon

Mix the two flours together in a bowl and rub in the butter, using the fingertips. Add the sugar, eggs and lemon rind, then knead well together until smooth.

Put the mixture into a piping (pastry) bag, fitted with a 1 cm/½ inch plain nozzle, and pipe small rings onto a baking (cookie) sheet. Bake in a preheated moderate oven (180°C/350°F/Gas Mark 4) for 20 minutes or until golden. Leave on the sheets for 5 minutes, then transfer to a wire rack and cool completely.

MAKES 25 TO 30

PRUS MARTIN AL VINO

Pears Cooked in Wine

The Piedmontese most frequently use the locally produced Barolo wine for this dish, but it is equally good with medium white wine.

Metric/Imperial	American
750 g/1¾ lb firm cooking pears, peeled	1¾ lb firm cooking pears, peeled
450 ml/¾ pint medium red or white wine	2 cups medium red or white wine
100 g/4 oz sugar	½ cup sugar
4 whole cloves	4 whole cloves
pinch of ground cinnamon	pinch of ground cinnamon

Stand the pears in an ovenproof dish, pour over the wine, then sprinkle with the sugar, cloves and cinnamon.

Bake in a preheated moderate oven (160°C/325°F/Gas Mark 3) for 45 minutes or until the pears are tender and the liquor is thick and syrupy. Serve hot or cold.

SERVES 4 TO 6

PESCHE RIPIENE

Baked Stuffed Peaches

Metric/Imperial	American
4 ripe peaches, halved and stoned	4 ripe peaches, halved and pitted
4 blanched almonds, finely chopped	4 blanched almonds, finely chopped
8 macaroons, crushed	8 macaroons, crushed
75 g/3 oz sugar	⅓ cup sugar
25 g/1 oz cocoa powder	¼ cup unsweetened cocoa
7 tablespoons dry white wine	7 tablespoons dry white wine
40 g/1½ oz butter	3 tablespoons butter

Scoop out a little flesh from the hollows in the peaches and reserve. Mix together the almonds, macaroons, half the sugar, the cocoa, 1 tablespoon wine and the reserved peach flesh. Fill the peach halves with the mixture and top each one with a small piece of butter.

Arrange the peach halves in a buttered ovenproof dish, pour over the remaining wine and sprinkle with the remaining sugar. Bake in a preheated moderate oven (180°C/350°F/Gas Mark 4) for 25 to 30 minutes until the peaches are tender. Serve hot.

SERVES 4

Desserts and puddings as we know them figure rarely at the end of Italian meals, and recipes for these are not usual. The few Italian desserts listed under 'I Dolci' on Italian restaurant menus are probably there to pay a kind of lip-service to those of us who are used to a dessert course at the end of a meal. These desserts usually include a selection of rich and rather heavily decorated gâteaux, and it is rare to see an Italian choosing from this section of a menu. Most Italians prefer to end a meal with cheese or fresh fruit.

AMARETTI
Macaroons

If bitter almonds are not available, use all blanched almonds instead and decrease the amount of sugar by 2 tablespoons.

Metric/Imperial	American
225 g/8 oz blanched almonds	2 cups blanched almonds
50–75 g/2–3 oz bitter almonds	1 cup bitter almonds
350 g/12 oz caster sugar	1½ cups superfine sugar
25 g/1 oz plain flour, sifted	¼ cup all-purpose flour, sifted
4 egg whites	4 egg whites
few drops of vanilla essence	few drops of vanilla extract
¼ teaspoon grated lemon rind	¼ teaspoon grated lemon rind

Grind all the almonds together, using a pestle and mortar.

Place in a bowl with all except 2 tablespoons of the sugar and the flour; stir well to mix. Lightly whisk the egg whites with a fork, then add the vanilla and lemon rind. Add to the almond mixture gradually, until a smooth soft mixture, which holds its shape, is obtained.

Place small spoonfuls of the mixture on a greased and floured baking (cookie) sheet, spacing them well apart. Sprinkle with the remaining sugar and bake in a preheated moderate oven (180°C/350°F/Gas Mark 4) for about 20 minutes or until lightly browned. Transfer to a wire rack to cool completely before serving.

MAKES 35 TO 40

CRUMIRI
Crescent-shaped Biscuits (Cookies)

Metric/Imperial	American
250 g/9 oz fine maize flour	2¼ cups fine maize flour
200 g/7 oz coarse bran flour	1¾ cups coarse bran flour
275 g/10 oz butter, softened and cut into small pieces	1¼ cups butter, softened and cut into small pieces
175 g/6 oz sugar	¾ cup sugar
4 egg yolks	4 egg yolks
2 tablespoons honey	2 tablespoons honey
¼ teaspoon grated lemon rind	¼ teaspoon grated lemon rind

Mix the two flours together on a work surface and make a well in the centre. Add the remaining ingredients and work together, using the fingertips, to give a smooth, firm dough. Form into a ball, cover and chill for 30 minutes.

Put some of the mixture into a piping (pastry) bag, fitted with a 1 cm/½ inch plain nozzle, and pipe 7.5cm/3 inch long pieces onto a baking (cookie) sheet lined with greased greaseproof (wax) paper. Bend the pieces gently into crescent shapes. Repeat with the remaining mixture. Bake in a preheated moderate oven (160°C/325°F/Gas Mark 3) for 15 to 20 minutes until golden brown. Transfer to a wire rack to cool before serving.

MAKES 30 TO 35

BACI DI DAMA
Orange Almond Cookies

Metric/Imperial	American
100 g/4 oz blanched almonds, ground	1 cup ground blanched almonds
100 g/4 oz sugar	½ cup sugar
100 g/4 oz candied orange peel, minced	½ cup minced candied orange peel
100 g/4 oz plain flour, sifted	1 cup all-purpose flour, sifted
6–8 tablespoons milk	6–8 tablespoons milk
50 g/2 oz plain chocolate, melted	⅓ cup semi-sweet chocolate pieces, melted

Put the ground almonds in a bowl with the sugar, orange peel and all but 1 tablespoon of the flour. Mix well, then stir in enough milk to give a smooth, firm dough.

Roll into small balls and place, well apart, on a baking (cookie) sheet lined with greased greaseproof (wax) paper. Sprinkle with the remaining flour, and bake in a preheated moderate oven (180°C/350°F/Gas Mark 4) for 15 minutes or until golden brown.

Transfer to a wire rack to cool. When cold, sandwich the biscuits (cookies) together in pairs with the melted chocolate. Chill in the refrigerator for 1 hour before serving.

MAKES 12 TO 15

BICCIOLANI
Spiced Biscuits (Cookies)

Metric/Imperial	American
575 g/1¼ lb plain flour	5 cups all-purpose flour
200 g/7 oz sugar	1 cup sugar
1 tablespoon ground cinnamon	1 tablespoon ground cinnamon
20 coriander seeds	20 coriander seeds
pinch of salt	pinch of salt
pinch of grated nutmeg	pinch of grated nutmeg
5 whole cloves, ground	5 whole cloves, ground
350 g/12 oz butter, softened and cut into small pieces	1½ cups butter, softened and cut into small pieces
5 egg yolks	5 egg yolks

Sift the flour onto a work surface and mix in the sugar, cinnamon, coriander seeds, salt, nutmeg and cloves. Make a well in the centre, add the butter and egg yolks and work the ingredients together with the fingertips. Knead well together until smooth and quite soft. Cover and chill in the refrigerator for 3 hours.

Put some of the mixture in a piping (pastry) bag, fitted with a large plain nozzle, and pipe long 'ribbons' onto a baking (cookie) sheet lined with greased greaseproof (wax) paper. Repeat with the remaining mixture.

Bake in a preheated moderate oven (160°C/325°F/Gas Mark 3) for 15 to 20 minutes until golden brown. Cut into 9 cm/3½ inch lengths and transfer to a wire rack to cool before serving.

MAKES 30 TO 40

RIGHT: **Baci di dama; Amaretti; Bicciolani; Crumiri**

The Italians, renowned for their sweet tooths, have been fond of biscuits (cookies) for centuries – sugar was first brought to Europe via the Venetian traders. Pastry shop windows are full of different varieties, many of which are purely local to the area in which they are made. These are eaten at odd times in Italian homes – always offered to visitors with a glass of wine, no matter what time of the day they call. *Amaretti* are even eaten with aperitifs before a meal.

TORTA SBRISULONA

Almond Cake

Metric/Imperial	American
300 g/11 oz plain flour	2¾ cups all-purpose flour
100 g/4 oz maize flour	1 cup maize flour
100 g/4 oz butter, cut into small pieces	½ cup butter, cut into small pieces
100 g/4 oz lard, cut into small pieces	½ cup shortening, cut into small pieces
200 g/7 oz blanched almonds, chopped	1¾ cups chopped blanched almonds
200 g/7 oz sugar	1 cup sugar
2 egg yolks	2 egg yolks
finely grated rind of 1 lemon	finely grated rind of 1 lemon
few drops of vanilla essence	few drops of vanilla extract

Sift the flours into a bowl and rub in the butter and lard (shortening) until the mixture resembles fine bread-crumbs. Stir in the almonds and sugar, then add the egg yolks, lemon rind and vanilla. Knead to a smooth, stiff dough.

Put the mixture into a greased 23 cm/9 inch shallow round tin (pan) and smooth the surface. Bake in a preheated moderate oven (160°C/325°F/Gas Mark 3) for 45 minutes.

Leave to stand for 10 minutes before turning out of the tin (pan). Transfer to a wire rack to cool. Cut into wedges before serving.

MAKES ONE 23 CM/9 INCH CAKE

MONTE BIANCO

Chestnut Purée with Cream

There are many versions of this dessert, ranging from elaborate restaurant confections to this simple recipe which seems to resemble the snow-capped Mont Blanc better than most. Serve this dish soon after preparing for optimum flavour.

Metric/Imperial	American
450 g/1 lb chestnuts	1 lb chestnuts
2 tablespoons milk	2 tablespoons milk
175 g/6 oz icing sugar, sifted	1⅓ cups confectioners' sugar, sifted
pinch of salt	pinch of salt
150 ml/¼ pint double cream	⅔ cup heavy cream
2 tablespoons brandy, rum or Strega liqueur	2 tablespoons brandy, rum or Strega liqueur

Cut a cross at the pointed end of each chestnut with a knife. Put them in a pan, cover with water, bring to boil and simmer for 15 minutes. Drain and leave until cool enough to handle. While still quite hot, peel off the shells and inner skins.

Return the chestnuts to the pan, cover with cold water and bring to the boil. Simmer for 45 minutes or until soft. Drain and purée the chestnuts with the milk in an electric blender, or mash using a fork. Stir in the sugar and salt.

Pile the chestnut purée into a mound on a serving dish. Whip the cream with the brandy, rum or liqueur until thick but not stiff. Swirl lightly over the top of the mound, leaving the base uncovered.

Alternatively, spoon the chestnut purée into individual glass dishes and swirl the flavoured whipped cream on top.

SERVES 4

TORTA GENOVESE

Genoese Sponge

Metric/Imperial	American
4 eggs	4 eggs
175 g/6 oz caster sugar	¾ cup superfine sugar
100 g/4 oz plain flour, sifted twice	1 cup all-purpose flour, sifted twice
100 g/4 oz butter, melted	½ cup butter, melted

Put the eggs and 125 g/4½ oz/½ cup sugar in a heatproof bowl standing over a pan of gently simmering water. Whisk until light and fluffy and double its original volume. Remove from the heat and continue whisking until cool.

Add the flour all at once and fold gently into the mixture until evenly blended, then fold in the melted butter.

Spoon the mixture into a lined and greased 20 cm/8 inch round cake tin (pan). Bake in a preheated moderate oven (180°C/350°F/Gas Mark 4) for about 40 minutes or until golden and firm to the touch. Turn out onto a wire rack and leave to cool. Sprinkle with the remaining sugar before serving.

MAKES ONE 20 CM/8 INCH CAKE

Chestnuts are used extensively in Italian recipes, both in sweet and savoury dishes. Once harvested, they are piled into baskets and sold in the markets and food shops all over Italy. So fond are the Italians of this nut that they even go to the trouble of drying them, for use in winter. Canned chestnuts can be used if fresh ones are not available here.

Fritole and *frittelle* (both types of fritters), are typical festive fare in Italy. They are usually sold in the street from kiosks or stands. Carnival fritters are sold on Carnival Night, the day before Lent. Years ago, Carnival Night was a great celebration, particularly on the island of Sicily, where *cannoli* were eaten. These are sweet pastries filled with ricotta cheese and candied fruits; they are still eaten in Sicily, but the tradition of eating them on Carnival Night seems to be gradually dying out.

LEFT: **Monte bianco**
BELOW: **Torta genovese;
Frittelle di mele**

FRIULI-VENEZIA GIULIA

FRITOLE DI CARNEVALE

Spicy Carnival Fritters

Metric/Imperial	American
300 ml/½ pint dry white wine	1¼ cups dry white wine
50 g/2 oz butter	¼ cup butter
400 g/14 oz plain flour, sifted	3½ cups all-purpose flour, sifted
2 teaspoons ground cinnamon	2 teaspoons ground cinnamon
2 teaspoons grated nutmeg	2 teaspoons grated nutmeg
pinch of salt	pinch of salt
finely grated rind of ½ lemon	finely grated rind of ½ lemon
7 tablespoons Maraschino liqueur	7 tablespoons Maraschino liqueur
1 tablespoon dried yeast, dissolved in 2 tablespoons warm water	1 tablespoon active dry yeast, dissolved in 2 tablespoons warm water
vegetable oil for shallow-frying	vegetable oil for shallow-frying
50 g/2 oz caster sugar	¼ cup sugar

Put the wine and butter in a heavy pan and heat gently until the butter has melted. Remove from the heat and gradually stir in the flour. Beat until smooth, then add the spices, salt, lemon rind, liqueur and yeast. Mix well, then cover and leave to stand for 1 hour.

Heat the oil in a frying pan (skillet) to a depth of 5 mm/¼ inch. Add tablespoonfuls of the batter and fry until golden brown on both sides. Drain on absorbent kitchen paper and keep hot while cooking the remaining fritters. Sprinkle with sugar and serve immediately.
SERVES 6 TO 8

TRENTINO-ALTO ADIGE

FRITTELLE DI MELE

Apple Fritters

Metric/Imperial	American
50 g/2 oz butter, melted	¼ cup butter, melted
50 g/2 oz caster sugar	¼ cup sugar
150 ml/¼ pint milk	⅔ cup milk
50 g/2 oz plain flour	½ cup all-purpose flour
3 eggs, beaten	3 eggs, beaten
1 teaspoon dried yeast, dissolved in 2 teaspoons warm water	1 teaspoon active dry yeast, dissolved in 2 teaspoons warm water
8 dessert apples	8 dessert apples
vegetable oil for deep-frying	vegetable oil for deep-frying

Put the melted butter in a bowl with half the sugar, the milk, flour, eggs and yeast. Beat to a smooth batter.

Peel and core the apples, then slice into thin rounds and sprinkle with the remaining sugar.

Heat the oil in a deep-fryer. Dip the apple slices a few at a time into the batter, then deep-fry in the hot oil until golden brown. Drain on absorbent kitchen paper and keep warm while frying the remainder. Serve immediately.
SERVES 6 TO 8

Nearly every region in Italy seems to have its own version of a celebration cake, although these have a texture and flavour more like sweetened bread than cake. They are eaten throughout the year with a cup of coffee or maybe dunked in a glass of wine (they are rather dry), but on feast days and other special occasions they appear in the shops in profusion. *Panettone* appears in Milan at Christmas, *Colomba* at Easter. *Pandoro* is a New Year speciality cake from Verona.

BUCCELLATO
Sweet Yeast Ring Cake

Metric/Imperial	American
400 g/14 oz plain flour	3½ cups all-purpose flour
200 g/7 oz caster sugar	1 cup sugar
2 eggs, beaten	2 eggs, beaten
100 g/4 oz butter, softened and cut into small pieces	½ cup butter, softened and cut into small pieces
2 teaspoons bicarbonate of soda	2 teaspoons baking soda
2 teaspoons dried yeast, dissolved in 2 tablespoons lukewarm milk	2 teaspoons active dry yeast, dissolved in 2 tablespoons lukewarm milk
pinch of salt	pinch of salt
few tablespoons warm milk to mix	few tablespoons warm milk to mix
beaten egg to glaze	beaten egg to glaze

Sift the flour into a bowl, stir in the sugar and make a well in the centre. Add the eggs, butter, soda, yeast and salt. Knead ingredients together, adding enough milk to form a soft dough. Knead well until smooth and pliable, shape into a ball, place in a bowl and cover with a damp cloth. Leave to rise in a warm place for 1 hour or until doubled in bulk.

Knead the dough on a work surface, then shape into a ring with your hands. Place on a baking (cookie) sheet lined with greased greaseproof (wax) paper. Brush with beaten egg. Bake in a preheated moderately hot oven (200°C/400°F/Gas Mark 6) for 40 minutes until risen and firm to the touch. Transfer to a wire rack to cool before serving.

SERVES 4 TO 6

PANFORTE DI SIENA
Siena Cake

This flat 'cake' with a nougat-like texture, rich in candied peel, toasted nuts and spices, is a particular speciality of the town of Siena.

Metric/Imperial	American
75 g/3 oz hazelnuts	½ cup filberts
75 g/3 oz blanched almonds, coarsely chopped	½ cup coarsely chopped blanched almonds
175 g/6 oz candied peel, finely chopped	1 cup finely chopped candied peel
25 g/1 oz cocoa powder	¼ cup unsweetened cocoa powder
50 g/2 oz plain flour	½ cup all-purpose flour
½ teaspoon ground cinnamon	½ teaspoon ground cinnamon
¼ teaspoon ground mixed spice	¼ teaspoon grated nutmeg
100 g/4 oz sugar	½ cup sugar
100 g/4 oz honey	½ cup honey
TOPPING:	TOPPING:
2 tablespoons icing sugar	2 tablespoons confectioners' sugar
1 teaspoon ground cinnamon	1 teaspoon ground cinnamon

Spread the hazelnuts (filberts) on a baking (cookie) sheet and put into a preheated moderately hot oven (190°C/375°F/Gas Mark 5) for 5 to 10 minutes. Rub the nuts in a clean cloth (napkin) to remove skins, then chop coarsely.

Place in a bowl with the almonds, candied peel, cocoa, flour and spices. Stir well.

Put the sugar and honey in a pan and heat gently until the sugar dissolves, then boil until a sugar thermometer registers 115°C/240°F, or until a little of the mixture dropped into a cup of cold water forms a ball. Take off the heat immediately, add to the nut mixture and stir until well mixed.

Turn into a 20 cm/8 inch flan ring (pie pan) lined with non-stick parchment. Spread flat, making sure the mixture is no more than 1 cm/½ inch thick. Bake in a preheated cool oven (150°C/300°F/Gas Mark 2) for 30 to 35 minutes.

Turn onto a wire rack, peel off the paper and leave to cool. Sprinkle the top thickly with the icing (confectioners') sugar sifted with the cinnamon. Serve cut into small wedges.

MAKES 8 TO 10 WEDGES

BOMBOLONI
Doughnuts

Metric/Imperial	American
450 g/1 lb plain flour	4 cups all-purpose flour
175 g/6 oz caster sugar	¾ cup sugar
finely grated rind of 1 lemon	finely grated rind of 1 lemon
pinch of salt	pinch of salt
75 g/3 oz butter, softened and cut into small pieces	⅓ cup butter, softened and cut into small pieces
15 g/½ oz fresh yeast, dissolved in 2 tablespoons warm water	½ cake compressed yeast, dissolved in 2 tablespoons warm water
vegetable oil for deep-frying	vegetable oil for deep-frying

Sift the flour into a bowl and stir in 75 g/3 oz/⅓ cup sugar, the lemon rind and salt. Make a well in the centre and add the butter and yeast. Mix the ingredients together, adding a little lukewarm water to form a soft dough. Knead well until smooth and pliable, shape into a ball and cover with a damp cloth. Leave to rise in a warm place for 1 hour or until doubled in bulk.

Flatten the dough with a rolling pin and roll out into a sheet about 1 cm/½ inch thick. Cut into circles, about 5 cm/2 inches in diameter, using a pastry (cookie) cutter. Place on a baking (cookie) sheet and leave to rise in a warm place for 1 hour.

Heat the oil in a deep-fryer and deep-fry the doughnuts a few at a time until golden brown. Drain on absorbent kitchen paper while frying the remainder. Sprinkle with the remaining sugar and serve immediately.

MAKES 15 TO 20

ABOVE: **Panforte di siena**

PINOCCATE

Pine Nut Candies

Metric/Imperial	American
150 g/5 oz candied orange peel, chopped	scant 1 cup chopped candied orange peel
7 tablespoons Maraschino liqueur	7 tablespoons Maraschino liqueur
200 ml/7 fl oz water	1 cup water
450 g/1 lb sugar	2 cups sugar
150 g/5 oz pine kernels	1⅓ cups pine kernels

Soak the orange peel in the liqueur.

Put the water and sugar in a pan over low heat until dissolved, then boil rapidly until the syrup thickens and reaches the 'thread' stage. To test, place a teaspoonful of the syrup in a cup of cold water to cool slightly, then draw the syrup between the thumb and forefinger. If it forms a thread the syrup is ready.

Remove from the heat and stir vigorously with a wooden spatula until white and soft. Drain the orange peel, then immediately add to the sugar with the pine kernels. Spoon small heaps of the mixture onto a sheet of buttered foil and leave to cool before serving.
MAKES 20 TO 25

GELATO DI RICOTTA

Ricotta and Rum Bombe

Metric/Imperial	American
5 egg yolks	5 egg yolks
100 g/4 oz sugar	½ cup sugar
5 tablespoons rum	⅓ cup rum
450 g/1 lb fresh ricotta cheese*, sieved	2 cups fresh ricotta cheese*, sieved

Line a 1.2 litre/2 pint freezerproof mould with foil.

Put the egg yolks in a bowl with the sugar and whisk until light and fluffy. Fold in the rum, then fold in the ricotta a little at a time.

Spoon the mixture into the prepared mould, smooth the surface, then cover with foil. Freeze until solid. Unmould onto a serving plate and serve immediately.
SERVES 4 TO 6

CALCIONI ALL'ASCOLANA

Little Cheesecakes

Metric/Imperial	American
PASTRY:	PASTRY:
450 g/1 lb plain flour	4 cups all-purpose flour
4 eggs	4 eggs
2 tablespoons olive oil	2 tablespoons olive oil
pinch of salt	pinch of salt
FILLING:	FILLING:
250 g/9 oz pecorino cheese★, grated	2 cups grated pecorino cheese★
25 g/1 oz sugar	2 tablespoons sugar
finely grated rind and juice of ½ lemon	finely grated rind and juice of ½ lemon
4 egg yolks	4 egg yolks

Sift the flour onto a work surface and make a well in the centre. Add 3 eggs, the oil and salt and mix the ingredients together to form a soft dough, adding 1 to 2 tablespoons lukewarm water if necessary.

Knead the dough until smooth and pliable. Shape into a ball, cover and chill for 30 minutes.

Meanwhile, prepare the filling. Place the cheese, sugar, lemon rind and juice and the egg yolks in a bowl and mix thoroughly.

Flatten the dough on a work surface and roll out to a thickness of 5 mm/¼ inch. Cut into circles, about 7.5 cm/3 inches in diameter, using a pastry (cookie) cutter. Put a little of the filling in the centre of each circle and fold over one half of the dough to enclose the filling. Press the edges firmly together to seal, making semi-circular shapes.

Brush each cake with the remaining egg and place on an oiled baking (cookie) sheet. Bake in a preheated moderate oven (180°C/350°F/Gas Mark 4) for 30 minutes or until puffed and golden. Serve hot.

MAKES 15 TO 20

MARITOZZI

Raisin and Candied Peel Buns

Metric/Imperial	American
350 g/12 oz plain flour, sifted	3 cups all-purpose flour, sifted
25 g/1 oz fresh yeast, dissolved in 2 tablespoons warm water	1 cake compressed yeast, dissolved in 2 tablespoons warm water
2 eggs	2 eggs
3 tablespoons olive oil	3 tablespoons olive oil
salt	salt
50 g/2 oz caster sugar	¼ cup sugar
100 g/4 oz seedless raisins, soaked in lukewarm water for 15 minutes, drained and dried	⅔ cup seedless raisins, soaked in lukewarm water for 15 minutes, drained and dried
50 g/2 oz pine kernels	½ cup pine kernels
50 g/2 oz candied lemon peel, chopped	⅓ cup chopped candied lemon peel

Sift half the flour into a bowl and stir in the yeast mixture, 1 egg, 1 tablespoon oil and a pinch of salt. Mix

well, then knead until smooth. Place in a bowl, sprinkle with a little flour, cover with a damp cloth and leave to rise in a warm place for about 1 hour.

Place the dough on a work surface and knead in the remaining flour and oil, the sugar, a pinch of salt and the remaining egg. Continue kneading until the dough is fairly soft, adding a little lukewarm water if necessary. Add the raisins, pine kernels and lemon peel to the dough and continue kneading for a further 10 minutes.

Divide the dough into 12 pieces and shape into small oval buns. Place on an oiled baking (cookie) sheet. Cover with a damp cloth and leave to rise in a warm place until doubled in size.

Bake in a preheated moderately hot oven (190°C/375°F/Gas Mark 5) for 20 minutes. Transfer to a wire rack to cool before serving.

MAKES 12

PAN ROZZO

Spiced Almond Cake

Metric/Imperial	American
50 g/2 oz plain flour	½ cup all-purpose flour
50 g/2 oz potato flour	½ cup potato flour
pinch of ground cinnamon	pinch of ground cinnamon
4 eggs, separated	4 eggs, separated
75 g/3 oz sugar	⅓ cup sugar
50 g/2 oz ground almonds	½ cup ground almonds
40 g/1½ oz butter, melted	3 tablespoons butter, melted
2 tablespoons amaretti di sarrono or other liqueur	2 tablespoons amaretti di sarrono or other liqueur
75 g/3 oz plain chocolate	⅔ cup semi-sweet chocolate pieces
1 tablespoon water	1 tablespoon water

Sift the two flours together with the cinnamon. Put the egg yolks in a bowl with the sugar and whisk until light and frothy. Fold in the flours and the almonds, with the butter and liqueur. Beat the egg whites until stiff, then carefully fold into the mixture.

Spoon into a lined and greased 18 cm/7 inch cake tin (pan) and smooth the surface. Bake in a preheated moderate oven (180°C/350°F/Gas Mark 4) for about 1 hour until well risen. Transfer to a wire rack to cool.

Melt the chocolate with the water in a bowl over a pan of simmering water. Spread over the cake to cover completely. Leave until the chocolate has set before serving.

MAKES ONE 18 CM/7 INCH CAKE

RIGHT: **Pan rozzo**; Maritozzi; Calcioni all'ascolana

ABOVE: **Ricotta fritta;
Nepitelle**

NEPITELLE
Fig and Nut Pasties

Metric/Imperial

PASTRY:
400 g/14 oz plain flour
150 g/5 oz caster sugar
165 g/5½ oz butter, softened
  and cut into small pieces
3 eggs
1 egg, separated
pinch of salt
FILLING:
300 g/11 oz dried figs
150 g/5 oz shelled walnuts,
  ground
150 g/5 oz blanched
  almonds, toasted and
  ground
100 g/4 oz seedless raisins,
  soaked in lukewarm
  water for 15 minutes and
  drained
200 g/7 oz marmalade
finely grated rind of 3
  oranges
¼ teaspoon ground cloves
1 teaspoon ground cinnamon

American

PASTRY:
3½ cups all-purpose flour
⅔ cup sugar
⅔ cup butter, softened and
  cut into small pieces
3 eggs
1 egg, separated
pinch of salt
FILLING:
2 cups dried figs
1¼ cups shelled walnuts,
  ground
1¼ cups blanched almonds,
  toasted and ground
⅔ cup seedless raisins,
  soaked in lukewarm
  water for 15 minutes and
  drained
scant ¾ cup marmalade
finely grated rind of 3
  oranges
¼ teaspoon ground cloves
1 teaspoon ground cinnamon

To make the pastry: sift the flour into a bowl, stir in the sugar, then make a well in the centre. Add the butter, 2 eggs, 1 egg yolk and the salt. Work the ingredients together with the fingertips to form a soft dough, then knead well until smooth and elastic. Shape the dough into a ball, cover and chill while making the filling.

Cook the figs in boiling water for 10 minutes. Drain thoroughly, then chop. Place in a bowl with the remaining filling ingredients and mix thoroughly.

Flatten the dough with a rolling pin and roll out to a sheet, about 5 mm/¼ inch thick. Cut into 10 cm/4 inch circles, using a pastry (cookie) cutter. Put a little filling in the middle of each circle, then fold the dough over the filling to form half-moon shapes. Moisten the edges with a little beaten egg white, then press firmly to seal.

Make a few cuts in the surface of each pasty and place on a greased baking (cookie) sheet. Brush with the remaining beaten egg to glaze. Bake in a preheated moderate oven (160°C/325°F/Gas Mark 3) for 25 to 30 minutes until puffed and golden. Serve hot or cold.
MAKES 6 TO 8

VECCHIARELLE

Honey-coated Fritters

Metric/Imperial	American
400 g/14 oz plain flour	3½ cups all-purpose flour
15 g/½ oz fresh yeast, dissolved in 3 tablespoons lukewarm water	½ cake compressed yeast, dissolved in 3 tablespoons lukewarm water
pinch of salt	pinch of salt
vegetable oil for deep-frying	vegetable oil for deep-frying
175 g/6 oz thin honey	½ cup thin honey

Sift the flour onto a work surface and make a well in the centre. Add the yeast and salt and work together with the fingertips. Add lukewarm water gradually, kneading until a smooth, pliable dough is obtained. Shape into a ball and place in a bowl. Sprinkle with a little flour and cover with a damp cloth. Leave to rise in a warm place for about 1 hour until doubled in bulk.

Knead the dough on a floured surface, then shape into small sticks, about 1 cm/½ inch thick and 6.5 cm/2½ inches long. Heat the oil in a deep-fryer and deep-fry the sticks, a few at a time, until golden brown. Drain on absorbent kitchen paper and keep warm while frying the remainder.

Put the honey in a saucepan and heat gently until it has melted, stirring constantly. Dip the sticks into the honey to coat and serve immediately.

SERVES 4 TO 6

PANINI DOLCI

Almond Yeast Cakes

Metric/Imperial	American
450 g/1 lb plain flour	4 cups all-purpose flour
pinch of salt	pinch of salt
pinch of ground cloves	pinch of ground cloves
pinch of ground cinnamon	pinch of ground cinnamon
50 g/2 oz blanched almonds, toasted and chopped	½ cup blanched almonds, toasted and chopped
200 g/7 oz caster sugar	1 cup sugar
1 teaspoon dried yeast, dissolved in 3–4 tablespoons warm water	1 teaspoon active dry yeast, dissolved in about ¼ cup warm water

Sift the flour, salt and spices into a bowl and make a well in the centre. Add the remaining ingredients and work together with the fingertips. Add warm water gradually, mixing until a soft dough is obtained. Knead until smooth and elastic.

Form the dough into a ball, place in a bowl and cover with a damp cloth. Leave to rise in a warm place for 1 hour or until doubled in size.

Flatten the dough with a rolling pin and roll out to a sheet, about 1 cm/½ inch thick. Cut into small shapes, using different shaped pastry (cookie) cutters. Place on a greased and floured baking (cookie) sheet and bake in a preheated moderately hot oven (190°C/375°F/Gas Mark 5), for 15 minutes or until risen and golden brown. Transfer to a wire rack to cool before serving.

MAKES ABOUT 20

In 1533, when Catherine de Medici travelled from 'the court of Turin to France to be married to the Dauphin, she took her own pastry cooks with her. She feared the French pastry cooks would not be able to meet her high standards. Even today Italian housewives tend to leave pastry-making to the experts, seldom making pies and tarts at home. They prefer to buy them at their favourite pâtisserie, where they are bound to be spoilt for choice.

RICOTTA FRITTA

Ricotta Cheese Fritters

Metric/Imperial	American
450 g/1 lb fresh ricotta cheese*	1 lb fresh ricotta cheese*
plain flour for coating	all-purpose flour for coating
2 eggs, beaten	2 eggs, beaten
vegetable oil for deep-frying	vegetable oil for deep-frying
100 g/4 oz caster sugar	½ cup sugar

Cut the cheese into sticks, 4 cm/1½ inches long and 1 cm/½ inch across. Coat lightly with flour, taking care not to break them, then dip into the beaten eggs.

Heat the oil in a deep-fryer and deep-fry the ricotta slices, a few at a time, until golden brown. Drain on absorbent kitchen paper and keep warm while frying the remainder. Sprinkle with the sugar and serve immediately.

SERVES 4 TO 6

ZABAIONE

*This most famous of all Italian desserts is very quick
and simple to make, but make it immediately before
serving as it is apt to separate if left to stand for more
than a few minutes. A superb light dessert to complete
a meal.*

Metric/Imperial	American
4 egg yolks	4 egg yolks
4 tablespoons caster sugar	$\frac{1}{4}$ cup sugar
1 tablespoon warm water	1 tablespoon warm water
7 tablespoons Marsala	7 tablespoons Marsala
sponge fingers to serve	lady fingers to serve

Place the egg yolks, sugar and warm water in a bowl
over a saucepan of hot water. Beat with a balloon or
rotary whisk (not an electric beater) until pale in colour
and frothy.

Whisk in the Marsala a little at a time and continue
whisking over heat for 5 to 10 minutes until the
mixture increases in volume, becomes thick and foamy
and holds its shape in a spoon.

Remove from the heat and spoon into tall wine
glasses. Serve immediately with sponge fingers (lady
fingers).

SERVES 3 TO 4

MANTECATO DI PESCHE

Peach Water Ice

*A typical Sicilian fruit-based water ice. Melon ice can
be made the same way, by replacing the peaches with
750 g/$1\frac{1}{2}$ lb ripe, peeled and deseeded ogen melon flesh.*

Metric/Imperial	American
100 g/4 oz sugar	$\frac{1}{2}$ cup sugar
150 ml/$\frac{1}{4}$ pint water	$\frac{2}{3}$ cup water
4 large peaches	4 large peaches
juice of 1 lemon	juice of 1 lemon

Put the sugar and water into a small pan and heat
gently until the sugar has dissolved, then boil for 3 to 4
minutes. Leave until quite cold.

Immerse the peaches in boiling water for 1 minute,
then drain and remove the skins and stones (seeds).
Immediately, purée the flesh in an electric blender or
press through a nylon sieve (strainer), then mix with
the lemon juice to prevent discolouration. Stir in the
cold syrup, pour into a shallow freezer tray and freeze
until half firm.

Turn into a bowl and whisk vigorously for a few
minutes, then return to the tray and freeze until firm.

Transfer to the refrigerator 30 to 40 minutes before
serving to allow the ice to soften a little. To serve,
scoop the water ice into individual glasses.

SERVES 4

ABOVE: **Zabaglione;**
Mantecato di pesche

The Italians were the first
Europeans to learn to
make water ices and
sherbets, but whether
they learnt the art from
the Arabs way back in the
ninth century, or later
from the Chinese during
Marco Polo's time, is
open to question. The
Romans even had a
rather crude form of
water ice; it was a simple
mixture of ice from the
mountains with crushed
fresh fruit.

PÀRDULAS

Cream Cheesecakes

Metric/Imperial	American
PASTRY:	PASTRY:
400 g/14 oz plain flour	3½ cups all-purpose flour
pinch of salt	pinch of salt
100 g/4 oz lard, cut into pieces	½ cup shortening, cut into pieces
4–6 tablespoons water	4–6 tablespoons water
FILLING:	FILLING:
350 g/12 oz fresh cream cheese, sieved	1½ cups fresh cream cheese, sieved
175 g/6 oz caster sugar	¾ cup sugar
3 eggs, beaten	3 eggs, beaten
finely grated rind of 1 lemon	finely grated rind of 1 lemon
50 g/2 oz plain flour	½ cup all-purpose flour
pinch of saffron powder	pinch of saffron powder
pinch of ground cinnamon	pinch of ground cinnamon
pinch of salt	pinch of salt

To make the pastry: sift the flour and salt into a bowl
and rub in the lard (shortening), using the fingertips.
Mix in enough water to give a fairly stiff dough. Knead
lightly until smooth. Cover and chill for 30 minutes.

Meanwhile, make the filling. Beat the cheese with
the sugar, then gradually beat in the eggs. Add the
lemon rind and sift in the flour with spices and salt. Stir
well until thoroughly mixed.

Flatten the dough with a rolling pin and roll out to a
thin sheet. Cut into circles about 10 cm/4 inches in
diameter, using a pastry (cookie) cutter.

Put a little filling in the centre of each circle, then
raise the edges of the dough around the filling and
pinch them together with the fingertips to resemble
tartlets with curly rims. Stand the pastries on a lightly
oiled baking (cookie) sheet and bake in a preheated
moderate oven (180°C/350°F/Gas Mark 4) for 30
minutes or until golden brown. Transfer to a wire rack
to cool before serving.
MAKES 25 TO 30

Index

SUPPLIERS OF SPECIAL ITALIAN FOODS AND COOKING EQUIPMENT ★ indicates cooking equipment suppliers

BLOOMINGDALE'S★
1000 Third Avenue
New York, N.Y. 10022
BRIDGE KITCHENWARE CORP.★
214 East 52nd Street
New York, N.Y. 10022
MACY'S★
Herald Square
New York, N.Y. 10001
PAPRIKAS WEISS
1546 Second Avenue
New York, N.Y. 10021
TODARO BROS.
555 Second Avenue
New York, N.Y. 10016
PETRINI'S
Delicatessen Department
Masonic and Fulton Ave
San Francisco
California 94117
WILLIAMS-SONOMA★
P O Box 3792
San Francisco
California 94119
THE CULINARY ARTS★
Gateway Shopping Center
Wilton
Connecticut 06897
COOK'S MART★
609 North La Salle Street
Chicago
Illinois 60610

IL CONTE DE SAVOIA
555 West Roosevelt Road
Chicago
Illinois 60607
RIVIERA ITALIAN FOODS
3220 North Harlem Avenue
Harwood Heights
Illinois 60656
LA CUISINE CLASSIQUE★
631 Royal Street
New Orleans
Louisiana 70130
NEIMAN-MARCUS
P O Box 2968
Dallas
Texas 75221
FIGI'S, INC.★
The Cook's Collection
Marshfield
Wisconsin 54449

ACKNOWLEDGMENTS

Special photography by Robert Golden
Food prepared by Caroline Ellwood
Photographic stylist: Antonia Gaunt

The publishers would also like to thank the following individuals and organizations for their kind permission to reproduce the location photographs in this book:—
Adespoton Film Service 42; J. Allan Cash Ltd. 16, 28–29; Peter Baker Photography 20–21, 23; Bullaty Lomeo (The Image Bank) 11; Douglas Dickins 8; Fabbri Editore 6, 7; Robert Harding Associates 37; Raymond Pask 18–19; M. Pedone (The Image Bank) 25; G.N. Petrini (The Image Bank) 26; The Photographers Library 12, 41; G. Rossi (The Image Bank) 44; Spectrum Colour Library 13, 15, 40; A. Vergani (The Image Bank) 33.

The publishers would also like to express their gratitude to the following companies for the loan of accessories for photography:—
Sam Birrel; Craftsmen Potters Association, William Blake House, Marshall St, W.I.; Elizabeth David Ltd, 46 Bourne St, SW1; Divertimenti Cooking and Tableware, 68 Marylebone Lane, W1; Kings Cross Continental Stores Ltd, 26 Caledonian Rd, N1; Pietro Negroni Ltd, Negroni House, 24 New Wharf Rd, N1; Figlio G. Parmigiani Ltd, 43 Frith St and 36A Old Compton St, W1; United Preservers Ltd, 8–10 Eldon Way, Abbey Rd, NW10; Vinorio, 8 Old Compton St, W1.